# Ritual and Ethnic Identity

A Comparative Study of the Social Meaning of Liturgical Ritual in Synagogues

Jack N. Lightstone and Frederick B. Bird
with Simcha Fishbane, Victor Levin, Marc P. Lalonde,
Louise Mayer and Madeleine Mcbrearty

Wilfrid Laurier University Press

**Canadian Cataloguing in Publication Data**

Lightstone, Jack N.
  Ritual and ethnic identity : a comparative study
of the social meaning of liturgical ritual in
Canadian synagogues

Includes bibliographical references and index.
ISBN 0-88920-247-8

1. Judaism – Canada – Liturgy.   2. Jews – Canada –
Social life and customs.   I. Bird, Frederick B.
(Frederick Bruce), 1938-   .   II. Title.

BM227.L54   1995      296.4'0971      C94-932341-1

Copyright © 1995

WILFRID LAURIER UNIVERSITY PRESS
Waterloo, Ontario, Canada
N2L 3C5

Cover design by Jose Martucci, Design Communications

Printed in the United States of America

*Ritual and Ethnic Identity: A Comparative Study of the Social Meaning of Liturgical Ritual in Synagogues* has been produced from a manuscript supplied in camera-ready form by the authors.

All rights reserved. No part of this work covered by the copyrights hereon may be reproduced or used in any form or by any means—graphic, electronic or mechanical—without the prior written permission of the publisher. Any request for photocopying, recording, taping or reproducing in information storage and retrieval systems of any part of this book shall be directed in writing to the Canadian Reprography Collective, 214 King Street West, Suite 312, Toronto, Ontario M5V 3S6.

# TABLE OF CONTENTS

Preface v

## PART 1
### Method, Theory and the Larger Context

1   Introduction: Liturgical Drama and Social Location: The Performance of Sabbath Morning Services in Several Canadian Synagogues,
*Jack N. Lightstone*   3

2   Ritual as Communicative Action,
*Frederick B. Bird*   23

3   The Religion of Jewish Peoplehood: The Myth, Ritual and Institutions of the Civil Religion of Canadian Jewry,
*Jack N. Lightstone*   53

## PART 2
### Congregational Liturgical Ritual

4   Ritual, Reality and Contemporary Society: The Case of a Reconstructionist Synagogue,
*Jack N. Lightstone*   65

5   The Use of Non-vernacular Language in the Sabbath Morning Service of a Reconstructionist Synagogue,
*Madeleine Mcbrearty*   81

6   Ritual Performance in a Reform Sabbath Service,
*Marc P. Lalonde, Louise Mayer and Jack N. Lightstone*   89

7   The Synagogue as a Symbol of Ethnic Identity: The Case of a Sephardi Congregation,
*Madeleine Mcbrearty*   109

| 8 | Back to the *Yeshiva*: The Social Dynamics of an Orthodox Sabbath Morning Service,<br>*Simcha Fishbane* | 123 |
|---|---|---|
| 9 | Sabbath Morning Services in a Traditional Conservative Synagogue,<br>*Victor Levin* | 135 |

## PART 3
## Between Congregation and Family

| 10 | Contemporary Bar Mitzvah Rituals in Modern Orthodoxy,<br>*Simcha Fishbane* | 155 |
|---|---|---|
| 11 | Jewish Mourning Rites: A Process of Resocialization,<br>*Simcha Fishbane* | 169 |
| 12 | Family Rituals and Religion: A Functional Analysis of Jewish and Christian Family Ritual Practices,<br>*Frederick B. Bird* | 185 |

| **Glossary** | 197 |
|---|---|
| **References** | 203 |
| **Index** | 216 |

# Preface

This volume emerged from the collaboration of the authors of its constituent essays within the context of a single research project conducted between 1986 and 1989. Perhaps the best way to describe in broad strokes the main subject matter of this book, then, is to describe briefly the origin and nature of the project, which I co-directed with Frederick Bird.

Our research attempted to document and interpret ritual practices among contemporary Canadian Jews, primarily from the perspectives of anthropology and the sociology of religion. A principal strength of what follows is our search for the meaning, including the social meaning, of these practices (as opposed to mere bean counting). By this, I refer to the documentation of what is practised and the frequency with which it is practised. The social scientific study of mainstream religious denominations in the West has focused overwhelmingly on changing rates of participation in traditional religious rites, such as church and synagogue attendance; these figures are taken as indicators of increasing secularization. By contrast, we treated the ritual of contemporary Canadian Jews as complex symbolic systems. To be sure, any anthropologist of so-called primitive religion will find in this approach nothing new. But anthropologists have tended not to approach the religious practices of contemporary Western societies (with the possible exception of new religious movements or small groups and sects). What makes this book not only different but important is our attempt to do so and, as a result, to solve problems that arise from the study of "mainstream" ritual phenomena in a complex, pluralistic (post-) industrialized milieu.

A second strength of our approach is its openness to a wide variety of phenomena. Where we observed both traditional ritual observances as well as seemingly secular ones, practices performed for their own intrinsic value, we tried to treat both traditional and "secular" together as a single ritual system. Patterns of handshaking and greeting among participants in a Sabbath morning service, for example, were described and interpreted together with the liturgy itself. We examined not only ritual acts themselves, moreover, but their settings as well. Thus we considered, among other things, the architecture of the sanctuary hall—that is, how its organization of space structured the actions and sensations of participants, quite apart from any behavioural prescriptions and proscriptions attached to the ritual acts themselves.

While the larger project dealt with ritual in the contexts of both the family and communal institutions, the evidence collected for the latter proved more coherent and detailed across the groups studied. This book, therefore, concentrates on the synagogue. Even so, as our research indicated, what happens in the synagogue cannot always be separated neatly from what happens in the family context. Two essays bring together the private realm of the family and the public realm of the synagogue, showing how particularly important moments in the former become transferred to the latter. One of these essays deals with the bar mitzvah, a personal rite of passage performed in large part in the public setting of the synagogue service. The other deals with death and mourning, rituals that in the contemporary Orthodox and traditional Conservative settings move from the public realm (the funeral) to the private (home) and back to the public (synagogue). Since even Jews who have drifted away from regular synagogue attendance tend still to observe these mourning rituals, including those that demand regular synagogue attendance for 12 months, we considered the phenomenon worth discussing in a volume concerned with liturgical ritual in the synagogue. The final chapter treats with broad strokes the meaning and role of ritual practices among the families observed. In addition, since rituals performed at home and at synagogue fit into a larger pattern of behaviour among Canadian Jews, most of whom seldom attend synagogue services, the last essay in Part 1 looks at that larger pattern, what I call the "civil religion" of Canadian Jewry.

These essays, which treat different parts of a unified project, have never appeared together. Four of them have been published previously in English; one, originally published in French, appears here in English for the first time. Complete bibliographical information concerning the first printing of each is given toward the end of this preface. The first two chapters, moreover, are newly written specifically to integrate the whole, synthesize the results and offer a coherent methodological and theoretical framework for this type of research. As a result of these integrative chapters, we believe, the whole is greater than the sum of the parts.

This research project and the resulting book would have been impossible without a generous grant from les Fonds FCAR (Formation de chercheurs et aide à la recherche) of the Province of Québec and financial support from the Faculty of Arts and Science of Concordia University. We are grateful for their help. Concordia University in general and our colleagues at the Department of Religion in particular continue to provide the type of environment that any researcher would envy. Fred Bird and I are particularly grateful to Michael Oppenheim, who regularly attended our meetings and advised us and other collaborators. A sabbatical leave granted me by Concordia enabled me, together with Fred Bird, to complete this volume.

Special thanks are reserved for the congregations and individual families who suffered our presence, our questions and our exploratory interpretations of their behaviour and attitudes. To allow such intrusions is a mark of tremendous courage and tolerance.

We want to thank the journals and publishers concerned for permission to reprint the previously published essays. In the order of their appearance here, they are:

J. Lightstone, "Mythe, rituels et institutions de la religion civile de la communauté juive canadienne," in Y. Desrosiers, et al., *Religion et culture au Québec: figures contemporaines du sacré* (Montréal: Fides, 1986): 119-36, appearing in English for the first time in this book;

J. Lightstone, "Ritual, Reality and Contemporary Society," *Journal of Ritual Studies* 2, 2 (1988): 195-216;

M. Mcbrearty, "The Use of Non-Vernacular Language in the Sabbath Morning Services of a Reconstructionist Synagogue," *Journal of Religion and Culture* 2, 1 (1987): 202-15;

S. Fishbane, "Contemporary Bar Mitzvah Rituals in Modern Orthodoxy," *Journal of Religion and Culture* 2, 1 (1987): 166-89;

S. Fishbane, "Jewish Mourning Rites, a Process of Resocialization," *Anthropologica* 31, 1 (1989): 65-85.

All of these previously published essays have been slightly revised for the current context. Specifically, the methodological and theoretical sections of each have been eliminated or shortened; the newly written synthetic and introductory chapters of this volume make these sections redundant.

Dr. Paul Nathanson did a masterful job copy editing the volume and preparing the Index. Wilfrid Laurier University Press—its director, editorial and production staff—deserve much gratitude. The Press continues to be a major force promoting the academic study of religion and culture in Canada.

Finally, a note on the transliteration of Hebrew and Yiddish words: the system chosen is purely phonetic; every vowel should be pronounced and silent consonants have been dropped.

Jack N. Lightstone
30 October 1993

# PART 1

## Method, Theory and the Larger Context

# 1

# Introduction—Liturgical Drama and Social Location: The Performance of Sabbath Morning Services in Several Canadian Synagogues

## JACK N. LIGHTSTONE

**The origins and constituent parts of this volume**

This volume focuses on the public performance of liturgical ritual, its character and meaning, at several synagogues in the greater metropolitan area of a large Canadian city. The individual studies all emerged from a collaborative research project. Conducted between 1986 and 1989, the project operated under a broader mandate than indicated by the title of this work: to study the ritual life of contemporary Canadian Jews in both the private and public spheres, both at home with the family and at synagogue or other communal institutions. To collect the data, we relied primarily on interviews, participant observation and, to a lesser extent, on questionnaires. Our aim was, first, to document ritual practice and, second, to interpret its meaning in the lives of practitioners.

This volume, then, concentrates on the performance of Sabbath liturgies in the synagogue as one aspect of a larger project. It also tries to frame and complement the examination of synagogue ritual with some synthetic accounts of ritual life beyond the synagogue. To that end, Part 1 (chaps. 2 and 3) offers two general essays. These provide an introduction and intelligible context for the studies, in Part 2, of liturgical rituals in synagogues associated with the Orthodox, Conservative, Reconstructionist and Reform movements, a large Sephardic congregation and a house-*yeshiva/shtibl* (rabbinic academy/small synagogue). Chapter 2 provides a general theoretical and methodological essay on the study of ritual. Chapter 3 presents an account of what we have called the "civil religion" of Canadian Jews. That overarching set of beliefs and practices seems to be shared by a significant proportion of Canadian Jews, those who attend synagogues on an episodic, but by no means haphazard and random, basis. Part 3 complements the studies of synagogue ritual. Chapter 12 offers a general account of the character and function of Jewish family rituals viewed in comparison with non-Jewish, primarily Christian, ones. Chapters 10 and 11 examine two sets of important life-cycle rites, those surrounding the death of a close relative and the bar mitzvah (coming of age, at 13, of a Jewish male). These rituals overarch both the private sphere of the home and the public one of the synagogue, serving at once a complex of interrelated purposes for both the family and the community. In the context of this volume, with its focus on public, liturgical ritual in the synagogue, the public, communal aspects of these family rites are privileged.[1]

This first chapter tries to place in context and synthesize what we have concluded about synagogue ritual. In light of our research, I shall spell out a conceptual framework by which to understand the character of a Sabbath morning liturgy, with associated rituals, and its significance for participants. This synthetic essay, like the ensemble of related studies, is intended to be illustrative and suggestive, not comprehensive. It illustrates an approach to what transpires during a synagogue service and suggests the meaning communicated to participants. An ironic fact indicates how timely this exercise is. The most famous study of behaviour at synagogue (Heilman 1976), assiduously avoids examining actual ritual. I do not mean to imply that Samuel Heilman staged Hamlet without the Prince. His interests lay elsewhere, specifically in a Goffman-inspired study of social interaction among participants. The synagogue provided a setting and its service the principal occasion for this interaction. But Heilman's agenda underscores the impression that social scientists have shown minimal interest in the study of contemporary ritual in the synagogue (or, for that matter, in the church).[2] Not surprisingly, therefore, they have done little to map out useful methodological and theoretical frameworks for the analysis and interpretation of liturgical ritual. This introductory essay, building on the individual studies in Part 2, provides a map of this kind and illustrates its general usefulness in the attempt to synthesize and interpret some of the data we have collected.

## Conceptual, methodological and theoretical issues

Chapter 2, as I have just noted, provides an extended methodological and theoretical discussion of the character and meaning of ritualized behaviour beyond but including synagogue liturgical ritual, the focus of this essay. It proposes several generalizations about ritual practice and its study in light of both the data collected for this research and evidence from other sources. Here, I discuss methodological and theoretical issues of a more limited character. What follows offers a basic conceptual framework, in other words, for the study of contemporary synagogue liturgies in Canada.

### Recurrent patterns and communication

The basic approach derives from the most pervasive traits of our evidence. Contemporary Canadian synagogue rituals, specifically the Sabbath morning liturgy, constitute stylized, structured behaviour by a group of voluntary participants. They are, for the most part, familiar with liturgical conduct. This stylized, structured behaviour involves the utterance of prescribed prayers or readings and the performance of actions or gestures authorized by tradition. All this takes place within a physical setting, of course. Many of its features are dictated by religious law and tradition. Even its architectural and aesthetic characteristics, though not always legislated, channel the

*Introduction* 5

actions and affect the experience of the participants. Some of these points warrant further explication.

First, as I have already noted, regular participants know and expect with precision and in detail what will happen in the course of any service. This is not to say that all of them, even those who regularly attend, are equally knowledgeable in all components of what weekly transpires. Quite the contrary, levels of virtuosity vary greatly among even those who attend regularly. Some roles in the service are reserved for officers of the synagogue; participants at most synagogues, for example, recognize the rabbi's right to offer a sermon. Other roles are reserved for either men or women; the opening and closing of the ark has become the prerogative of women in a number of congregations. Still other roles are reserved for either adults or children; in some synagogues, a concluding hymn is led by one or more children. Each of these differentiated roles and functions demands specialized knowledge with which others might acquire only a vague familiarity. Someone can watch the synagogue's vice-president place a Torah scroll in the ark every week, therefore, but remain unaware that the officer in question always turns around to his right when taking the scrolls from the cantor. Familiarity does not extend, in other words, to the minutiae. My point is that all who attend regularly have specific expectations of what will take place, whatever their mode of participation as determined either by knowledge or by rules with regard to rank, sex or age. Participants expect the familiar. They expect variation and innovation to take place within known and predetermined parameters. They know the rules (albeit to various levels of specificity) as established by religious law, tradition or by the custom of their own congregations, and they expect those rules to be followed. It is clear to everyone, therefore, when things have been done correctly. When variation exceeds the established parameters or when outright innovation occurs, the result is distress.

My second point is about the notion of custom, consciousness of which appears everywhere as part of the liturgical experience. Participants are aware that their service is (1) their own accepted rendition of (2) an officially authorized version of (3) a classical rabbinic service prescribed by both religious law and long-standing custom. Participants know that other renditions have evolved in neighbouring congregations using the same official version. They also know that other local congregations are using quite different official versions.

Contemporary Canadian Judaism is pluralistic. As in North America generally, the vast majority of Canadian synagogues are affiliated with an institutionalized synagogue union or movements—Orthodox, Conservative, Reconstructionist or Reform. (Orthodoxy itself is a congeries of movements, institutionalized to varying degrees.) Based on and working from the classical rabbinic model, each movement has taken a specific stance on, among other things, what ought to transpire in a public worship service. Its stance is based on its own world-view, philosophy and theology as expressed in its own officially sanctioned prayer-book (several in the case of Orthodox congregations). This constitutes for every congregation the "authorized version" of the classical tradition. And congregants are aware that their prayer-book might differ considerably from the one used in a neighbouring, differently affiliated congregation (even though few are aware of precisely how these books differ).

All this is not to say that the service in one Conservative congregation, say, is identical to that in another one (that is, one that uses the same official prayer-book). A great deal of what must inevitably be fixed by rule and custom falls outside the official guidelines of the parent movement. Still other matters, especially controversial ones on which the movement has taken no firm stand, are settled at the congregational level. Some congregations, moreover, openly defy—and with impunity—the directives of their movements. Just as members of Conservative congregations are aware that their own service differs significantly from that of Reconstructionist congregations, the members of each are aware that the services of sister congregations with the same affiliation differ substantially from their own. In one Conservative synagogue, for example, women may open the ark; in another, they may not. Nor is this awareness of difference merely an abstract concept for those who attend services. Most Canadian Jews will, for various reasons, periodically attend synagogues other than their own.

This last point leads to one final one that is basic to my conceptual approach. In addition to (or, perhaps, notwithstanding) the sense that one's own congregational service is authorized by both rabbinic law and longstanding tradition, as officially interpreted by a movement and further adapted by the authoritative decisions of past and present congregational leaders, Canadian Jews—especially those in larger cities—believe that they have chosen a rendition of the "official" liturgy. They could have chosen other synagogues, after all, or exerted pressure within the organizational structure of their own congregations to revise aspects of the liturgy (within the limits set by their movements). Over two-thirds of Canada's Jews live in the metropolitan areas surrounding Toronto and Montreal. In some neighbourhoods, three to six synagogues of varying affiliations might be situated within the same square mile. Migration from one to another would pose little inconvenience and is not uncommon. The Jewish population in some urban areas is dense enough to support "breakaway" congregations.

Taken together, these basic facts have considerable importance for this conceptual framework and its methodological and theoretical perspectives. Any attempt to make sense of the way a Sabbath morning service is conducted must take seriously what it means for participants: a self-conscious and voluntary stance both with respect to the classical tradition and over against the practices of synagogues down the street (figuratively and literally speaking). That stance is constituted by the sum total of what constitutes the congregation's official liturgical rendition; the architecture of its sanctuary; the gestures, actions, dress and comportment of participants; role differentiation; any particular use made of the authorized prayer-book; and many other things.

These basic, conspicuous and pervasive traits of our data suggest that congregants, via their particular rendition of the liturgy "intend" to say something about themselves to themselves and to others. They make "statements" using the "language" (that is, the "vocabulary, morphology, syntax and grammar") provided by both their synagogue movement and the classical tradition, exploiting the possibility that this "language" allows for structured variation within limiting rules and conventions. These statements have meaning of a significant sort, because it is possible to say something quite different using the same medium—as attested to by other synagogues down the street. A statement has meaning, after all, only when it excludes other meanings.

The analogy of language is useful in yet another way: when language is used to create highly formalized or stylized texts in which one encounters time and time again the same structured patterns, attendant rules and literary formularies governing the way specific items of content are presented. These recurrent, structured patterns convey information about how certain types of content should be related to one another, quite apart from what is conveyed by idiomatic substance in any one case. The text is, in some sense, a ritualized way of writing. The implicit (non-discursive) meaning conveyed by a formal pattern, even the recognition that a pattern exists, derives from the combined weight of repetitions—the synchrony and homology of passage after passage.

The weekly Sabbath service, in every congregation observed, evinces traits analogous to those of a highly formalized textual tradition. On the one hand, every service has idiomatic items of substance. One verse of a prayer declares: "Blessed are You, YHWH, Who chooses His people, Israel, in love." A congregant kisses the cloth covering the Torah scroll as it is carried in procession within the sanctuary. Both the liturgical sentence and the kiss convey something. But idiomatic items of ritual behaviour or liturgy occur within recurrent, structured patterns. In Orthodox synagogues, men and women sit in separate sections with some physical boundary separating them. The Torah might be "undressed" and revealed only on a raised or otherwise demarcated area to which specific people (only men in Orthodox congregations) are "called." Without being called for an honour, they may not approach the open scrolls. The scrolls are opened and read in a central area; it is surrounded by sections for the men and, around the perimeter, by sections for the women. Here, basic patterns of controlled and exclusive access recur. The combined synchrony and homology in one patterned domain after another implicitly convey meaning, albeit of a non-discursive nature.

Highly formalized textual traditions provide an apt conceptual analogy to our data in yet another respect. The notion of tradition implies, at one and the same time, both continuity and change. The structured patterns of any one document stand within a tradition. Some patterns are replicated; others are changed. The slightly changed pattern might convey a subtly different implicit meaning. For any informed reader conversant with the tradition, moreover, the nature and direction of the shift bears meaning in its own right. When what we expect is systematically redirected, the resulting irony or tension encourages a critique, if you will, of the implicit significance of the earlier pattern. That is, the diachronic shift from the "traditional" pattern to a slightly varied one, together with the synchrony of repeated encounters with the revised pattern, bear significance.

The usefulness of this analogy is clear. As noted, all of these services are adaptations of classical traditions and various authorized versions of them. To a high degree, moreover, congregants are aware of how their synagogue differs from others down the street. It is significant, therefore, when one Conservative congregation allows women to open the ark of Torah scrolls in full knowledge that another local Conservative congregation forbids them from doing so. The former synagogue says something implicitly about gender boundaries, or about social boundaries in general, which could not be said as effectively without a foil provided by the latter synagogue.

It would be facile to say that communication is exhausted by implicit meanings that are conveyed by homologous patterns of ritualized behaviour in one structured realm after another. As I have observed, liturgical texts either make theological statements or presuppose them. In addition, they frequently allude to the seminal mythic, or identity-grounding, events in the community's origin and development. The liturgy reinforces awareness of these events and thus generates a sense of religio-ethnic identity. But it would be equally facile to conclude that meaning is restricted to information conveyed by words. First, texts are by no means the only canonical aspects of liturgy. Second, all synagogue services, even in Reform synagogues, make extensive use of Hebrew. This language, though read (phonetically) by virtually everyone, is actually understood only by a minority. Most prayer-books of whatever affiliated movement provide facing English translations, it is true, but participants seldom actually read the English. Most tend to invest their effort primarily in following (or merely pronouncing) and chanting the Hebrew text. One is forced to conclude that much of the cogency has to do with what is communicated non-verbally.

My stress on implicit communication (through recurring homologous patterns and diachronic shifts) must be qualified in two further respects. First, congregations can offer explicit rationales for their particular adaptations of the authorized versions. They might say that separating men and women was abolished in their synagogue a decade or two ago, for example, because segregation by gender was deemed degrading to women, or because they wanted to promote the (nuclear) family by permitting whole families to sit together, or because doing otherwise would have discouraged potential new members from joining the synagogue. My claims about what is implicitly communicated are not intended to diminish the importance of explanations of congregants themselves.

This leads to a final qualifying claim. That which is communicated (the sum total of behaviour, gestures, spatial organization, texts and readings) is multivocal. Many things can be communicated simultaneously—some explicitly, others implicitly. Even with respect to the latter, several different but complementary meanings can be imparted. Indeed, the service permits contradictory meanings to co-exist in what is experienced as an integrated whole, the Sabbath morning service. Thus liturgical texts might refer to the People of Israel's chosenness and exclusivity while other behaviour signals an openness to crossing or even removing the boundaries that separate them from other peoples. For an ethnic minority in Canada's multicultural society, the value of both sentiments seems obvious. One might propose that the peculiar cogency of the service derives to some significant degree from its fundamentally multivocal character.

Let me sum up matters to this point. I have argued that recurrent structured patterns in service are communicative. They communicate meaning in terms of both synchronic and diachronic relations. Synchronically, homologous patterns exist in connection with similarly patterned behaviour encountered repeatedly throughout the service. Diachronically, participants experience many of these patterns as deliberate and controlled variations of the classical tradition as mediated by the "official version" of their synagogue movement. These are all the more communicative because participants know of, and have often directly experienced, alternative renditions in other synagogues. In relation to these other renditions, they view the practice of their own synagogue as more appropriate for themselves.

*Cogency and social commitments*

The fundamentally voluntaristic character of participating in one synagogue's service rather than that of some other one presupposes the cogency for regular participants of that which is communicated explicitly and implicitly by their own synagogue's particular rendition of the Sabbath morning service. One relevant factor, as I have said, is the theological or conceptual stance of participants. Some experience their own synagogue service as better, even if not ideally, suited to their own religious beliefs and policies. Members of a Conservative congregation might identify themselves explicitly with the theological stance of Conservative Judaism, which asserts that the classical tradition evolves continually in step with the historical experience of the Jewish people. This explains the appeal for them of a (that is, their) Conservative synagogue and its service.

But theological or conceptual stance takes us only part of the distance in understanding why a particular congregation evinces its idiomatic adaptation of the service, why the meanings encoded in that particular service are especially cogent for its members, or why its members have joined that congregation rather than some other one of either the same or a different affiliation. In defence of this last claim, we need appeal only to the fact that different Conservative synagogues in the metropolitan area produce significantly different renditions of the Sabbath morning service. It is difficult to see how the explicit world-view shared by everyone in the

Conservative movement gives rise to the unique features of any one service. In fact, the congregants themselves would be unable to account for more than a few aspects of their own synagogue's service.

For regular participants, therefore, other things must account for the character and cogency of their liturgical ritual. Particularly well-informed ones can offer "historical" anecdotes to account for some aspects of the service. When the new rabbi came, for example, this or that practice was changed at the rabbi's request. Or, an increasing number of members wanted mixed seating, and the board believed that they would join some other synagogue unless things changed. In these responses, social, political and financial aspects are given as the underlying causes of change.

Other people have explained that their parents, uncles, aunts and grandparents were active members of the congregation. The cogency of their synagogue's service lies, at least partially, in some kind of identification with family, the sense of trans-generational allegiance. Others say, likewise, that they "grew up" in a similar congregation elsewhere. Still others say that they joined a particular synagogue because their friends were members, or because they felt a great deal in common with other members. For some, the personality and style of the rabbi is given as a major factor. Less explicit responses are also forthcoming. Some congregants say simply that the "style" of the service suits them and/or their families; they feel "comfortable" at their congregation's service.

Explicit appeals to previous involvement of parents and grandparents, or to current participation of friends with whom they have much in common, point to the social dimension as a factor in the preference for one synagogue over another. By attending a particular service, individuals reinforce social ties to family and to people "like" themselves. In addition, their own sense of who they are and where they fit into the larger world (that is, their internalized social map) is bolstered by identification with similar people.

Remarks about the suitability of a liturgical "style" and statements about the "comfort" of that style refer to the positive emotional impact of the service as a whole. Those who provide these accounts must often be pressed for specifics. And, more often than not, questioners meet with minimal success. I propose that feelings of cogency, of self-evident appropriateness, are related to two things: what is explicitly communicated by the service and, equally, what is implicitly conveyed by what I have defined as the synchronic and diachronic relations of structured patterns within the service. As the studies of individual congregations repeatedly demonstrate, recurrent patterns usually have something to do with defining categories, establishing boundaries and acknowledging regions where categories may overlap. We have found that similar patterns occur in the formal ritual, per se, in the organization of sanctuary space and in the many other realms that, considered together, constitute the Sabbath morning service. To say that one is comfortable with the liturgical style, *grosso modo*, is to indicate that these patterns—along with the implicit and normative but non-discursive meanings thereby communicated—are experienced as particularly "fitting." Wherein, then, lies this sense of "fitness," of the cogency and self-evident appropriateness of a mapping effected by the service's structured patterns?

Informed by the work of Clifford Geertz (1966) and Mary Douglas (1973; 1975), I suggest that the cogency of implicit meanings (communicated in the sum total of a service's patterns) has to do with the homological fit between these patterns and others experienced by participants, especially their mapping of the social world. Some people try in other aspects of life to maintain hard and fast social categories, to make the boundaries between social groupings relatively impermeable. Not surprisingly, they often experience as "fitting" a service in which strict categorization and boundary maintenance recurs in feature after feature. Other people "grow up" in synagogues where services constantly open up, or soften, boundaries that are traditionally maintained and defended. Their social maps, relatively open to inter-group communication and concourse, seem self-evidently appropriate in light of what they have experienced at synagogue. Whether their social maps often predispose people to seek out synagogue services with certain styles, or whether the vectors often run in the opposite direction, I cannot and need not categorically state.

This, then, is the general conceptual framework of the larger research project from which the essays in this volume derive. The remainder of this essay accounts for a large swath of our findings in terms of it.

## Modalities of mapping the world implicit in the Sabbath morning services of Canadian synagogues

Anecdotal evidence already noted suggests that the particular Sabbath morning service of each congregation represents for regular participants a satisfying expression of Judaism, of Jewish ethnic identity and of more general social commitments, values or allegiances. I shall discuss this first in abstract terms and then with reference to some concrete data presented and analyzed in the essays that follow in Part 2.

Each congregation's service explicitly and implicitly expresses distinctive modalities of identity in both Canadian Jewish and Judaic terms. And each corresponds to a map of the social terrain in terms of both the local community and the larger one. This is not to say that individual services communicate a set of meanings corresponding to some comprehensive map of the social world. Quite the contrary. Our evidence suggests that the patterns indicated by any one synagogue's controlled variation of the "classical" and/or "authorized" liturgy, coupled with the awareness of variation from one synagogue to another, more often effects *in relation to those others* a revision, rejection or introduction of some key element in an existing, presupposed and common mapping. This sense of having a different stance is balanced by a correlative apprehension of what all stances have in common. One cannot be aware of varying some things without at the same time remaining cognizant of what does not vary. In this manner, congregants experience the patterns of their synagogue's liturgy as different from, but substantially like, that of other synagogues. Each patterning of the liturgy communicates sets of meanings that represent a *particular modality of* what, at some other level, participants consider *one substantially unitary and unified family of mappings*. (Only among Orthodox Jews of the extreme right wing are there groups that do not recognize as Judaism the practices of Reform, Reconstructionist or Conservative Jews of the left wing.)

In abstract terms, then, my first general observation is that our evidence indicates particular modalities of what participants experience as some unified class of mappings of the world, particularly of the social world—the class of mappings I call "being Canadian Jews." My second general observation, again expressed in the abstract, is that each patterning of the liturgy explicitly or implicitly tends to communicate sets of meanings relating to the issue of inclusion and exclusion from social categories. In our evidence, at least, these latter issues above all others seem to be the principal problematic being "worked out" in each synagogue's controlled variation of the Sabbath morning liturgy. For some synagogues, the main issue seems to be including different types of Jew within a single framework: within the congregation and, by analogy, within the larger Jewish community. In other synagogues, it is participating in the larger non-Jewish world, or integrating non-Jews and things non-Jewish generally into the Jewish world. Who may have concourse with whom, under what circumstances and in what realm? The goal, of course, is both to maintain a meaningfully unitary Jewish "world" and to allow for meaningful participation in the non-Jewish one. These appear in one instance after another of the liturgies which we studied. I turn now to some concrete data that illustrate and explicate these abstract observations. A discussion of the evidence for three congregations in particular—a Reconstructionist synagogue, a Reform temple and a *shtibl* (an Orthodox house-*yeshiva*/synagogue)—will serve my purpose aptly.

In chapter 8, Simcha Fishbane argues that the *shtibl*'s service attempts to (re)create for its participants the experience of membership in a small, elite and bounded world of the rabbinic academy (*yeshiva*). Well-institutionalized, well-structured and, often, fairly large rabbinic academies based on this "classical" eastern European model continue to function in many large cities of both Israel and North America (but also, to a limited extent, England and western Europe). These institutions represent within right-wing Orthodoxy the locus par excellence of power and authority; they are the only "true" centres of "Torah learning" (that is, mastery of classical rabbinic texts and codes). The *yeshiva*'s students and faculty represent the elite. To be a "true" rabbi is to have been educated within and, ideally, to stay within that milieu as a member of its teaching staff and/or as a perpetual student. Whether or not they attain the title of rabbi (*rav musmak*), those educated at a *yeshiva* and earning a living elsewhere are expected to contribute to its maintenance (including that of its students) and to participate regularly in its study sessions. One explicit goal of participation in the extra-*yeshiva* and extra-Jewish domain is to provide the economic wherewithal to maintain a primary focus throughout their lives on *yeshiva*-based Torah study.

The world of the "classical" *yeshiva*, even in its contemporary versions, is an entirely male domain. Its participants observe a strict code of dress and grooming (beards, black suits, often with three-quarter length jackets, black fedoras and white shirts with or without ties). Consequently, they are immediately identifiable as a class apart. These institutions actively exclude any influence, especially by cultural products, of the outside world. Secular productions such as newspapers, magazines, literature—especially movies and television shows—are considered either frivolous or corrupting. This exclusion encompasses not only the cultural world of non-Jews, but also, and perhaps especially, that of non-Orthodox Jews.

For members of the classical *yeshiva*, prayer takes place within the academy itself, typically in its *bet midrash* (study hall). An ark holding the Torah scrolls is situated on an eastern wall of the room. The same long reading tables and benches (or chairs) used at other times for study provide seating for male participants in the service. The head of the academy has a designated place at one of the tables. Instead of a professional cantor, several members of the community lead the service from a lectern or table designed to hold the Torah scrolls as they are unrolled for reading.

Women are present on Sabbaths and festivals. To accommodate them, temporary changes are made to the room. Their space is seldom defined by a permanent architectural feature; a curtain is usually drawn to set off one end of the room for their seats. Whatever the means used, the separation of women from men is complete. This eliminates the possibility that members of one sex might see members of the other. The women often do sit at long tables in their separate space, but in chairs set up in rows. A dress code stressing appropriate "modesty" is observed by all women. They must wear longish dresses with sleeves. Married women must wear some covering to hide their hair: a kerchief, hat or wig. Their clothing exhibits considerable variety in style and colour. Women often try to be "fashionable" within the limits of their dress code; they do not wear a female version of the men's "uniform." As temporary entrants into the *yeshiva* world, women are excluded from the institution's primary activity: Torah study. It should surprise no one to find that non-Jews are also excluded. Their presence is virtually beyond the imagination of those who attend services at a *yeshiva*, those who generally prefer not to pray in synagogues—even Orthodox ones—where participants invariably include Jews who are not fully Orthodox in observance.

The house *yeshiva* studied by Fishbane attempts to replicate a classical rabbinic *yeshiva*, in miniature, for its regular participants. Yet in a number of important respects it is patently not a classical *yeshiva*. Formed when a distinguished senior faculty member from a local *yeshiva* split with his colleagues, it has a single rabbinic "master." Some six to ten Orthodox members of the Jewish community, none of whom would be classified as the right-wing Orthodox associates of a classical *yeshiva* and its encompassing social sphere, have set up in a duplex this breakaway *yeshiva* for a senior rabbinic scholar. This rabbi lives in the upstairs apartment. Downstairs, he operates his *yeshiva* for some dozen or so part-time students. None of them, in appearance or ethos, would be taken as a classical *yeshiva* student. Some are the sons of the benefactors and pursue, in addition, studies at local universities. Both they and their fathers dress like most other people of their age and socio-economic status, except for small knitted skull-caps in the case of the "boys" and fashionable men's hats in the case of the adults. A few students hope to be granted the title of rabbi, although they are not necessarily studying at the *yeshiva* with that in mind. The senior rabbinic scholar provides them with post-secondary talmudic studies as an ongoing complement to their secular studies. From time to time, he takes on students for the express purpose of granting *smika*, Orthodox ordination as a rabbi. These latter students tend to come from outside the close circle of those associated in an ongoing way with the maintenance of and regular attendance at the *yeshiva*. Those seeking ordination tend to be professionals elsewhere in the Jewish community, men who would greatly enhance their career opportunities by attaining the title of rabbi.

The part-time students and the adult male benefactors (for the most part parents of the former) number 20 at the most and are the core of those who serve and are served by the house-synagogue's services and its resident senior scholar. At Sabbath and festival services, they are joined by the women of their households. The living room of the ground-floor apartment is set up as a classical (but small-scale) *bet midrash*. During the service, the students and male benefactors sit at tables according to an established pecking order, as they would at a classical *yeshiva*, but with the foremost adult benefactors sitting near the senior scholar. As in a classical *yeshiva*, there are no professionals charged with liturgical functions. The latter are carried out by the males in attendance. The women in attendance sit on chairs in an adjacent, smaller room. They can hear but not see the service in progress.

Here, then, is a community of those who, though patently not part of the classical *yeshiva* world, have constructed its likeness in miniature. But they have not done so in every respect. Missing is the expectation that its (male) adherents will commit themselves to *yeshiva*-based Torah study as the *summum bonum*, conform to a uniform set of behavioural patterns (that include, among other things, the wearing of a "uniform"), isolate themselves from most "alien" expressions of culture, and limit social involvement in the outside world to economic activities necessary for the financial viability of their families, their community and their *yeshiva*. None of the above characterize the patrons and participants in our *shtibl*'s services. Both students and benefactors have meaningful social relations (not merely of an economic nature) in the outside world, although close social relationships are invariably limited to other Jews. Both students and benefactors are regular consumers of Canadian culture: movies, television shows, magazines, literature and clothing (but on the modest, conservative side of what is "fashionable"). The students pursue studies at secular universities. Neither they nor their parents would promote Torah-learning to the detriment of university studies. They would, however, ascribe to the study of rabbinic documents a special and sacred status.

Our *shtibl* can be located on a continuum. On the right are "real" classical *yeshiva*-centred communities. On the left are modes of being Jewish that display greater and more meaningful participation in the general secular "world." The patrons of our *shtibl* have adopted and adapted the *yeshiva* model rather than the synagogue model (even the Orthodox synagogue). In doing so, they express an affinity for the former and a rejection of the behaviour and/or values they associate with the latter.

In short, our *shtibl*'s patrons explicitly and strongly identify with Torah learning (that is, the status accruing to those involved in ongoing Torah study with the aim of Torah mastery). On the other hand, the variety they permit in dress communicates their rejection of the classical *yeshiva* community's demand for uniformity and control, its negation of individually defined standards of personal development, advancement and status in the outside world. Only the senior scholar still wears the dress of the *yeshiva* faculty member. Only he devotes himself full time to the study and teaching of classical rabbinic texts. It is the senior scholar, then, who lends the authority and status of the classical *yeshiva* world to this community of his patrons and clients.

In the last analysis, the part-time students and their senior scholar preserve, at least partially, the notion of a community of the elite, the latter being defined by the importance of and ongoing participation in the study of classical texts. The adult benefactors themselves might not engage in ongoing study, but they lay claim to membership in the elite community by making it possible within their *yeshiva-shtibl*. At services, therefore, they are given all the kudos and honours (such as physical proximity to the head of the institution) that, in a classical *yeshiva*, would be bestowed only on Torah scholars.

What have the members of our *shtibl* community communicated in avoiding the model of the synagogue, even the modern Orthodox synagogue? Some facts about the latter are germane to any response. First, most modern Orthodox synagogues are no longer associated with classical Torah learning. This had been the case among first-generation immigrants from eastern Europe; they gathered in their synagogues several times a week or even every day to study small sections of classical rabbinic texts (the *hevra shas* and *hevra mishnayos*). Second, even Orthodox synagogues in the metropolitan area under discussion do not, by and large, boast of members who are serious observers of rabbinic legal proscriptions and prescriptions (that is, the observance of *halaka*). Even Orthodox synagogues are mainly heterogeneous and pluralistic in the sense that members differ vastly in their observance of and familiarity with Judaism (let alone its classical rabbinic texts). In Canada, for example, many members of most Orthodox synagogues do not observe the principal proscriptions associated with the Sabbath and festivals, do not adhere to rabbinic dietary laws and do not, for that matter, regularly attend synagogue. By contrast, the "members" of our *shtibl* and those who attend services regularly cannot be differentiated; they are one set of people. Virtually all are halakically observant in accordance with what might be considered modern Orthodox standards. In comparison with the average Orthodox synagogue, our *shtibl* is a rather homogeneous community.

In the social world as mapped by our *shtibl* members, a community of halakically observant Torah learners and supporters of Torah learning defines the inner circle. This inner circle is surrounded by other Jews and by non-Jews. As individuals, members of this inner circle might take from and seek achievement within the realms outside their own domain—so long as social and cultural intercourse does not result in the adoption of characteristics that undermine their membership in it. This mapping of the world remains decidedly different from that of both the classical *yeshiva* and the average synagogue (even the average Orthodox synagogue) as the members of our *shtibl* perceive it.

In terms of social mapping, the evidence from our Reform synagogue explicitly and implicitly communicates a set of meanings congruent with an entirely different social topography. The principal Sabbath service at this Reform synagogue (described in chap. 6 by Marc Lalonde, Louise Mayer and me) is held on Friday evening, not Saturday morning. In this respect, the synagogue adheres to what has been the norm for most of the last 50 years among Reform congregations in North America. Other typical characteristics include: the use of an organ accompaniment, prohibited on Sabbath and festivals in all Orthodox and virtually all Conservative synagogues; the mixed seating of men and women, an arrangement preferred in Reform, Reconstructionist and virtually all Conservative synagogues; and the extensive use of English in the liturgy, a practice that diminishes in popularity along the continuum from Reform to Reconstructionist to Conservative to modern Orthodox synagogues. The conduct of the service is left to professionals; this is typical of most large congregations, though, whatever the affiliation.

In our Reform congregation, the professionals included a male rabbi and a female cantor (*hazanit*). The latter was always referred to as "the soloist" in connection with her liturgical function. This is interesting not only because the title *hazan(it)* or its translation, cantor(ess), was explicitly avoided but also because the term "soloist," unlike the terms *hazan(it)* and cantor (or, for that matter, rabbi), did not function as a formal title at all. In direct conversation, the rabbi was generally addressed as "Rabbi [Surname]," as would be the case in virtually any other synagogue of any affiliation. In virtually all synagogues the cantor would be addressed as either "Cantor or Hazzan [Surname]" or "Reverend [Surname]." In direct conversation at our Reform synagogue, though, the soloist would be addressed as "Soloist [Surname]" no more than the soloist of a choir or orchestra would be. In other words, "soloist" remains a common noun describing a function discharged at a particular moment and in a limited context. It never becomes a salutary title referring to some inherent, reverential status or quality permanently affixed to someone who, by virtue of that status or quality, is deemed appropriate to perform certain sacerdotal functions. This refusal to recognize any inherent, reverential status or quality in their soloist provides an apt homology for other aspects of the service.

The sanctuary is spatially organized as an auditorium. The ark (containing Torah scrolls) occupies the centre of a raised stage (*bima*) that cuts across the width of the sanctuary. The rabbi's lectern-pulpit stands on one side of the ark, the soloist's table on the other. Rows of auditorium-like seats extend from the front of the stage (*bima*) to the rear of the sanctuary-hall. This spatial arrangement has become the norm in most North American synagogues, whether Reform, Reconstructionist or Conservative. A good many modern Orthodox synagogues have adopted this arrangement (though it is adapted, by means of a physical barrier, to accommodate separate seating for men and women). But in our Reform synagogue the auditorium or concert hall layout fosters one of the principal roles assumed by those who attend services: that of the engaged audience.

We were struck by three recurrent features of the Friday evening service. First, we noticed the relatively high degree of "controlled" change. On a week-to-week basis, different selections are made from the *Union Prayer Book*. So, too, the soloist regularly offers different musical renditions of texts. In the classical service of an Orthodox congregation, of course, prayers change according to the time of year. Indeed, readings from the Pentateuch and books of the prophets change from week to week. But these changes occur in accordance with a regular liturgical calender and in accordance with set rules. In other words, the "changes" are entirely predictable; they are not really changes at all from the perspective of an annual cycle rather than a weekly one. Innovation is primarily restricted to the rabbi's weekly sermon (formally, not part of the liturgy itself), which congregants expect to be newly composed for each Sabbath or festival service. In our Reform synagogue, the weekly changes are intended to be unpredictable; regular participants expect something new and different to happen every week.

Second, some features of the service did not vary from one week to the next. Among those that are invariably retained is the *kadish*. This doxology is recited by individuals as memorials on anniversaries marking the deaths of close relatives and within the mourning period immediately following these events. Also retained are rituals that, in the classical Orthodox and most Conservative traditions, are carried out at home within the context of family life. These include the lighting of Sabbath candles and related rites.

Third, our description highlights the degree to which the service is designed to foster congregational passivity. It is largely an observed liturgy rather than a performed one. This remains true even though most of those who attend the service do so regularly.

We have concentrated on the first feature. Especially interesting are the sharp contrasts with evidence adduced by Frida Furman in her studies of an American Reform synagogue (Furman 1987). By comparison, orchestrated change constitutes a principal feature and defines the character of the Friday evening services in our synagogue. This penchant for constant, unpredictable innovation aptly supports the third feature, namely, the penchant for congregants to observe and take in the liturgical performance rather than to participate actively in its performance. Regular change coupled with the presence of a "solo performer," after all, demand that they simply listen for what will happen next. What implicitly communicated "statements" about the world are supported by such regularized irregularity? More specifically, what social mapping is created by a liturgy to be "observed" silently (or at least quietly) by congregants?

Our data suggest that a significant proportion of those who attend on Friday evenings "perceive" an objective and autonomous Judaic realm outside of which they generally operate but from which they episodically derive "sustenance" (as opposed to locating themselves within and participating in it). Their religio-ethnic identity, in other words, is one that they take on occasionally as individuals and on a voluntary basis. Normally, however, they locate themselves outside this Judaic realm.

How does the synagogue service provide a synchronic homology for this mapping? The synagogue hall, located below and in front of the *bima*-stage, is adjacent to but beyond the Judaic realm proper. And, as our description makes clear, congregants in the hall do not ascend the *bima* for liturgical honours as they do in most other Canadian synagogues. All participants in the liturgy, including congregants to be honoured during the service, enter the sanctuary with the clergy at *bima*-level and are present on the *bima* from the service's beginning. Congregants in the hall limit their role primarily to watching and hearing what transpires on the *bima*. The *bima*-stage, especially the ark, is a portal to the Judaic realm. The values and teachings of Judaism are passed down to them by professionals and honoured participants on the *bima*. The rabbi, always known as "Rabbi [Surname]" has permanent access to this realm or permanently inhabits it. Interestingly, the soloist does not. When not performing her liturgical role, she is known simply as "Ms, Miss or Mrs. [Surname]."

In view of the social mapping at this Reform synagogue, it should be helpful to reconsider the importation of rituals—such as lighting the Sabbath candles—from home to synagogue. This phenomenon originates in the realization that many regular participants do not perform these rituals at home. But surely the experience of watching them done by professionals for and before one in a public setting differs substantially from performing them personally within the "normal" setting of one's own home. Again, participants are placed in the position of engaged observers within a special context, the synagogue, in which they "consume" things Judaic. This is consonant with the fact that some or many participants define their normal "social location" (including home life) entirely in terms of general, non-Judaic "territory." In this regard, it is interesting to note that regular attendance at the Friday evening Sabbath service surely discourages them from having Sabbath meals at home with their families. The foregoing takes on increased significance in view of our research on family-based rituals. Jewish families in the larger metropolitan area consistently identified the family meal on Friday evening as the most important family ritual. This was the case no matter what the level of traditional Sabbath rites they performed during the meal, and no matter what synagogue movement they had joined. Our evidence suggests, moreover, that the same is true of many members of our Reform synagogue (though not necessarily those who attend services on Friday evenings).

Entirely consistent with this interpretation are other data about this synagogue, its history and its policies. For many years the board asked its rabbis to perform mixed marriages (that is, marriages in which one partner had neither been born Jewish nor converted to Judaism). Indeed, we were told that a previous rabbi had co-officiated with Christian clergy at mixed-marriage wedding ceremonies. In fact, the performance of mixed marriages is contrary to the policy of the Reform movement. And expecting rabbis to perform weddings of this kind severely hampered the synagogue's recruitment of clergy through the 1970s and early 1980s (after the retirement of a rabbi who had served for over 40 years). The implicit assumption was that the life of the home and family could lie outside the "Jewish world" (that is, in the highly differentiated and heterogeneous secular world). Jewish partners in such homes might nevertheless "consume" the Judaic "substance" accruing from *personal* access to the Judaic sphere as mediated by Jewish professionals.

While Jews have privileged access to the Judaic via the synagogue, whether by birth or through conversion, they do not enjoy exclusive access. We thought it noteworthy that one of the regular participants on Friday evenings was a local Christian clergyman. He considered this permitted access to the Judaic realm essential to his appropriation of Christianity's Jewish roots. What better expression could be given to this hall in which individuals, qua individuals, come to consume whatever might be had from the Judaic realm? This Christian clergyman's regular attendance is consonant with other longstanding trends and traits of the congregation. The previously mentioned rabbi of 40 years devoted much energy to maintaining close relations with Christian clergy, and the synagogue planned many opportunities to host Christian clergy within its walls. Were the Christian cleric not a real person, he might have been invented.

In sum, the Friday evening service of our Reform synagogue implicitly communicates and accommodates a certain map of the social world. According to it, regular participants can "normally" inhabit general, non-Judaic, territory; at the synagogue, though, they can inhabit a distinctively Jewish territory, privileged access to its "goods and services" being attained through the mediation of professionals. People exercise this right of access voluntarily as individuals. And as individuals, they integrate into their "normal" lives the "goods" gained from the Judaic realm.

I turn, finally, to our Reconstructionist congregation. Again, the sets of meanings implicitly conveyed by its Sabbath morning liturgy can be seen to derive both from two sources: its diachronic relation to the "demands" of classical rabbinic tradition and law; and the synchronic contrast with the quite different adaptations of that tradition found in other congregations (especially local ones). Indeed, a salient feature of this congregation is the value it placed on becoming increasingly knowledgeable and conscious of its own stance and that of the Reconstructionist movement over against those of both other contemporary forms of Judaism and the classical tradition. As with the two congregations already discussed, the Reconstructionist congregation's service indicates patterns, and these communicate implicit meanings. These are particularly well suited to the way participants locate themselves as Jews, socially and culturally, within both the Jewish community and the larger non-Jewish one. For them, the fit is deeply satisfying; it confirms their complex array of social allegiances.

As described in my own essay (chap. 4) and in Madeleine Mcbrearty's (chap. 5), the Reconstructionist synagogue's Sabbath morning service repeatedly gives expression to basic norms and values. These are communicated in homologous patterns: the physical arrangement of seating; the architectural features of a multipurpose sanctuary; the flow and timing of the service; relations between the rabbi and the congregation during the service; and a controlled variation of the liturgical rules that attenuates the classical service's differentiation of participants by "caste" or gender.

First, we found repeated expressions of openness to and inclusion of the "other." As in Conservative and Reform congregations, men and women sit together, generally as family units. Because the congregation has embraced the view (now supported by both the Reform and Reconstructionist movements) that either matrilineal or patrilineal descent suffices to define children as Jews by birth, and because the congregation has for an even longer time permitted non-Jewish spouses of Jews to be full members, those who attend on a regular basis include several non-Jews as active participants (albeit with some limitations). The seating arrangement in the relatively small, multipurpose sanctuary requires people to sit closely together. This, combined with the way services are led by the rabbi (who also acts as the cantor), encourages a high degree of active participation. In this way, it is unlike the Reform synagogue.

Several conspicuous variations on the classical service give symbolic expression to the value placed on reducing differences that would otherwise divide people and on including the other. Utterly ignored are the traditional honours due to male descendants of the ancient priestly and levitical castes. Utterly ignored, in addition, is the tradition of reserving liturgical honours exclusively for men. After the rabbi has delivered his discourse/sermon, in a manner similar to that of his rabbinic colleagues in most modern Orthodox and Conservative synagogues, congregants are permitted to comment on, add to or even take exception to his remarks during a short period of open discussion. Respect is given to the rabbi both as a person and as a result of his rabbinic expertise. Consequently, he is usually addressed or referred to as "rabbi." Due to a sense of warmth toward him and, I would maintain, a sense of permissiveness born of the congregation's essential commitment to egalitarianism, he is often addressed or referred to as "Rabbi [First name]" rather than "Rabbi [Surname]." Even the ark's construction expresses this reaching out across "traditionally" maintained difference and distance. Its doors are made of transparent lucite and its back is actually the room's main window. Everyone can see through the doors, therefore, into a *sanctum* reserved for the Torah scrolls. Light from outside shines through the ark's interior and into the hall. We were struck by the maintenance of community with so little internal differentiation. In this respect, our Reconstructionist congregation is reminiscent of the *shtibl-yeshiva*. But the former radically differs from the latter in its fundamental openness to the other and its relaxation or elimination of distinctions. In our *shtibl,* of course, these distinctions constitute the *sine qua non* of membership in a bounded, quasi-elitist community of Torah scholars and their benefactors.

This fundamental difference—the attenuation of traditionally ascribed distinctions according to birth, caste and gender—is implicitly communicated in the liturgy's cadence. The chanting is interrupted on several occasions for other readings, commentaries and explications. The flow is interrupted, in other words, to include materials from outside. For those used to a traditional Orthodox service, these interruptions and inclusions are jarring; they break up an otherwise homogeneous and inviolate realm. But for those used to a Reconstructionist service, these pauses constitute an apt homology of the underlying commitment to "openness." Implicitly communicated here, as elsewhere, is the perception that homogeneous realms must allow entry to realms beyond them.

A second pervasive feature of this liturgy is its appeal to and valuing of critical analysis. Already explicit in the Reconstructionist movement's official prayer-book is the idea that traditional liturgical language must be examined, understood, critiqued and revised in view of contemporary, North American, liberal values. The Reconstructionist prayer-book has revised the traditional one wherever it seems to conflict with these values. Many congregants are aware, moreover, of exactly where these changes have been made. And such matters are often discussed. I have already observed that the rabbi's sermon (which, in style and use of classical rabbinic texts, generally resembles those of his modern Orthodox and Conservative colleagues) is followed by an open discussion. Great value is ascribed to discussion, debate and critical re-examination by everyone present.

Again, the various aspects of this liturgy communicate implicitly a fundamental mapping of the world, one that is particularly well suited to the social allegiances of congregants. A great many of them are professionals. Collectively their level of education is high. Virtually all have university degrees; many have post-graduate degrees. As highly educated professionals, their participation in the non-Jewish cultural and social spheres is decidedly more significant than would be the case for other members of the Jewish community. Yet these people maintain a strong sense of belonging to a specifically Jewish realm. It is a realm that remains fundamentally open to entry from the outside, however. At the same time, it is a realm from which individuals must make serious forays to participate meaningfully in the heterogeneous and non-differentiated realm of non-Jewish society and culture.

By way of summation, I have in this essay laid out a methodological and theoretical framework for collecting, organizing and interpreting the seemingly disparate types of information associated with liturgical conduct in individual congregations. In addition, I have attempted a synthetic rendering and analysis of the evidence from three of the six congregations discussed in the essays that constitute the bulk of this book. My analysis highlights three fundamental points. First, each congregation's liturgy is unique. Second, the various patterned realms that together make up the liturgical experience implicitly communicate sets of meanings, especially when viewed in two ways: on the diachronic axis, as controlled variations and adaptations of the classical liturgical tradition; and, on the synchronic axis, over against the adaptations found in congregations "down the street." Third, these sets of meanings fit a distinctive mapping of the social world; in view of this, the liturgy can be experienced by regular participants as particularly apt and satisfying.

With all this in mind, we turn in the next chapter to Fred Bird's general theoretical account of ritual as communicative action. This is followed, in the last chapter of Part 1, by my own attempt to describe the larger common context of a Canadian Jewish "civil religion." This is the backdrop for our discussions of meaning in synagogue liturgies for people who attend on a regular basis.

## Notes

1 A study of either bar/bat mitzvah or mourning rituals focusing more specifically on the home and family settings would legitimately result in complementary empirical studies with, in all likelihood, substantially different results. That is because a complex ritual operating in multiple contexts may have meaning within each context's system. Indeed, the practitioners themselves may not always be aware of, or agree upon, which context is the most salient at any one moment. On bar/bat mitzvah viewed in other, more broadly defined contexts, see Schoenfeld (1988; 1990; 1992).

2 Compare as well essays by Jick (1987), Gurock (1987) and Wertheimer (1987). This volume's concerns receive some attention, but are by no means the focus of, work by Prell (1989). Particularly telling of the lacuna to which I refer is the section on synagogues and communal rituals in the survey essay by W.P. Zenner and J.S. Belcove-Shalin (1988) on the study of North American Jewry from the perspectives of cultural anthropology.

# 2

# Ritual as Communicative Action

## FREDERICK B. BIRD

Rituals play a large and distinctive role in our lives. They affect the way we greet each other—kissing on both cheeks, shaking hands, making eye contact and so on—bury our dead, celebrate birthdays, mark the seasons and move from one stage of life to the next. They facilitate and colour the ways we interact with authorities, ancestors or gods. They influence the gestures by which we eat especially important meals and the ways certain days become genuine holidays rather than simply days off from work.

To discover why people perform rituals in so many settings, it is necessary to ask two different but related questions. First, how do ritual acts differ from non-ritual ones? Second, how do variations in the performance of these affect their meaning and impact? To these questions, another must be added: how can rituals—which occur at some of the most engaging, festive and memorable times in our lives—sometimes become annoying, bothersome or even boring?

The following essay[1] addresses these questions by focusing on only one aspect of ritual behaviour: its communicative character. This aspect is not always emphasized by ritual actors themselves. Inherent in ritual, nonetheless, is communication. The essay is divided into three major parts; these are about (1) the characteristic features of ritual; (2) ritual as communication; and (3) variations in performance and how they affect the appeal of rituals.

## Characteristic features: Ritual as drama

Scholars have adopted both narrow and broad definitions of ritual. According to the former, ritual is a formal liturgical act. According to the latter, it is an expressive, often dramatic aspect of all behaviour (Wuthnow 1987, 109). My definition is based on a mediating position (see Bird 1979). Ritual elements, as I have just observed, play a decisive role in almost all aspects of daily life: the way we greet each other, conduct trials, observe sports events, attend concerts and so forth. Nevertheless, confusion results from classifying all of these activities as a single phenomenon. I define rituals as symbolic acts that are intrinsically valued and usually repeated, ritual actors trying to behave in keeping with expected characters and roles by using stylized gestures and words.[2]

Whenever we act ritually, we use prepared oral or written scripts that, in varying detail, spell out how we should speak, gesture and place ourselves. Rather than acting discursively to choose our own words and movements, we follow guides that prescribe precisely what words we ought to say and what movements we ought to make. Although some rituals allow for moments of discursive speech—when sermons are delivered, for example, testimonials uttered or announcements made—these departures from text are highly stylized. As alternatives, they call attention to (and thus reinforce) the scripted character of ritual.

Special festivals or ceremonies often call for a mixture of actions that are scripted to varying degrees: reciting well-known chants, rereading texts, uttering familiar prayers and so on. These are interspersed with set pieces that allow for some extemporaneous speech or gesture, for the exchange of familiar stylized greetings as well as for opportunities to engage in fully discursive actions either between scenes or off-stage. Ritual, in short, is like drama. It involves acting according to scripts in stylized ways that, nevertheless, permit ad-libbing or other forms of personal rendition.

In ritual, people play the roles of characters required by their scripts. These characters vary according to the type of ritual. In greetings and formal interactions, for example, people take on the roles of "gentlemen" and "ladies" as these characters have been defined by traditions of courtly life in Europe, say, or China. Other modes of speech and gesture are intended to help people protect themselves and others from shame, to signal that they recognize and honour each other's status (Goffman 1963; 1967; 1969; Elias 1979, vol.1; see also Castiglioni 1959). Jews celebrating Passover are expected to play Israelites about to flee from bondage in the land of Goshen. Christians celebrating communion are expected to act in some ways as if they were sharing a last meal with Jesus. Those attending funeral services follow scriptural cues to act as mourners. Muslims at prayer assume the character of worshippers submitting to God. These examples could be multiplied many times. To express identification with these characters, ritual actors use various techniques: wearing special clothes, putting on make-up or masks, covering or uncovering their heads, wearing broad or narrow shawls and assuming whatever tones of voice or mentalities are considered appropriate. These characters are the personae people play as they enact diverse rituals during the course of their lives.

Sometimes, rituals call for the re-enactment by specific people of historical or legendary events. On Purim, for example, Jews re-enact the story of Esther, Mordecai and Haman. On Christmas, Christians re-enact the story of Jesus' birth. Except when they are deliberately re-enacting a story, ritual actors seldom identify themselves with specific historic individuals. More often, they identify themselves with generic characters. On Palm Sunday, Christians briefly take on some features of the crowd that waved palm branches to greet Jesus when he arrived in Jerusalem shortly before his death. On Sukot, Jews build huts as their ancient ancestors had done during the harvest season. Usually, in fact, the characters called for by ritual scripts are even more broadly defined. They are expected to act as "children of God," "devotees," "citizens" or "lords and ladies."

Mircea Eliade captured the mind-set of ritual actors when he argued that they view their ritual acts primarily as re-enactments (1957). He overgeneralized this insight in arguing that they typically try to re-experience the foundational events of primordial time. It is true that many rituals make indirect references to cosmological events (as they do in connection with Passover, Christmas and Ramadan) or formative events (when the Buddha was born, the Declaration of Independence signed or the Bastille stormed). But references like these are, in many rituals, either absent or elusive. The more pervasive phenomenon is simply the sense of following a script and identifying with the characters in it.

Basil Bernstein has made a useful distinction between elaborate and restricted communication codes. Elaborate codes allow people to express unique or idiosyncratic meanings. Such communication is characterized by pauses, personal qualifiers, and rephrasing as they search for gestures and words suitable not only for what they themselves want to do or say but also for what their audiences expect to see or hear. Restricted codes, on the other hand, use symbols and gestures that are heavily weighted with commonly assumed meanings (Bernstein 1973). When people act ritually, I maintain, they use restricted codes, not elaborate ones. Even if they offer particular interpretations or renditions, in other words, they do so in keeping with scripts created by restricted speech codes.

Since rituals can be either complex, longlasting ceremonies (such as spring and winter festivals) or very brief ones (such as greeting people, departing, courting, eating ordinary meals and going to bed), there is considerable variation in the degree to which people are aware of the several ritual roles to be enacted on a regular basis. Unless they are explicitly governed by religious codes, the brief rituals associated with eating, departing, courting, greeting or going to bed are seldom even acknowledged as such.

Rituals do not happen accidentally. They are scheduled for special times. These times might be determined by the passing seasons, days of the week, hours of the day or stages of the life cycle. Rituals often take place at moments of transition between activities. Even in connection with random encounters, ritualized greetings based on scripts often provide helpful ways of handling what would otherwise be awkward exchanges.[3]

The characteristic features of ritual can be seen by comparing ritual behaviour with non-ritual behaviour. Non-ritual behaviour is primarily (1) strategic; (2) customary; and (3) expressive. Ritual behaviour, on the other hand, is not.

Strategic acts are instrumental; people mobilize their energies, resources and connections, they threaten or reward others, in order to achieve goals. Strategic acts, moreover, are self-interested; people choose whatever means are most likely to serve their own needs. Strategic action, finally, is practical; people act, without undue concern for duty or obligation, in whatever ways seems to work (Habermas 1984; 1990). Max Weber referred to this as the "purposive rational" way of acting characterized by conscious attempts to weigh means, ends, and secondary consequences in order to maximize benefits against costs (1978).

Ritual, however, is not strategic. In ritual, people feel compelled to use words and gestures in ways that honour oral or written scripts. They feel constrained to imitate models (Durkheim 1961, 378-381). To pursue strategic objectives, it is true, they sometimes make use of rituals—ceremonies, taboos, honorifics—because of their power to influence or discipline. This use of ritual remains strategic, or instrumental, whether it is the result of cynical manipulation or deference to local customs.

Customary behaviour often includes ritual. Because observers occasionally use the words "customary" and "ritualized" in close connection to describe traditional routines, it is necessary to make clear the specific character of each. Acts are customary to the degree that they are the result of engrained and unreflective habits (Weber 1978, 25). Unselfconsciously, people follow customs with respect to the clothes they wear, the food they eat, the preparation of their food, the harvesting of their crops, the care they provide for their animals, the games they play and so on. Customary behaviour involves no conscious recognition of choice; no alternatives are seriously considered. Moreover, it involves no desire to excel according to some standard of performance; the best way to do something is simply the way it has always been done.

Ritual, however, is not customary. It is conventional. Unlike customary conduct, conventional conduct is deliberately chosen and consciously valorized as preferred and worthwhile (Weber 1978, 34). People feel compelled to comply with conventions—stylized forms of behaviour that conform to shared expectations—and feel obliged to offer rationales for failing to do so. And they consider this intrinsically worthwhile. At least for the duration of a ritual, they adopt the orientation of dramatic actors. Although many rituals are incorporated in social traditions, moreover, not all rituals are traditional. Some have been created very recently. These include rituals associated with modern political movements, religious communes, complex organizations and even cohabiting couples.

Expressive behaviour corresponds to what Max Weber identified as affectual action that is "dominated by the actor's special affects and feeling states" (Weber 1978, 25). Jürgen Habermas uses the term "expressive" to categorize actions influenced primarily by feelings (Habermas 1984, 23). Expressive acts include any that are shaped by individual taste, personal feelings (rage, envy, lust, joy, bravado and so forth) or aesthetic sensitivities. When acting expressively, people tune into their own feelings, moods or perceptions in ways that allow them to be themselves. Although they might respect and defer to accepted conventions with respect to artistic styles, they still want to reveal their own visions and convictions.

Ritual, however, is not primarily expressive (even though it can provide a powerful vehicle for the expression of strong feelings). In ritual, people act in accordance with scripts based on expectations set largely by others (although they sometimes create scripts for themselves). People worship, greet each other, honour authorities and respect taboos in stylized ways that call for them to express their feelings through the words and gestures of scripts. By using these scripts, ironically, they are often able to express their feelings more effectively than by doing so extemporaneously. Just as a script—which is to say, its art or poetry—limits the range of expression, it also increases the intensity of expression.

Even though rituals make use of scripts, there is no reason to conclude that they are necessarily traditional. People continually create new rituals. Sometimes, they do so purposefully; rituals might be created to celebrate recent achievements, say, or newly designated holidays. At other times, people do so incidentally and casually; rituals might be created as by-products of emergent interaction patterns in the organization of weekends, say, or meetings. A fiftieth wedding anniversary can be a very complex affair. It might include both traditional and emergent ritual acts such as the blowing out of candles on a cake or toasts for the fêted couple. It might also include non-ritual ones such as spontaneous socializing or spur-of-the-moment celebrations (Grimes 1992).

It is true that ritual can be used to achieve strategic goals, out of customary deference or to express feelings. But the state of mind characteristic of ritual, as such, corresponds to none of these. While performing rituals, people become actors. They call on valued scripts as the vehicles by which to realize their aims, defer to conventions and/or express their feelings. They become actors in particular dramas. This is true of momentary greetings no less than of prolonged ceremonies, of healing arts and ethnic festivals no less than of religious worship. Even representing their own individuality in these dramas, they follow scripts that provide appropriate words and gestures.

Ritual involves make-believe, as Richard Hayes has observed, in a double sense. During rituals, for one thing, people pretend to be the characters called for by scripts. Momentarily, they suspend the beliefs that govern non-ritual behaviour. Doing this over and over again, though, tends to reinforce and make real the beliefs that correspond to them, whether these invoke a supreme being, the unique character and status of a group or an idealized objective such as enlightenment or salvation (Hayes 1992).

In short, once again, ritual performances are very much like theatrical ones. Nevertheless, they differ in several significant ways. Rituals never consist simply of retelling older stories. When retelling does occur, as it does in many congregational rites, the narrative presentation is always associated with a current enactment that is experienced by participants as both compelling and worth doing. When people enact a ritual, in other words, they do so not only because they think of it in terms of drama, something desirable or entertaining, but also because they think of it in terms of morality, something that ought to be done (Durkheim 1974, part 2).

In his analysis of synagogue services, Samuel Heilman used Goffman's framework to identify the dramalike character of these rituals. He examined several aspects: the setting; differences between on-stage performance and backstage activities; and the roles played by several groups of people constituting the dramatis personae (1976). This kind of analysis can be extended much further. To appreciate fully the dramatic character of all ritual acts (and not just congregational ceremonies), it is necessary as well to analyze the dramatic tensions and developments within the scripts themselves, the ways particular groups stage and perform these scripts, and the ways individuals render their characters. The next step in the process of developing a more nuanced appreciation of the drama-like character of ritual acts, then, is to examine in greater depth their communicative character.

**Ritual as a medium of communication**

Whatever else people might be doing when they engage in ritual acts, they are communicating with each other and with themselves. Depending on the particular ritual, they communicate feelings, recognitions, codes for conduct, beliefs, legends, myths, philosophies and so forth. Ritual is a unique medium of communication. Typically, it is both compact and multidimensional. Through ritual, people communicate in several different ways at the same time. As a result, ritual is a particularly rich medium. Failure to recognize this has led to many misleading and reductionistic accounts. Rituals cannot be understood adequately, for example, as the mere enactments of beliefs and legends, even though they have often been treated this way. Challenging this overly cognitive interpretation of ritual, I could argue with equal validity that myths and philosophies are the aetiological and discursive elaborations of ritual dramas. Still, even this account would be too narrow. These opposing accounts, even if reconciled, represent no more than a few of the many ways in which ritual communicates. Both fail to explore the more immediate ways in which it facilitates communication among the ritual actors themselves.

Rituals often use several different media at the same time: word, gesture, rhythm, music, setting, staging and so forth. Typically, there is no correlation between the uses of these media and the different kinds of communication they transmit. Rather, the former characteristically reinforce, intensify and heighten the latter—that is, meanings, self-representations and feelings (Tambiah 1979). I refer in what follows to five forms of communication associated with ritual: (1) constitutive; (2) self-representative; (3) expressive; (4) regulative; and (5) invocative.[4] The first four are found in all ritual acts; the fifth is found only in religious ones. Although all religious rituals can be analyzed in terms of each form, particular rituals are likely to highlight one or more of them.

*Constitutive communication in ritual*

Ritual acts bring certain realities into being or into play. This statement is obviously true of a few rituals in particular; weddings, inaugurations and ordinations explicitly announce and initiate new conditions in which people enjoy new statuses. It is also true, though, of rituals in general. As a form of speaking, rituals function as what John Austin calls "performatives" (1961). By means of these words and gestures, actors give rise to situations that focus their attention. Their scripts, more precisely, provide outlines of the new realities much as the basic rules of football, hockey and chess do (Searle 1969, 34). When two people embrace and kiss each other on both cheeks, for example, they reconstitute themselves in a particular kind of friendship no less than they call attention to the existing friendship. Changes in the form of greeting mark developments in the relationship, but they also create these developments. When people who had once been heterogenous individuals worship together, as members of the early Christian movement in Antioch did, the act of doing so constitutes (or reconstitutes) them as a group just as it symbolizes their commitment to one another. When two acquaintances engage more and more often in sexual intercourse, which can be a highly stylized and ritual-like activity, they not only affirm what was already a special friendship but also constitute and reconstitute themselves as a couple.

It is important to think about all this because of the pervasive tendency to consider ritual merely decorative. To be sure, ritual can be decorative. Examples include the formal prayer that begins a public meeting, say, and the perfunctory grace before a domestic meal. It could be argued that few people present pay much attention to these acts or enter very far into the worlds of thought represented by their words and symbols. Are these rituals not like the applause after someone sings the national anthem at a baseball game? The burst of enthusiasm and conviviality that arises after largely decorative rituals often seems to express nothing more than relief that this bit of solemnity is now over and everyone can get on with whatever it is that really matters. But this line of reasoning can easily become superficial. Even in these cases, after all, ritual invokes the social membership shared by all participants.

For most participants, ritual is something more than a decorative frill. Rituals are constitutive to the degree that events would be markedly different without them. Consider a family that celebrates the Sabbath at home. Doing so reconstitutes it as a Jewish family. It also asserts that they the family has decided to become more observant. Regular re-enactment of this ritual introduces family members to dimensions of their Jewishness not previously experienced. As William James observed (although he focused on inner feelings more than external events) the regular practice of a stylized and ritually conditioned activity, such as prayer, not only provides an occasion for people to think about God but also fundamentally qualifies their experience of reality so that God seems real and present to them (1961, chaps. 3; 19). Without this action, he argues, one has philosophy but not religion.

By means of congregational rites, individuals signify the groups of which they are part. They also reconstitute these groups with themselves as members (Jay 1992, chap. 1). Rituals of this kind bring about states of consciousness that are integral to, and the necessary condition for, any sense of groups as living realities. By means of collective sacrifices and communal festivals, congregations establish and re-establish themselves not only as identifiable groups but as groups with specific qualities. Consider, once again, my analogy between ritual and theatre. If they act well, the individuals staging *Romeo and Juliet* reconstitute, first for themselves and then for their audience, the fictive world of Shakespeare's Verona. Likewise, ritual actors reconstitute the world-view envisioned by their scripts. Unlike thespians, though, ritual actors typically view the world thus created—its statuses, social contours and interrelationships—as fundamentally real (Geertz 1973, chap. 4)—even "more real," in some cases, than the ordinary workaday world.

*Self-representative communication in ritual*

By means of ritual, people represent themselves to themselves. To be sure, rituals also represent them to others. People adopt the clothes they wear, the forms of polite address they assume or the stylized deportment they exhibit partly to show themselves favourably to others involved in the same rituals. I will examine this further when I discuss the expressive character of ritual. Here, I want to analyze the intrinsically reflexive, self-representing aspect of ritual. As people engage in rituals, they make statements about who they take themselves to be. Momentarily, they identify themselves with the character/roles called for by their scripts. In doing so, they assert the importance of various character traits. According to Edmund Leach: "We engage in rituals in order to transmit collective messages to ourselves" (1976, 45).

This reflexive, self-representing character can be observed easily enough. When people shake hands after an argument, for example, they are representing themselves as civil and reasonable beings. When Jewish families mark their meal on Friday evening with a ceremony, they are representing themselves as one of many families doing the same thing at the same time; they are thus bound together with other families of the past, present and future. Variations in congregational rituals can reflect differences in theological beliefs. But variations also reflect (often more decisively) differences in how these groups think about themselves. When churches assign families to designated pews, they reaffirm the church as a community of families. When churches offer worship marked by the skilled performances of professional choirs and organists, they reaffirm the church as a community of professionals who are used to hiring other professionals in order to get their work done and their families tended. This reflexive self-representing can be seen very clearly in the ritualized practices of meditation. Transcendental meditators, for example, represent themselves to themselves as fundamentally single persons, defined not by thoughts or feelings, however tortured or idealized, or by any relationships, however stressful or fulfilling, but by their own affirmation of themselves as living and breathing selves grounded ultimately in the creative intelligence of Being. The ritual of meditation allows individuals distance not only from the expectations of both themselves and others but also from their own drives and appetites; they can thus represent themselves as self-constituting and autonomous egos (Bird 1978).

In ritual action, this reflexive self-representing typically occurs immediately and unselfconsciously. By means of ritual, people identify themselves directly, without discursive reflection, as (temporarily) the characters whose parts they take. This immediate self-representing to themselves can be seen in the various forms of congregational worship. In some cases, people remain relatively passive, like the audience at a drama staged by others. In other cases, they participate more actively (either because they are like members of a Greek chorus or because they respond movingly and often vocally to the roles played by central characters). By taking more or less active roles, by gaining more or less skill in singing, chanting, and reciting, people not only affect the character of worship but also represent themselves as being, in different ways and to varying degrees, consumers of these activities: audiences; constitutive members of self-constituting associations; adepts staging their own dramas; students; disciples and so on.

The significance of ritual as a medium for self-representation is affected by the relation of particular rituals to others in which they also participate. Household rituals (such as grace at meal time, evening prayers and holiday celebrations) often assume added meanings by echoing symbols and miming gestures that were enacted in congregational or communal rituals. The opposite is also true: congregational rituals often allude to and incorporate elements from domestic ones. Ritual self-representations can be fully understood only by examining the full range of their enactments.

Whenever choices are made among different types of ritual—whether these be in congregational, family or individual settings—the meaning of ritual as a means of self-representation can be discerned by considering the kinds of ritual gestures that are excluded. When people choose to participate in rituals using non-vernacular languages, for example, their choice is a way of representing their own sense of identity in relation to scriptural or sacred languages.

*Expressive communication in ritual*

Ritual provides an opportunity to express intense and highly charged emotion. This expressive character of ritual is evident not only in emotionally voluble contexts (such as funerals, weddings and births) but in almost any context. Stylized greetings transmit strong affection. Stylized cheers and handshakes after a football game, for example, provide a way of expressing either elation and pride or despondency, frustration and resolve.

Ritual expresses feelings in particular ways. These are neither simple, however, nor direct. Thomas Scheff has argued that ritual enables people to acknowledge and express feelings in ways that avoid the extremes of having to repress them or of allowing them to become overwhelming. He studied the ways people use ritual to express grief, fear, embarrassment and anger at a fitting aesthetic distance; through ritual, they avoid both the pain of those engulfed by these emotions and the emotionlessness of those denied permission to express emotion (Scheff 1977). Building on Freud's theory of hysteria (Freud and Breuer 1974) and Jacklin's theory of re-evaluation, Scheff argues that rituals often facilitate the cathartic release of distressing feelings by actions that allow those involved to retain a strong sense of themselves as individuals. Just as puppets sometimes allow children the freedom to express their own feelings, rituals allow people the opportunity to express feelings that might otherwise be either unacknowledged and unexpressed or all-encompassing and overwhelming. Rituals allow people to channel and express their grief in connection with losses as well as their hopes or anxieties in connection with healings. Although rituals do this sort of thing, Scheff's moderate and Aristotelian account is too simple. It provides an inadequate basis for understanding sacrificial rites, for example, or the relation between ritual and pleasurable emotions.

Mary Douglas' analyses nicely complement those of Scheff. She argues that ritual fosters the expression of feelings wherever people would otherwise be likely to babble or remain inarticulate. At weddings, funerals and encounters with casual acquaintances, ritual characteristically provides a vehicle for people to speak up and communicate congratulations, condolences and so forth (Douglas 1974). When these forms are not readily available, people often worry about not knowing quite what to say. This is obviously true when they encounter suffering or grieving people, for instance, and when they encounter people they meet only occasionally. Geertz has described a Javanese funeral at which the temporary unavailability of ritual forms led not only to confusion but to considerable hostility as well (1973, chap. 7).

People often use ritual to communicate intimacy. Observe the degree to which they address their intimates using both nicknames and common stylized phrases such as "dear," "Mommy," "sweetie" and "brother." As Bernstein argued with respect to restricted speech codes generally, repeated and stylized terms of this kind are used not to convey information but to re-invoke feelings. These terms of address along with the stylized gestures that ordinarily accompany them—hugging, looking in each other's eyes and smiling, caressing each other, placing hands on shoulders or waists—provide opportunities to communicate recognition and love, to re-affirm the relationship's value and importance. Discursive talk in these settings can be experienced as distracting noise that calls attention to one of the people involved or to a particular problem rather than to the relationship itself. Discursive speech is likely to abolish the state of intimacy and replace it with the state of processing information or making choices. To avoid these distracting conditions, people often resort to shared silence. By itself, however, silence neither creates nor evokes the sense of intimacy in the way that stylized and ritually uttered terms of endearment do.

We seldom recognize the ritual character of intimate address. This is partly because these forms of communication seem so natural, so familiar, so personal. It is also partly because we tend to associate rituals with more formal settings. Nonetheless, people do use these stylized forms. In doing so, they identify themselves with generic characters invoked precisely because they are so well suited to the expression of intimacy. As Erving Goffman has demonstrated with personal encounters in general, these stylized gestures and forms of address enable people to perform simply and harmoniously a number of exchanges: recognizing other people; acknowledging their status and the claims they might make; re-asserting their own status and claims; and invoking earlier exchanges (Goffman 1967; see also Fingarette 1971).

If worship is an intimate interaction with whatever people consider sacred, then, by extension, rituals enable them to be articulate when they would otherwise be silent or speak up in ways likely to be distracting and alienating. It is true that philosophical and theological discourse provide fitting ways to think about sacred realities and to communicate whatever theories emerge. And the gods of philosophers and theologians might well be the same gods that ordinary people worship through their traditional liturgies and other forms of piety. But the discursive speech patterns of philosophy and theology are fundamentally misunderstood if they are thought to be ways of interacting with the gods. That is what stylized and repetitious liturgies are for. They provide the terms of endearment that communicate closeness to the gods or to any other form of the sacred. To be sure, the vocabulary of worship varies from one tradition to another—from simple Quaker meetings to highly elaborate Orthodox Jewish liturgies. Each expresses a distinctive experience of the relationship. All, however, are rituals.

So people use ritual to express intense and intimate feelings. In doing this, however, they often express multiple or even disparate feelings. Ritual provides vehicles for the expression not only of simple and isolated feelings—unadulterated joy, sadness, affection or anger—but also of more complex and inter-related feelings that involve ambivalence and tension. Consider funeral rituals. These typically provide vocabularies and settings for the expression not only of sadness itself but also (usually in sublimated forms) disappointment, anger, uncertainty over how to cope and affection for other members of the community. Funeral rites structure settings in which people can act out both the love they feel for the deceased and the revulsion they feel for the corpse. Now consider the ceremonies associated with royalty. These typically provide ways of expressing admiration for rulers because of their status, accomplishments and power. At the same time, they provide ways of expressing envy and anger caused by the fact that rulers enjoy privileges denied to everyone else. As Freud observed, these ceremonies both honour rulers and cut them off from ordinary social intercourse (Freud 1950). The same is true of wedding ceremonies. The families involved usually feel most of the following: bravado at getting their children married; sadness over the childhoods—and supposed innocence—that are being left behind; sadness over the departure of children establishing homes of their own; and discomfort as well as pride over the alliance with strangers being established. Funerals, royal ceremonies and weddings set forth fairly complex scripts with both plots and subplots, both texts and subtexts.

Rituals of many other kinds enable participants to express multiple, strong and conflicting feelings (Lévi-Strauss 1979a). The handshake, after all, is at once a form of greeting, a testing of strength or forthrightness and a demonstration that no weapons are hidden. Freud argued perceptively that almost all taboo rituals exhibit simultaneously both attraction to and distance from an object: directly, they express rejection and/or denial; indirectly, though, they bear witness to secret desires (Freud 1950).

Several observers have pointed to the characteristic ambivalence of sacrificial rites (Girard 1977; Jay 1992; Freud 1950; Burkert 1985; Mack 1987). Through sacrifice, participants engage, whether directly or symbolically, in the act of killing. They witness and tacitly approve the killing of an animal or even a human being. The victim is offered to a god, usually through some form of burning or cooking. Then, at a ceremonial feast, parts of the sacrifice are either directly or symbolically consumed by participants. Because sacrifice involves giving something up to a god, it has an element of self-sacrifice. But because participants are either directly or symbolically nourished by the substance being sacrificed, this is usually balanced by gratitude. Sacrifices embody ambivalence toward the fundamental and universal phenomena of living and killing. In order to live, people must kill or destroy. They do so either by hunting animals or by killing other people (often those most likely to strike first). Sacrificial rites provide opportunities to express ambivalence toward a supreme authority and also toward the sacred objects through which they hope to influence this authority. The tension is especially evident when people use ritual to honour totemic creatures as symbolic representatives of themselves. These totemic creatures are taboo with respect to ordinary hunting and are thus preserved. When sacrificed, of course, they are killed and consumed. Freud and others have found strong hints that these rites allow people to do two things at once: to project onto sacrificial victims anger at being controlled and manipulated by the gods; and to express veneration of and identification with these same gods (Freud 1950; Girard 1977). Sacrifice allows people to express their feelings and, at the same time, to achieve an inner balance. They become neither openly rebellious nor slavishly compliant. They remain loyal subjects and supporters but also autonomous beings.

But ritual communication is seldom direct and discursive. It rarely makes feelings self-evident on a cognitive basis. Instead, disclosure is balanced by closure. By the latter, I refer to privately coded gestures and words whose meaning is recognizable only indirectly to participants. It is possible to acknowledge feelings that would otherwise have to be suppressed as dangerous, anti-social or troubling—feelings such as loss, shame, jealousy, remorse and resentment—precisely because they are acknowledged safely (that is, symbolically). Like poetry and music, ritual both arouses and stills the emotions. Like poetry and music, ritual intensifies emotions but does so by channelling them through standardized aesthetic phrases, rhythms, and tonal signals that translate subjective feelings into objective forms.

*Regulative communication in ritual*

Ritual is a primary vehicle for communicating the highly valued beliefs and moral codes that, together, regulate communal life. The most immediate context for learning these is a cycle of rituals in which legendary or mythic lore is propagated through recitation, music and dance. To participate regularly in these rites is to hear of, recognize and reaffirm these stories and the beliefs they embody. Different beliefs might be cited at weddings and births, at spring festivals and new year ceremonies, at weekly services and daily prayers. But the cumulative impact is to assemble a larger collection of myths and beliefs as they are popularly recognized and understood. These are regularly cited, in turn, to justify communal mores. In this way, ritual plays a pedagogical and socializing role. As children participate, they become aware of the beliefs and standards of their elders.

Clearly, rituals are very important when it comes to moral education. To be sure, moral education can also take place either formally at school and informally at home. Much attention has been given to the effective ways of promoting moral education in these settings. Sometimes, formal education is instituted to prepare people for particular rites, especially those associated with puberty, initiation and marriage. Participants are often thoroughly trained not only to perform the expected rituals with skill and aplomb but also to know communal lore. This kind of preparation still constitutes formal schooling. Participation itself, though, can be considered a powerful form of moral education; it gives people a lively sense of communal mores.

This pedagogical function can be illustrated by looking closely at many rituals. Think of the way weekly synagogue services enlighten children with regard to the reasons for allocating honour and status, the importance of traditional stories and language as points of reference for everyday life, the deference to be shown toward learning and wisdom, the importance of observance, as well as the freedom enjoyed by individual participants to talk during some parts of the service as long as they continue to express loyalty and compliance during other, highly valued, parts. Many other illustrations could be discussed—weddings, funerals, Thanksgiving, Passover and so forth. One is particularly interesting in the context of moral education: the *kadish*, a prayer adult male Jews recite daily for one year after the death of a parent. Three times a day, the son is expected to join with at least nine other men, thus forming a *minyan*, to repeat this standardized Aramaic prayer. In doing so, he expresses solidarity with other bereaved men of his own generation and, in addition, with that of his parents. Moreover, they put themselves in a position to develop their liturgical skills. Finally, they learn the value of cooperation: being ready to help another mourner by taking part in the *minyan* (without which the *kadish* could not be said as a public ritual). As a result, many middle-aged Jewish men become much more active participants at synagogue. In practical terms, this ritual often brings back into the Jewish milieu men whose careers had led them away from it.

Rituals are models for how men and women, parents and children, and members of the community should interact. Life-cycle rituals help define and order life through stages from birth through adolescence, marriage, middle age, old age and death. Seasonal rituals establish a pattern for the year, setting aside certain periods as especially important. Weekly rituals organize everyday life in terms of weeks and weekends. In all of these ways, rituals establish patterns and thereby regulate social interactions.

*Invocative communication in ritual*

Some rituals are practised in order to bring about desired states of being by invoking gods, spirits, powers or other sacred realities. The best examples are shamanistic rituals. By singing and dancing, beating on drums or reciting incantations—all highly stylized activities—shamans invoke spirits in order to heal. In the process, they might communicate from a distance or even transport themselves spiritually to another world. Shamans enable their clients to visualize, and thereby express in mythic language, either the malady that is distressing them (Lévi-Strauss 1979b) or the events that led to it (Turner 1969). At one level, these rites unlock healing powers simply by allowing subjects to confront otherwise repressed feelings. At another level, they enable subjects to focus their consciousness intensely on gaining help from powers that would otherwise be inaccessible.

Invocative communication is present in many other kinds of ritual as well. Consider thaumaturgical formulae or incantations. These are used widely in rituals for divining, healing, fortune-telling and charming. In some cases, they are uttered by respected seers, palmists or astrologers. In other cases, they are uttered by untrained, ordinary people as they say prayers before sports contests or battles. Formal invocations are often made before public meetings, especially political gatherings, as a form of polite civility. The idea is to ensure that these occasions are peaceful and successful. Then, too, invocative communication plays a major role in meditation. By focusing one's mind in this way, it is hoped, higher states of consciousness will be attained.

People participate in religious rituals partly because they hope to gain blessings. By "blessing," I refer to the sense of possessing some extraordinary, charmed power that enhances well-being or attracts good fortune and wards off forces or circumstances likely to produce the opposite result. In secular terms, "blessing" refers to the sense of enhanced self-confidence or of being lucky. Either way, people believe, participating in a ritual can lead directly to good fortune. Blessings assume many forms: the sense of peace or grace after receiving the eucharistic elements, say, or the sense of healing after shamanistic rites. Blessings are associated with pilgrimages, moreover. They can be attained merely by being in a holy place. They can be "caught" by contagion from others at the same place. And they can be sustained by returning with souvenirs—vials of holy water, copies of ancient sacred scrolls, amulets and so forth—that embody the holy place. In Jewish liturgies, blessings are transmitted from the Torah scrolls by those who carry them, read from them and kiss them (or touch them first and then kiss their fingers).

In all of these examples, people who come in contact with sacred objects—whether by eating eucharistic elements, circumambulating holy shrines or touching revered scrolls—gain in social status by doing so. Their sense of gain is proportionate to the difficulty in making contact and the proximity of contact. But augmented social esteem is only one feature of these ritual interactions, probably a minor one. Most important is the sense of gaining privileged access to an otherwise distant or unavailable power.

The extent to which religious rites seem to transmit blessings is directly correlated with the degree to which these rites are invocative. Their invocative character results from the integration of two quite different perspectives: the sense that sacred objects are close (relatively accessible) and the sense that they are remote (relatively inaccessible). Emile Durkheim argued that sacred objects, if they are to remain sacred, must be sealed off from ordinary access by fortified walls (taboos and other restrictions); if they are to become a source of blessing, on the other hand, some leaks (but not too many) must be allowed. The use of non-vernacular language in rituals can help preserve this aura of otherness (see Mcbrearty 1987) as can the use of special clothing.

In all these examples of invocative ritual, once again, gestures and words are used to establish communication with sacred realities. The latter, of course, are considered capable of bringing about desired states of being. People do not seek this result directly by using ordinary methods of altering social interactions or biological conditions (even though the desired result might be defined in terms of social and biological changes such as the healing of a disease, the finding of water, the winning of a battle, the resolution of a conflict and so forth). Instead, they seek the desired result indirectly by using stylized gestures and utterances.

These gestures and utterances consist of iconic symbols that seem to have unusual power. Symbols of this kind are not signs for which one figure might easily be substituted for another; they are representations that are integrally and intimately linked to sacred realities (Tillich 1957). If used casually, they would lose their significance. Using them is taboo, in fact, except under specific circumstances. They are charged with special significance because those who use them have already been blessed by doing so on earlier occasions. These empowering experiences might result from the collective effervescence that arises from collective participation in ceremonies (Durkheim 1961, book 2, chap. 7); from the releasing of otherwise subconscious feelings (James 1961, chap. 19); and/or from the resolution of otherwise intractable conflicts (Lévi-Strauss 1979a). The symbols themselves, with their corresponding ritual practices, assume a special aura. They are invocatively powerful.

Ritual scripts often call for repetitive acts performed in prescribed sequences. When performed well, they raise and reinforce expectations. These expectations, in turn, facilitate effective performances (Tambiah 1979).

*Ritual communication and feasting*

Many rituals include some form of feasting, either directly or symbolically. At morning worship, or *puja*, Hindus offer bits of food to their gods. At the eucharist, similarly, Christians share small portions of bread and wine. Once meat or produce is offered to the gods in sacrificial rituals, participants usually feast on what has been sanctified. Often, to be sure, the feasting occurs not as part of the formal ritual but as an accompaniment. After the formal rite of circumcision, for example, Jewish parents host a feast for their guests. Elaborately prepared food is served either by or for a bereaved family. Wedding ceremonies are almost everywhere followed by feasts. Following a formal bar mitzvah or bat mitzvah, Jewish parents present a *kidush* (feast inaugurated by the blessing over wine) for their guests. At both churches and synagogues, weekly morning worship is often followed by an informal gathering at which refreshments are served.

In all these settings, serving and eating food is a communicative activity and not just a means of consuming nourishment (Douglas 1984). As Douglas has observed: "Food is not feed" (1982, 117). In connection with ritual in particular, eating assumes considerable symbolic significance. It is worth exploring in more detail the very interesting ways in which special foods are used in particular rituals, such as bread and wine in the eucharist, and how they are associated with specific meanings. What follows is a study of the relation between food and ritual. Of particular importance are the ways in which eating together reinforces and embodies the communicative aspects of ritual.

To begin, I must note several characteristics of the relation between food and ritual. People serve food, for example, that in some way represents themselves as a group: food they especially like; food of the kind they have eaten previously at well-remembered celebrations; and food they associate with their ethnic heritage. On ritual occasions, moreover, people serve foods that would be classified as special treats. Food of this kind often includes items, such as wines or cakes, that are somewhat more expensive than daily fare. Outsiders are excluded from these feasts. (Sometimes outsiders exclude themselves; they might dislike the food served or be unfamiliar with it.) Ritual food is served by some for others. It is a gift. Like all gifts, though, it is part of an exchange (Mauss 1967; Titmuss 1970). At weddings, funerals, circumcisions, bar mitzvahs and bat mitzvahs, the gift is extended partly in exchange for the attendance of guests. Still, there is another aspect of this exchange to consider: those who willingly accept the gift of food in these settings assume an open-ended obligation to return the invitation (Gouldner 1960).

Eating together—eating in the presence of each other, serving food to each other, receiving food from each other—establishes and reinforces the sense of intimacy. Those who eat together regularly are either families or like families. By eating together, people reconstitute themselves as identifiable groups, represent themselves to each other as such and express their sense of connectedness. This kind of communication occurs immediately, whether or not the occasion involves deep conversation. Small talk, in fact, is cherished precisely because it does not distract from the sense of being part of a larger gathering.[5]

*Thick communication*

Ritual facilitates several forms of communication at the same time. These differ from ordinary, discursive forms of communication in being both richer and less direct. They are both multilayered, in other words, and compact. Typically, their function is not so much to transmit information but to communicate self-recognition, intense and ambivalent feelings, moral principles and invocations. These forms of expressive communication play a vital role in human interactions—a role no less vital than strategic communication used to accomplish particular ends or discursive communication used to achieve understanding or agreement.

The dense, multidimensional character of ritual communication can be appreciated by analyzing any one of numerous examples. Think of the very simple act of saying grace before a family meal. From a theological perspective, this ritual is considered a form of communication with God. As social scientists, of course, we can neither accept nor reject theological claims. But we can observe the several ways in which this ritual fosters other forms of communication. In the first place, it obviously plays a constitutive role in family life. By saying grace together, individuals constitute themselves as a family for the purpose of this meal. Not incidentally, they also establish a clear beginning for the meal. At a time when family members seldom eat all their meals together, or when they seldom begin or finish eating at the same time, saying grace together constitutes meals not simply as an individual activity of biological importance but as a collective activity of symbolic importance (see Bellah et al., 1991, 93; 260).

Saying grace is also a self-representative act. By virtue of the grace, people represent themselves to themselves both as a group engaged in a significant collective activity and also as a family that has been constituted in the first place by ritual activities of a specific religious and/or civil tradition. Meals inaugurated by grace are special. They usually include at least one of the following: extra courses; special foods, drinks or deserts; and unusual decorations (Douglas 1975). This observation does not apply to families that say grace at all meals, of course, but these families use the grace in even more extensive ways. By saying grace, they acknowledge their association with a larger religious tradition, which is the origin of specific symbols and gestures—bowing heads, holding or folding hands, invoking "God," the "Lord," the "Heavenly Father" and so on. They acknowledge a religious identity, no matter how vague, that is shared among themselves and with others. And they call to mind, no matter how distantly, the fact that these same symbols were used ceremonially at the wedding that formally constituted their family in the first place.

By saying grace, family members also express their sense of being bound up with each other through shared obligation, risk and affection. Saying grace expresses the fact that they are both part of a collectivity and subordinate to it. This is symbolized by a gesture expressing both gratitude and submission to a deity. The household division of labour, which results in collecting and preparing food, is deliberately obscured. No one is allowed to assume special credit. No one is allowed to feel either superior to and independent of or inferior to and dependent on the others. Instead, the family as a whole expresses gratitude—directly for the meal and nourishment and indirectly for the family and its identity. Corresponding to the collective character of saying grace are the conversations that take place. These tend, in stylized ways, to address shared concerns in ways that everyone can understand and discuss. The saying of grace typically occurs at meals that discourage dyadic withdrawal (intimate exchanges between two family members).

Regulative communication, too, takes place in this context. When grace is said, family members recognize that they must wait before eating until everyone has been served. They are made aware that this is a time set aside for the family, not just a time to eat. Saying grace, moreover, makes them aware of a structure of authority; even when everyone is invited to participate in the saying or singing of grace, one parent is assigned the task of signalling the time to start. Saying grace, finally, calls attention to gratitude as a cardinal virtue and ingratitude as a cardinal vice. No matter what is served, no matter how much is available, saying grace calls on everyone present to be grateful for givens of the moment. These are understood to include not only the food itself but also those who provided it and prepared it.

Something similar could be said of invocative communication in this context. The words said or sung at grace usually call quite directly for the blessing of God's spirit. But they also convey indirectly the unspoken wishes of those present that their meal will be a peaceful and enriching experience for all.

It might be objected that this account of grace at meal-time errs by reading too much into a simple, usually absent-minded and perfunctory activity. Such a criticism might be valid for the way grace is performed in some homes; in the next section, I discuss at length how the actual performance of rituals affects their communicative activity and experienced significance. But if this criticism assumes that ritual participants are fully cognizant of the meanings they are communicating, it is likely to be off the mark even with respect to many off-handed performances. I have argued that ritual communication is like poetic or musical communication without commentary. Those who listen or dance to music, for example, experience directly the significance of what they hear even though they might not be able to provide a completely intelligible account. Because ritual communication is a form of aesthetic communication (Scheff 1977), it is unlikely that participants will be fully cognizant of what they are communicating. After all, ritual communication is thick, condensed, multidimensional and figurative.[6]

## Variation in ritual performance

How rituals are actually experienced depends in large part on how they are performed. Because rituals are like dramas, their actual enactments can be understood by examining them as dramatic performances. In gross terms, the front stage (where ritual action occurs) can be distinguished from the back stage (which supports the actors as the place from which they emerge and to which they return after performing). A corresponding distinction can be made between the main ritual roles and how those chosen to portray them interpret the script. A director is in charge of the timing, cuing and harmonizing the ritual production. Costumes vary according to the venue. Even though the ritual script itself seldom varies, every group of ritual actors brings its own interpretation to the performance. Attention can be focused not only on generic features of ritual at the Passover *seder*, for example, but also on features that vary according to both the idiosyncrasies of family life and the passage of time.

Also worth considering is the fact that ritual performances vary according to the level of expertise attained by their actors. Some know their lines well; others do not. This can be an important factor, especially when liturgical changes are introduced. If performers fail to rehearse, they are likely to stumble over words in a disturbing way. Around 20 years ago, Christian congregations introduced a new ritual, "passing the peace," into morning worship services. The script called for lay participants to greet those nearest them by shaking their hands and saying "the peace of Christ" or "the peace of God be with you." Initially, many people experienced this as an awkward moment. Many still do. Others have adjusted by turning a formal gesture (with a theological emphasis on the transmission of divine peace) into an informal one (with a social and psychological emphasis on personal greetings or even friendly chatter). Over time, congregations have varied according to how they interpret this element and how smoothly and comfortably they integrate it into the service. In some, congregants perform it self-consciously, as if they were reading their lines. In others, they do so less self-consciously, as if they truly "own it." We can understand the difference, at least partly, by analyzing how well participants know and perform what is expected of them. Generally speaking, people vary according to the competence they demonstrate in performing the ritual roles assigned to them.

Because all rituals involve skilled performances, it is worth elaborating on this point. People often learn the requisite skills without being fully aware of doing so. They simply imitate the conduct of others. This is how they learn to perform many domestic rituals—such as birthday parties, saying grace and personal greetings. They learn how to act during seasonal and life-cycle rites the same way: by going along with whatever others are doing until they feel confident in their ability to perform autonomously. Sometimes, though, people see the need for training. This is often the case when it comes to using prayer-books, reading scripture aloud and chanting liturgical prayers. One ritual practice for which most people seek special training is meditation. Although meditating is a highly individual activity, it is typically undertaken according to specific guidelines. Not only are meditators instructed, but their skill is evaluated by teachers, masters or gurus.

It is naive to assume that people need no training to participate in rituals. It is also naive to assume that all people are equally competent, by nature, to perform rituals. Like, thespians, they vary in their skills as dramatic performers. Some are better trained than others. Some are more gifted than others at playing specific roles. Some have had more experience than others. Some simply have better direction than others. Whether direction is provided by someone designated for this purpose or not, after all, the quality of performance often reflects the amount of care given to activities such as timing, staging and cueing, not to mention personal encouragement and discipline.

From the perspective of lay participants, the quality of a ritual performance varies according to the kind and number of roles they themselves are expected and trained to play. In some settings, lay adherents are treated primarily as members of an audience; they witness (and pay for) the performances of professional choirs and clergy. Being fairly passive, they often expect stellar performances by official casts. In other settings, things are very different. Among Mormons or Quakers, for example, lay members are expected to perform all the roles (although, for the Quakers, ritual roles are quite simple and call for nothing more than speaking up from time to time). Lay involvement usually falls between these extremes. Lay members can often perform several different roles, each with its own degree of associated honour. For example, they can be ushers, choir members, refreshment servers or scripture readers. I think two quite different roles are worth discussing: ritual sponsors and ritual adepts. Ritual sponsors might not participate directly. Because of sizeable contributions in kind or in money, however, they make it possible to stage the ritual. Many people feel quite comfortable with this role. They might well gain a sense of blessing simply from the knowledge that a ritual takes place regularly, as it would in the case of a shrine, even if they themselves hardly ever participate. Ritual adepts play a quite different role. They are the people who participate regularly and with great skill. As the core of competent practitioners, they take pride in making rituals happen by showing others how to act and, indeed, by their very presence. In Jewish congregations, they are the men who, by regular attendance, constitute the *minyan* necessary for public (as distinct from private) worship.

For Jews, a particular attraction of traditional sabbath services is the variety of roles open to lay people. They might play several at different times or even at the same time. On the other hand, they might play only a single one. In connection with a bar mitzvah or bat mitzvah, for example, they might play the roles of sponsors, readers, friends or relatives. Even in connection with mourning, either during the first year or on subsequent anniversaries, they might play the roles of friends or relatives. They might act as core members of the daily *minyan*, as sponsors of a *kidush* or as lay readers. Although scripts for the Sabbath morning service as a whole are fairly well set by denominational and congregational traditions, variety is added by changes in the "cast."

Specific traditions distinguish theologically between recommended and discouraged or rejected rituals as well as between *felicitas* and *infelicitas* performances. Recommended rituals and *felicitas* performances bring about valued objectives. In particular, they cultivate and strengthen desired habits of mind and feeling as well as esteemed patterns of social interaction. Of course, these valued states and patterns vary enormously from one tradition to another. Buddhists, for example, value rituals that reinforce deference to the monastic community, or *sangha*, and psychological detachment (Hayes 1992). Confucians, on the other hand, value rituals that promote filial piety (Fingarette 1971).

To distinguish between satisfactory and unsatisfactory performances of ritual acts, Erik Erikson referred to "rituals" and "ritualisms" in connection with events that are, respectively, lively or fulfilling and deadly or dull (Erikson 1977). This distinction was an after-the-fact way of indicating that some ritual performances are far more engaging than others. It allowed Erikson to demonstrate that rituals have a useful function but also to acknowledge that many people find actual rituals arbitrary, stilted, officious and, in short, quite unengaging. Because actual performances vary in terms of both interpretation and competence, it is important to appreciate the particular way specific rituals are acted out.

Ritualism refers to a poorly performed ritual. With an eye both to evaluating actual performance and advising those concerned on how to improve their enactment, Ronald Grimes has listed several ways that rituals can be performed infelicitously. Following suggestions made by John Austin with respect to ineffective speech acts, Grimes reviews typical ways in which ritual performances go awry: misfires; abuses; ineffectual performances; violations; vague presentations; misframed staging; omissions; and contagion. As Grimes elaborates on these, he shows that ritual performances can be performed poorly by omitting features, by pacing or timing events too quickly or too slowly, by including too many elements that are unintelligible or unrecognizable, by insincere acting (especially by ritual leaders) and by introducing too many unconventional elements at once (Grimes 1990, chap. 9).

The mark of excellence in ritual performance is its ability to engage people as participants, not observers, people who have deliberately and satisfactorily chosen to take part.[7] This kind of ritual participation contrasts sharply with obsessive behaviour (even though both involve the repeated enactment of symbolic gestures and the utterance of symbolic words for intrinsically valued reasons that are not fully reducible to instrumental objectives). Obsessive behaviours—phobias, addictions, anorexia, compulsive habits—involve people who perform symbolic acts repeatedly; in doing so, they reduce anxiety and generate satisfaction but for reasons that usually remain inexplicable, either to themselves or to others. These obsessive acts are repeated because, though often self-destructive, they seem to work. They remain compelling, in other words, even when they give rise to illness, strained relations with loved ones and personal confusion or unhappiness. Freud noticed that ritual acts were like obsessive ones in several ways: they were repeated, intrinsically valued, highly symbolic and often personally compelling. Consequently, he considered ritual a form of obsessive neurosis (Freud 1950). While appreciating several characteristic features of ritual, he failed to appreciate several decisive differences between rituals and obsessions. Ritual action (unless it is also neurotic) is voluntarily chosen, often collective, culturally mandated and publicly explicable.

It is true that the cessation of ritual acts, like obsessive ones, can be disorienting and even lead to confused interactions. But the result is seldom intense anxiety or anger. This is because ritual acts, unlike obsessive ones, are voluntary. Most ritual acts, even those associated with meditation, involve cooperative interactions with others; obsessive ones, on the other hand, are private affairs. More importantly, ritual acts are culturally, not privately, mandated; ritual actors render their interpretations of oral or written scripts that have been created by others (their ancestors, for example, and their religious, ethnic or political communities). Finally, ritual acts are explicable; they can be legitimated in ways that are intelligible and coherent to people who share a cultural tradition. Poorly performed rituals, on the other hand, really are like obsessive acts to the extent that they are performed as mindless routines, do not connect people with others and can be explained only in terms of what people have always done. Most ritual performances are not like this.

So far, I have argued that rituals are thick, non-discursive and multidimensional communications. And I have identified five different dimensions of ritual communication: (1) constitutive; (2) self-representative; (3) expressive; (4) regulative; and (5) invocative. These same five dimensions can also be used as reference points for evaluating and comparing actual ritual performances.

First, ritual performances vary in connection with their constitutive dimension. They constitute or reconstitute social reality—a tribal gathering, say, or a dispersed family. In this case, ritual performances are indispensable. They cement relationships, bring about desired states of mind and foster sentiments that would arise either not at all or not as strongly without them. On the other hand, ritual performances might do nothing more than provide extraneous decorative flourishes. In this case, they are merely optional. They might even be distracting.

Second, ritual performances vary in connection with their self-representative dimension. They represent participants to themselves. They might, of course, present only distorted self-representations. Participants might not be able to see themselves in congregational rites or family rituals that present only heroic, self-sacrificing and highly idealized characters. On the other hand, participants might be unable or unwilling to recognize themselves in rituals that present only alien or evil characters. In that case, their performances are likely to be wooden, dispirited and merely perfunctory. Ritual performances are especially engaging to the degree that participants satisfy the narcissistic need to experience them as self-acknowledging. But rituals do not represent participants realistically. Instead, they represent participants in relation to what Durkheim called the moral or ideal self (1961, conclusion), or what Freud called the ego ideal (1973, chap. 3).

The extent to which any ritual provides genuine self-representation depends on the way performance establishes a fit between the script and the participants. This fit, in turn, does not depend only on what the script calls for and on how well it is directed. In his study of Australian Aboriginal rites Durkheim showed that participants see something of themselves in animals, gods, or mythical ancestors. Consequently, they can take on these parts during ritual performances. Their sense of connection, though, can dissipate for at least two major reasons: not enough adaptation of scripts to changing times (in which case they are boring) and too much adaptation (in which case they are unfamiliar).

Third, ritual performances vary in connection with their expressive dimension. The degree of expressiveness, of course, varies considerably. In some cases, rituals are too emotional; participants feel overwhelmed by enthusiasm. In other cases, rituals are not emotional enough; participants feel bored or disengaged. This general statement is true even of highly passionate rituals. Some generate acts such as speaking in tongues—that depart from ritual forms. Others generate acts—such as ecstatic dancing or fervent chanting—that are channelled by ritual forms. When performed well, these rituals allow people to experience and act out intense feelings in concert with others and in ways that are responsive to others. When not performed well, two things can happen. They might give rise to the same passions but in ways that destroy harmony or leave aroused individuals unconnected with others. Or, at the other extreme, they might allow little or no expressive communication and thus be experienced as boring.

With this in mind, consider rituals that call for at least some participants to speak in tongues. Jonathan Edwards found, in the 1730s and 1740s, that his congregations began speaking in tongues spontaneously (Edwards 1959; Marty 1984). This happens very seldom. Much more often, individuals speak in tongues when this is what everyone expects and when rituals are structured to facilitate this experience (Goodman 1972; Bourguignon 1974). Even then, the experience varies from one person to another. The apostle Paul complained of the way this experience, and the claims made by those who had it, became disruptive (1 Corinthians:13, 14). Many descriptions of revivals and camp meetings indicate that the emotions aroused by fervent rituals can easily get out of hand. Other descriptions, however, indicate that the opposite can happen: a congregational service can leave people so cold that no one speaks in tongues in spite of both desire and expectation (Westley 1978; see also Acts 18: 24-19:7).

Ritual performances lose their expressive quality either by becoming too formal or too noisy. They work best when people act as expected, following a script. Noise is sound out of place. Neither choreographed exuberance nor loud rhythmic music are noisy for participants who know what to expect; those who do not—that is, outsiders—might well find these events jarring or disturbing. Typically, ritual scripts circumscribe the range of spontaneous actions. When spontaneity is appropriate, as it is in the case of personal testimonials, tacit guidelines are followed in connection with the manner of speaking, the vocabulary to be used and the topics expected. The result is that testimonials—even though they represent the introduction of personal, unrehearsed discursive statements—are not considered noisy or out of place (Schwartz 1977). Noise reduces the expressive quality of ritual performances because it distracts participants. Attention is diverted from the flow of ritual, no matter how simple or complex.

Many collective rituals allow participants to step back from the ongoing performance. While officiants continue to enact the central rites, lay participants gravitate to the edges of the performing area. There, they catch a breath of fresh air, talk to their friends or simply take a break. This is characteristic of both Jewish and Eastern Orthodox liturgies, pilgrimages and family celebrations. Ordinarily, these breaks—even ones that involve talking—are not considered noisy disruptions by those who continue to follow the ritual. They occur at scheduled times and places, after all, and in ways that do not overshadow the primary ritual. It could be argued, in fact, that this contrast reinforces the seriousness of primary rituals. On the other hand, breaks can be distracting if they become too loud, invade or upset the more honoured aspects of the ritual or turn into competitive engagements. To avoid noise, then, rituals follow expected forms. They become too formal whenever this adherence itself becomes lifeless and mechanical or whenever attention shifts from the actual performance as a present activity to compliance with the script, whether this compliance is successful or not.

Under these circumstances, participants are likely to believe that they are fulfilling obligations—reciting scripts or miming gestures—rather than expressing themselves.

Successful ritual performances strike a satisfactory balance between formality and noise. They do so by using words and gestures that are standardized yet special and symbolic, not casual. They seldom use ordinary, vernacular expressions. This is especially true of religious rituals. Just as language in the dreaming state is different from that of the waking state, the language of religious ritual is different from that of everyday life. It is often less directly intelligible and less readily explicable in discursive terms. Ritual communication is multidimensional, after all, and its compact symbols facilitate several types of communication at once.

Fourth, ritual performances vary in connection with their regulative dimension. As ritual details are elaborated and ceremonies added, they can become too figurative. This kind of decorative flowering can usually be traced to the preoccupations of those who stage rituals. They might want to linger on specific elements. Then, too, they might simply want to expand their own roles. As a result, these rituals call attention to themselves (that is, to attractive aspects or to attractive performers) rather than serving as vehicles for the communication of beliefs and mores. On the other hand, ritual performances can become too didactic (too focused on transmitting proper lessons and useful instructions) or too regimented (too preoccupied with performing in the proper way). The aesthetic dimension can be overwhelmed and lost whenever those staging rituals turn them into pedagogical vehicles. An effective ritual performance is one in which the aesthetic and moral dimensions are balanced and the ritual takes place on its own terms; an ineffective ritual performance is one in which either dimension subverts the other due to a preoccupation with artful staging or moralistic utility.

Finally, ritual performances vary in connection with their invocative dimension. They can be evocative and special events or unevocative and ordinary ones. Symbols and gestures used to address sacred realities can become opaque with respect to either the participants or the sacred realities. As the symbols used to invoke sacred realities enter more fully into ordinary discourse, of course, they lose their aura. If these symbols are used by political regimes, moreover, their value is considerably diminished for those who form the opposition.

The capacity of religious rituals to convey tangible blessings depends on their ability to keep sacred objects both distant and exclusive but also accessible under specific circumstances. They become less engaging when blessings are too easily available, to be sure, but also when they are almost unavailable. By democratizing access to the sacred, liberal Protestants have created a situation in which both problems arise: blessings that are easily available through word or sacrament seem ordinary and common (that is, not real or not really religious); blessings that do seem real or really religious, on the other hand, are ignored and unavailable.

In an earlier section of this essay, I made a number of claims with respect to the communicative functions of ritual. How ritual actually realizes these functions depends on how they are interpreted and how well they are performed. Even poorly performed rituals can still be understood as a particular kind of thick communication. Nevertheless, communication is likely to be obscured and distorted in various ways so that those involved feel more like witnesses than participants. It is no wonder that poor ritual performances are so disappointing: several kinds of communication are frustrated, not just one.

## Conclusion: Making sense of ritual action

In trying to understand rituals, most people resort either to ideological or functional explanations. The former calls for accounts of ritual in relation to beliefs stated explicitly, through verbal and graphic symbols, in the rituals themselves. This approach has been widely and instructively used. Observers of and participants in the Christian eucharist usually try to make sense of it by analyzing theological statements. Characteristically, these statements include discussions of what the bread and wine signify and what the words mean. In this case, distinct traditions of interpretation have developed, each embodying different beliefs. Are the bread and wine actually transformed into the body and blood of Jesus or symbolically transformed? Is the ritual a symbolic meal or a sacrifice (Jay 1992)? Each tradition of interpretation has influenced performance. It is possible to identify similar traditions of interpretation with respect to central rituals in other religious, national, ethnic and political movements. Scholars could compare Orthodox and Reform interpretations of Sabbath liturgy, for example, and show that each has affected actual performances.

These interpretations focus especially on the substantive content of verbal scripts and graphic symbols. By following this approach, people make sense of rituals by deciphering the messages contained in the scripts themselves. They use various techniques to do this: theological constructs, literary analyses, phenomenological observations, structural diagnoses and so forth. These messages are understood in relation to prominent traditions of interpretation rooted in specific religious and social movements. Dissenting interpretations notwithstanding, these are what could be considered the official ones. If asked why they hold a *seder* on Passover, for example, most Jews would invoke stories from scripture. If asked why they celebrate the eucharist, most Christians would do the same.

Ideological interpretations make sense by identifying the covert messages that ritual scripts ostensibly transmit to participants. Accordingly, these interpretations focus on what Austin and Searle refer to as the "locutionary" aspects of communication and on participants viewed primarily as the recipients of these lucutionary messages. It is possible to distinguish between three dimensions of communication: (1) the locutionary dimension, which is the substantive content of communication; (2) the illocutionary dimension, which identifies the particular purposes of communication; and (3) the perlocutionary dimension, which refers to actual results of communication (Austin 1962; Searle 1969). Ideological interpretations make sense by identifying the overt messages, the locutionary communication, transmitted through rituals to participants. These interpretations are based on close analyses of the ritual scripts and on the idea that participants are members of an audience. The results are interesting and important for those who want to know how effectively scripted messages are transmitted and how particular audiences tend to hear and receive these messages in light of their own cultural settings and personal concerns.

But some social scientists, especially Marx and Durkheim, have questioned the reliability of this approach. The official explanations given by participants, they argue, often seem incredible. Do people really repeat a rite simply because Moses, who has been dead for three thousands years, said that people living a long time ago should do so? Both Marx and Durkheim claimed that official motivations divert attention from less noble but more influential ones. People might defend their official interpretation to defend their status and power no less than their supposedly theological convictions. In any case, as social scientists, both were methodological agnostics. All theological explanations were dismissed for lack of empirical evidence. Marx, Durkheim and their followers proposed an alternative hermeneutical strategy: to analyze rituals in relation to their social functions. Functional analysis corresponds to a focus on what Austin and Searle called the perlocutionary dimension of communication. Alfred Reginald Radcliffe-Brown elegantly summarized this strategy when he argued that it was possible to see what sense rituals actually make in people's lives by examining the consequences of ritual participation for social interaction. If you want to know what it means for people to attend Sabbath services or participate in a Passover *seder*, find out how involvement actually shapes, modifies and gives value to their lives (Radcliffe-Brown 1979). He argued that looking for the origins of taboos or sacrifices will do little to explain contemporary behaviour. To do that, scholars should look for the advantages derived by contemporary people from particular forms of behaviour.

Functionalist interpretations, too, are often instructive. Weber and Douglas have demonstrated the way in which food taboos identify and reinforce social boundaries (Weber 1978; Douglas 1966). René Girard notes the way sacrificial rites channel and limit social violence (1977). Observing that sacrificial rites have almost everywhere been performed exclusively by men, Nancy Jay looked at a number of cross-cultural studies to show how sacrificial rites have been performed, especially in agricultural societies, to strengthen intergenerational links between men (1991). Marxists have examined the way public ceremonies are used to legitimate and reinforce public authorities. Durkheim observed the way many rituals celebrate and strengthen social solidarity (1961). In varying ways, these social scientists observed that it makes sense to participate in rituals, even though the theological rationales for doing so might seem incomprehensible to non-participants, because rituals have the consequence of promoting identifiable social functions.

We can appreciate both strategies by showing how the act of saying grace before a meal might be interpreted from either an ideological or a functional perspective. The former would require a detailed study of the words and phrases uttered, their origins and meanings (praise for the deity and gratitude for the meal). The latter would examine the impact of this ritual on the social interactions of family members. Does the saying of grace make a difference when observant households are compared with unobservant ones, when elaborate graces are compared with simple ones, when extemporaneous graces are compared with standardized ones?

In this essay, I propose a third strategy. It examines rituals in terms of how they channel and facilitate communication among participants themselves. In relation to Austin's typology, this approach focuses on neither the locutionary substance of the scripts nor the perlocutionary results but on the illocutionary activity occasioned by actual ritual performances. The fundamental assumption of this approach is that when people participate in rituals they are communicating with each other and with themselves. Moreover, this communication is not primarily discursive and instrumental. It is multilayered, thick and immediate in ways that may make it seem opaque when analyzed in terms of overt or locutionary meanings. A communicative interpretation analyzes the extent to which rituals facilitate several kinds of communication. Actual performances can be experienced immediately, in other words, as making much or little sense depending on the degree to which they are constitutive, self-representative, expressive, regulative, and invocative.

This approach indicates that specific rituals can communicate immediately a fairly wide range of feelings and representations. But it will be abused if analysts try to discover too much cognitive information encoded in rituals. The ideological approach errs whenever it examines rituals primarily as vehicles for the transmission of beliefs, legends and philosophies. The functional approach errs, similarly, whenever it examines rituals primarily as vehicles for the encoding of information about social relationships. Very often, the symbolic expressions and gestures are there to evoke sentiments and recognitions more than to convey ideas. They represent tacit forms of knowing. My approach is less tied to cognitive interpretations than the others, but it, too, can err by assuming that the messages and impressions given off by some actors are necessarily received by others. After all, poorly performed rituals are especially characterized by miscommunication. Even when rituals are performed well, the feelings and representations expressed can remain opaque to many.

No one hermeneutical strategy suffices to make sense of ritual behaviour. Any one of them can become reductionistic if used exclusively. Each adds to our understanding. I have discussed at length the communicative approach in this essay for two reasons: to introduce it as a complement to the others and to show how it can explain several characteristic features of ritual, especially why some performances are so engaging, so highly revered, and so vital while others are so arbitrary, so contrived and so alienating.

## Notes

1   I am grateful to several people who, at various times, have helped me in thinking about and writing this essay. These include my wife, Frances Westley, and the other participants in this project, especially Jack Lightstone. I am also very grateful for criticisms and comments (on an earlier draft of this paper) by Susan Palmer, Ron Grimes and colleagues in the Department of Religion at Concordia University.

2   Wuthnow's definition of ritual is too broad. Although he recognizes the instrumental character of much ritual activity, he regards rituals primarily as forms of expression. He treats both traffic signalling and witch trials, for example, as rituals. In contrast, I would argue that traffic signalling is best viewed as a repeated, stylistic and culturally specific way of transferring information. We could easily include most communication under this generic description. Wuthnow's broad definition does not provide a discriminate means of distinguishing between acts that are either more or less ritualistic. I would argue that transferring information becomes ritual-like to the degree that the actors themselves consider this form of behaviour intrinsically valuable and try to behave in keeping with given "scripts" (that is, specific expectations). With respect to trials, I would argue that all trials contain ritual elements. These elements might be more or less vital and necessary. In the case of witch trials, the ritual elements probably take on considerable importance in relation to the discursive process of adjudication (Wuthnow 1987).

3   I am indebted to my colleague, Michel Despland, for calling my attention to the scheduled character of rituals.

4   In this essay, I do not analyze the overt and ideological meanings that are transmitted by ritual performances. Most religious and communal rituals convey specific cosmological, theological, ideological and ethnological beliefs. There is, as Tambiah argues, a relation between the substance of these beliefs and the form of ritual enactments themselves (Tambiah 1979). As I observe in the conclusion, many analyses have focused on this. Here, though, I want to focus on more immediate forms of communication among participants.

5   Just as feasting plays an integral role in many different types of ritual, so does fasting. Fasting (as distinct from starving) is almost invariably a ritualized activity. Fasting often takes place as a form of preparation for feasting. It often accompanies the ritualized aspects of meditation. Those who fast are expected to do so with certain mind-sets. Whatever else they might be doing, they represent themselves to themselves as people willing to undergo specific deprivations in order to achieve valued objectives. Anorexia is the name for a medical condition suffered by those who neurotically—but ritualistically—refuse to consume food; they do so for private reasons, not public ones.

6   So far, I have examined the ways ritual facilitates communication. But this analysis does not presume that rituals are always socially interactive. Some rituals are performed by isolated individuals. This is true of the ways in which isolated individuals ritualize selected aspects of their eating, dressing and walking, of the corresponding ways in which they represent themselves to themselves, express their own sense of selfhood, constitute and reconstitute their own sense of identity or purpose, regulate their own lives and even invoke self-transcending powers on their own.

   Sometimes, ostensively individual rituals are performed in group settings. This often happens with both prayer and meditation. The meditation practices of Buddhist nuns and monks, as well as Christian ones, are usually regulated by social rules and take place in social settings. Buddhist monks, for example, characteristically practice their meditation in halls set aside for this purpose. They do so in the presence of both other meditators and the masters who supervise. In this contexts, meditation reconstitutes and represents the solidarity of the Sangha. It also encourages the spiritual development of each meditator (Welch 1967).

   As behaviour undertaken by individuals, meditation can be further analyzed as an activity by which individuals communicate with themselves. Meditation typically consists of self-disciplined mental activity, usually combined with self-disciplined physical and emotional restraints or actions. Meditators might chant sutras, repeat mantras, observe their own breathing, consider perplexing conundrums, empty their minds or imagine themselves in particular settings. The techniques used make a considerable difference on the states of being and mind they achieve. In all these varied forms, though, the act of meditation can be understood and analyzed as an act of self-communication in relation to the five forms of communication already discussed.

   By meditating, individuals reconstitute themselves as selves who hope to realize higher, more valued states of mind and being. They represent themselves as unique beings defined primarily not by their possessions, social positions and social roles, but rather by those dimensions of selfhood especially valorized and brought into play by the act of meditation itself. By this activity, typically, they express immediately but indirectly considerable esteem for their own sense of personhood as cultivated by meditation. Depending on cultural traditions, this sense of personhood might be regarded as a selfless self (Theravada Buddhism), say, or as a soul or spirit (Christianity). This activity certainly regulates their days. It provides them with distance from specific responsibilities. And it gives value to those habits of mind and body that are conducive to excelling at meditation. By meditating, finally, individuals regularly try to invoke transcending beings that are often believed immanent within their own beings.

7   Each dramaturgical tradition has its own standards for evaluating performances; each places a different value, in other words, on correct diction, faithful historical reconstructions, expressivity, innovative renderings and so forth. The same is true of ritual traditions. Each calls in particular for some quality: formal correctness, emotional interpretation, personal piety or some other characteristic. But aside from these specific expectations, I think, are universally recognized ones (although these are not necessarily formally named as such).

# 3

# The Religion of Jewish Peoplehood: The Myth, Ritual and Institutions of the Civil Religion of Canadian Jewry

## JACK N. LIGHTSTONE

**The problematic**

Michael Harrington spoke of America's invisible poor (1963). One might well describe American and Canadian Jews as invisible too. They are often indistinguishable from others (Sklare 1971, 115; Liebman 1973; Schoenfeld 1981, 142; Broadbar-Nemzer, Cohen, Reitzes, Shahar and Tobin 1993; Woocher 1986). They remain deeply aware of being Jewish, nevertheless, seeking out others who share their identity (Sklare 1971, 100ff.; 194ff.). In these respects, Jews are products of the unarticulated consensus of assumptions and commitments that have directed the course of Canadian Jewry for some 80 years. Contemporary Jews are intent on maintaining, in some significant sense, their Jewish identity (Schoenfeld 1981; Broadbar-Nemzer, Cohen, Reitzes, Shahar and Tobin 1993). But they are equally intent on participating fully in the larger Canadian (and American) milieu (Sklare 1971, 193). That path, they are convinced, has assured economic security. It has also, they realize, divested most Canadian (and American) Jews of a traditional Judaic lifestyle (Sklare 1971, 193; Schoenfeld 1981, 142ff.; Broadbar-Nemzer, Cohen, Reitzes, Shahar and Tobin 1993; Woocher 1986; Kallen 1977; Luckmann 1967). The latter observation, recognized by all and bemoaned by many Jews, has not diminished their commitment to pass, unseen and undifferentiated, within the larger society of Canada. The divestiture of Judaism lies at the heart of a major fear among Jews: that assimilation will continue depleting their numbers.

"Outmarriage" is undoubtedly a persistent and increasing phenomenon within the Canadian (and the American) Jewish communities. Yet scholars have for decades disagreed on the prognosis indicated by the hard demographic evidence. Evidence may not fully substantiate the claim of those Jews who maintain that Jews are "doing themselves in" (Sklare 1971, 201; Morgan 1964a; 1964b; Weinfeld 1981)[1] through assimilation (Goldstein and Goldscheider 1968; Cohen and Goldscheider 1984; Weinfeld 1981, 374; Brym 1993). The contemporary generation of Jews should, according to earlier predictions of doom, have been lost to Jewry. But Jews of childbearing age still retain their Jewish identity. They might bear that identity more comfortably, in fact, than the previous one. What has happened? Why do contemporary Jews, many of whom were expected to have disappeared from

Jewish ranks, feel as Jewish as their parents and more at ease with the feeling? On the whole, they are no more Judaic. Indeed, they are generally less Judaic.[2] This generation might remain, for the most part, distant from *Judaism*. But, I contend, some structured whole has emerged. It gives meaning to, and effectively reinforces, a profound sense of Jewish being. This new "whole," then, deserves attention and analysis.

To restate my hypothesis and anticipate my conclusions: Yes, this generation might be lost to Judaism (in the classical sense of that word); indeed Judaism might well be beyond rehabilitation for most Canadian Jews. But something different has emerged in its place, something well integrated and structured even if unarticulated. It commands the loyalty of most Canadian Jews, even young ones. And it seems to be not entirely secular.

Cultural systems consist mainly of, and depend heavily on, shared views of reality, identity and mutual responsibilities (Geertz 1966). Members of the system re-create this complex of meanings by telling themselves and one another stories of what it means to belong to their group and by engaging in rituals geared to the same end. Changes in this complex of meanings (notions of "who the group is") entail, and are entailed by, changes in these stories and shifts in these rituals. The old stories and rituals, however, are never discarded; they are just changed subtly over time. Almost by definition, group identity and consciousness could not survive radical and sudden changes. To tell a story one day in response to the question, Who am I? and to tell an entirely different one the next day would involve the dissolution of group identity or allegiance in order to embrace another. It is, in short, to convert. But the phenomenon under discussion patently involves metamorphosis, not conversion. It involves a shift in the sense of "who we are" so contiguous with "who our grandparents or great-grandparents *were*" as to have happened imperceptibly—almost unconsciously. Consciousness of continuity remains intact. I examine here these shifts in story and ritual. How, why and with what effect have Jews changed these since their ancestors left the traditional world? This constitutes the problematic.

Let me acknowledge at the outset, though, my theoretical allegiances. Shared perceptions of ourselves, of the world and of our place within it are cogent, because they reflect our shared social experience (Douglas 1973; 1975a; 1975b; 1975c; Durkheim 1961). Will a world-view—whether formulated in discursive language or communicated in symbol and ritual—be taken up by many as a particularly plausible account of how things are? The answer depends on how well it fits the structure of communal life. In short, I follow that sociological and anthropological tradition, which sees ideas and shared perceptions as inextricably linked to structures and experiences within the social sphere, even if not wholly determined by social relations.

## Classical antecedents

Canadian Jews, with very few exceptions, find their immediate Jewish heritage in rabbinic Judaism. The latter emerged after 70 CE, following a

## Religion of Jewish Peoplehood

revolt of Jews against the Romans and the consequent destruction of their Temple in Jerusalem (see Neusner 1965-69; 1981a; 1984; Katz 1971). By the seventh or eighth century, rabbinic Judaism was the religion of almost all Jews in the Middle East, the Mediterranean basin and Europe. It remained the dominant form of Judaism in these areas up to and through the late nineteenth and early twentieth centuries. At that point, massive waves of Jews migrated to the United States and Canada. To understand the contemporary expressions of Canadian Jews *qua* Jews, then, is to understand what has become of rabbinic Judaism in Canada and to analyze new forms of activity and belief, along with the sherds of rabbinic Judaism, that have come to define the Jewish life of Canadian Jewry.

Rabbinic Judaism had provided the immigrants with a fairly comprehensive cultural system in their "homelands." According to the sacred story passed down to them by ancient rabbinic "masters," the God of Israel, YHWH, made a covenant with the patriarchs, liberated their progeny from Egypt and revealed a dual revelation, or Torah, to Moses "our Rabbi" at Sinai. One revelation, in written form, is the Pentateuch (the first five books of Hebrew scripture). The other revelation, in oral form, has been communicated by Moses to successive generations of Israel's leaders (see Mishnah Avot 1, 1; *Avot Derabi Natan*, version a, 1, ed. Schechter; Abraham Ibn Daud's *Book of Tradition*). The rabbis claimed mastery due to their knowledge of this whole Torah. Their writings—the Mishnah, the Palestinian and Babylonian Talmuds, subsequent codes and commentaries—are expressions of Torah. Ultimately, though, Torah resides in the person and pronouncements of rabbis and their disciples. In terms of content, the parameters of this whole Torah are open-ended. Included are not only such matters as prayer, synagogue, religious fasts and festivals, but also family, business, civil and criminal law, and the court system by which these are legislated and enforced. In this sense, then, rabbinic Judaism provided the immigrants with everything required by religion, society and culture (see Katz 1971; Handlin 1973).

### New socio-economic and cultural contexts and rabbinic Judaism

The Canadian context, like the American, provided the Jews and Judaism with a cogent challenge. The price of free and open participation by a Jewish minority in a secular society (overwhelmingly indebted to Protestantism for its culture) meant relegating their lives as Jews to something other than a total, all-encompassing cultural system. The latter was now defined by the surrounding Canadian or American milieu. A reasonable level of participation within that sphere was desirable in itself, but it was also necessary for economic survival (see Sklare 1971; Liebman 1973; Schoenfeld 1981). To be sure, Canada was and remains a pluralistic society in which cultural differences among minorities are tolerated, even encouraged. But societies, especially modern pluralistic ones, still depend for their cohesiveness and solidarity on shared norms and values. The cost of not conforming is social prejudice on the one hand and low economic potential on the other (although conformity does not always, of course, mean social acceptance and high economic potential). Jews overwhelmingly chose to remain Jews, in some significant sense, but also to become Canadians (that is, to participate fully in Canadian society). They perforce adopted distinctive definitions of Judaism. And they did so by means of an unofficial consensus, which was legitimated by contemporary "narratives" and rituals instead of traditional rabbinic authority.

Like their American counterparts, Canadian Jews generally practise rabbinic Judaism in only the most selective manner (Sklare 1971, 110ff.; Neusner 1972; Schoenfeld 1981; Kallen 1977; Broadbar-Nemzer, Cohen, Reitzes, Shahar and Tobin 1993). Rabbinic legal injunctions (the *halaka*, or "way" of Torah concerning such matters as refraining from all manner of labour on the Sabbath and festivals) are seldom honoured. Most Jews ignore the dietary laws, daily prayer, distinctive dress, menstrual taboos, regular Torah study and the like. Not surprisingly, the same is true of Jewish laws governing business, civil and criminal suits; all have been laid aside in deference to Canadian laws. Synagogues as the venues for communal prayer suffer infrequent and sporadic attendance, even though the rate of formal affiliation (membership as expressed through the payment of annual dues) remains relatively high (see Elinon, Haberman and Cell 1967; see also Sklare 1971; Neusner 1972; Schoenfeld 1981; Broadbar-Nemzer, Cohen, Reitzes, Shahar and Tobin 1993; Kallen 1977).

Even so, Jews appear remarkably consistent and persistent in which aspects of their traditional (rabbinic) religion they *choose* to practise (Sklare 1971; Neusner 1972; Schoenfeld 1981; Broadbar-Nemzer, Cohen, Reitzes, Shahar and Tobin 1993; Kallen 1977; Goldscheider 1986a and b; Cohen 1983; Goldscheider and Zuckerman 1984). Attendance at prayer services on the New Year and Day of Atonement (along with fasting on the latter), for example, are still considered *de rigueur*. Although the interdictions against leaven and other laws pertaining to the Passover are not widely or strictly observed, the family *seder* (a ritual performed at home in conjunction with a meal at the onset of the Passover) is widely, if not strictly, observed. Many families reunite for a Friday evening meal to usher in the Sabbath, which is otherwise hardly honoured. The festival of Hanuka also retains a considerable following; in the minds of most Jews, it commemorates a thwarted attempt at forced enculturation under the Seleucid (Hellenistic) Empire. Many Jews find similar significance in Purim, which recalls a thwarted attempt at the physical extinction of Jews. In addition, most Jews prefer to marry within the fold.

That Jews have largely abandoned their traditional patterns of behaviour and belief should surprise no one; most Canadians have done so. What calls for interpretation and explanation is the consistency, both individually and collectively, in what has been selected from rabbinic Judaism for continued observance.

A partial explanation is to be found in the commitment of Canadian Jews to participate fully in the social, cultural, political and economic life of North America. Jews want to pass invisibly in these spheres. Traditional practices that impinge on this passage remain honoured, if at all, in the breach (Schoenfeld 1981; Woocher 1986). But bear in mind, too, that the culture of contemporary Canada is secular; Canadians view the passionately devout of any religious persuasion with suspicion, even scorn. Canadian Jews want to remain Jews within socially sanctioned parameters and with a certain degree of invisibility. I will spell out more fully this social dimension, for it is integral to my analysis.

Because traditional Judaism does not reflect the social reality in which North American Jews live, they have largely abandoned it. Jews did not reason themselves out of a traditional Judaic lifestyle. The beliefs and rituals they retain simply reflect and serve their social situation. Indeed, these express their social aspirations and loyalties as Canadians or Americans. At the same time, they support a widely shared and sufficiently institutionalized Jewish polity.

Jews have abandoned whatever reflects an autonomous Jewish social system. The rightist Hasidic sects are exceptions that prove the rule for most of North American Jewry; wherever Jews retain a sectarian social location in America, the cogency of their halakic system remains intact and serves real social functions. Most Jews, however, have transformed their system of beliefs and rituals. Instead of celebrating the life of Torah as understood by the rabbis and expressed as *halaka*, they celebration their common ethnic-national—but fully North American—peoplehood. Not surprisingly, this new "Judaism" is devoid of any ritual that would render the Jews socially peripheral. But is there, nevertheless, a coherent mythic perception of reality that is communicated in whatever Jews have retained of rabbinic Judaism and in whatever they have appended to it?

**Ritual, symbol and myth**

As I have already said, much, if not all, of what is practised by Jews today patently stresses the importance of peoplehood and, within that context, of the family. The Passover *seder*, marrying within the faith, family meals on Sabbath eve—in all this, Jewish peoplehood and its constituent element, the family, are offered and reinforced as principal values. (I will consider later whether or not they are religious values.) God and Torah seem either conspicuously absent as symbolic foci or carefully hidden away.

The selective practice of traditional Judaism does not alone bear the burden of this "religion of Jewish peoplehood." New rituals have been incorporated into a wider context of the sacred story and holy action. Within the last three decades, the destruction of European Jewry (the "Holocaust") and the establishment of a Jewish state have come to constitute powerful symbols in the consciousness of Canadian and American Jews. Yom Ha'atzma'ut (Israel's Independence Day) and Yom Hasho'a (Holocaust

Memorial Day), along with numerous Holocaust-related events and Israel-focused activities comprise a new public ritual. The lay leaders of such activities command honour and respect. If synagogues are no longer houses of prayer, for the most part, they remain "houses of assembly" for these new Jewish activities.

That Israel (people and state) and Holocaust have displaced Torah at the symbolic centre of Jewish identity finds confirmation not only in what Jews do but also in what they are prone to say in their sacred stories. Over and over again, one hears Jews say that Israel is the guarantor of their continued existence; that they are proud to be Jews because of Israel; that the Holocaust, to a great extent, brought about the establishment of Israel; that the establishment of Israel after the Holocaust reaffirms their indestructibility; that the Holocaust commands them not to assimilate.

Surely these are elements of a new sacred story, albeit one that is generally left unarticulated. The message communicated is that Jews are an eternal people; when subjected (as in the Holocaust) to the most "advanced" techniques of mass destruction, the Jews *miraculously* survive and are renewed (as in the State of Israel). Holocaust and Israel constitute the paradigm of a Jewish situation that reflects centuries of miraculous persistence. Holocaust and Israel are prefigured in a litany of like (although perhaps lesser) events: Egypt and liberation; Haman and Mordecai; Antiochus and Judah the Maccabee. The paradigm culminates and finds its most perfect expression in Auschwitz and the re-united Jerusalem. "Miracles" continue in the Six Day War, the Yom Kippur War and so on. Again, cogency is not the result of philosophical or ideological concepts. It is a result of compatibility with the idiomatic social location of the vast majority of North American Jews.

Collectively, Jews set up distinctive institutions such as synagogues and community centres. Individually, they participate fully in the larger society. Intermarriage (in which there is no conversion to Judaism) is the only major social boundary that Jews are reluctant to cross (Weinfeld 1981; Sklare 1971, 201ff.).[3] They consider themselves members of a distinctive ethnic-national group that lacks, however, a distinctive culture. This reflects precisely the social position of Jews in America. As a community, they express themselves through rituals and institutions. As individuals, they do what everyone else does with everyone else. In other words, they recognize no idiomatic behavioural norms.

Jews have managed to invest this ambiguous and bimodal social location with the transcendent meaning accruing to a tradition thousands of years old. How? They perceive themselves and their place in the world in terms of symbols drawn from classical rabbinic Judaism, elevating some and downplaying others. They do not think about these symbols in connection with the analytic discourse of theology. They do so in connection with public ritual. That is what gives these symbols their power to shape shared perceptions. North American Jews have reached a remarkably consistent consensus concerning their ritual life. They have retained some, transformed others and added some of their own. As I have mentioned, the Passover *seder* is still very important and Hanuka has become very important. These festivals now symbolize the centrality and transcendent meaning of Jewish peoplehood, resistance to the forces of assimilation and vigilance against potentially genocidal anti-Semitism. New public rituals, such as Yom Ha'atmza'ut and Yom Hasho'a, have been added to the sacred calendar. But the Sabbath, the keystone of rabbinic Judaism, has been reduced to a celebration of the family (that is, the Jewish people). And Shavu'ot, celebrating the revelation of Torah and stressing Torah study, is simply ignored.

In all this, what symbols readily stand out as prisms through which they view themselves among others? Put simply, North American Jews are Israel without Torah. Israel, not Torah, stands at the centre of Jewish life. Israel, as both the state and the people, is the primary symbol that communicates a sense of reality to Jews. The words "Israel" and "the Jewish people" are neither invoked by nor do they evoke a systematically organized set of ideas. Experienced in ritual, they spark shared emotions, images and allegiances. They are symbolic, in short, not conceptual.

Ultimately, the images and emotions evoked by "Israel" sanction notions of who owes what to whom within the Jewish world. In this way, the symbol functions somewhat as it would in a systematically organized conceptual framework. Operating at a more subtle and implicit level, however, its symbolic content remains less open to debate, controversy and attack than it would otherwise.

It is not enough to explain that North Americans in general are essentially non-conceptual, a half-truth at best. It is more accurate to say that the substance conveyed by this symbol remains prior, both phenomenologically and historically, to any theology or way of thinking that might some day win the allegiance of most American and Canadian Jews. And if "Israel" were to lose its power to evoke these images and emotions, because it no longer adequately reflected the social reality of North American Jewry, no theology or way of thinking would long survive the transformation.

**The religion of Jewish peoplehood and Zionism**

The centrality of Israel as a symbol invites consideration of the nature and function of classical Zionist theories and institutions (Waller 1981b; Taras and Weinfeld 1993; Woocher 1986) in the North American context. Generally speaking, the relation between classical Zionism and the structure of myth, ritual and symbol elaborated above is one of symbiosis, not conflation or identity.

Many Zionists bemoan the demise among both Israelis and Diaspora Jews of classical Zionism. The spirit of the *yishuv* (pioneering settlement) has largely died in Israel, say Zionist intellectuals. Even in the *kibutzim* (cooperative agricultural settlements) a thirst for the good life is said to overshadow any ideal of building up the Land. In America, few involve themselves in Labour Zionist pursuits. Fewer still discuss matters of Zionist theory in its socialist, cultural or religious modes. Asher Zvi Ginzberg (Ahad Ha'am), Max Nordau, Nahman Syrkin and Samuel Hayyim Landau, all important thinkers of early Zionism, ring no bells for the vast majority of North American Jews. Not even North American Zionist thinkers, such as Ben Halpern, are household names; his books remain largely unknown.

As pertains to North American Jewry, however, one might well ask: If things are so bad, why are they so good? The United Jewish Appeal (UJA) or Combined Jewish Appeal (CJA), which among other things raise money for the State of Israel, might suffer in any one year for various reasons—the economy, for one. Since 1967, though, there has been an upward spiral of support and concern for Israel expressed in terms of dollars for Israel. The state and related matters, such as modern Hebrew language and literature, claim an ever-increasing proportion of so-called religious education in Jewish day and afternoon schools, where once traditional religious subjects exhausted the curriculum. Indeed, some classical rabbinic festivals, notably Tu Bishvat and Lag Ba'omer, gain attention today primarily because they have been successfully married to Israel. Yom Ha'atzma'ut, as I have said, now occupies an important place on the Jewish calendar of festivals; Israel's Independence Day engenders more extensive participation among North American Jews than Jewish holidays sanctioned by centuries of observance. Jews cringe when Israel is criticized and rejoice when it is lauded. They revel in its accomplishments and agonize over its shortcomings. They feel secure when it seems secure and threatened when it is threatened.

In short, the State of Israel today occupies a supreme place in the self-consciousness of North American Jews despite the lack of a shared, coherent Zionist way of thinking or even familiarity with classical Zionist thinking. Furthermore, it is difficult to see that the current place of Israel in Jewish life emerges directly from classical Zionist thinking. Indeed, a type of Zionism (for lack of any other term) flourishes in North America, even occupying a central location in the configuration of North American Judaism, without any basis in Zionist thinking, classical or otherwise. By contrast, Zionism held no privileged place among North American Jews from the 1920s to the 1940s, when classical Zionism was at its height.

Jews need no elaborate theories to bolster their commitment to Israel. The state is a central mythic symbol, not an idea, by which they understand themselves and their place in the world among others. As a result of Israel's mythic importance, their ties with the State endure. To the degree that classical Zionism might define relations between Israel and the Diaspora, indeed, it would strike at the centrality of Israel in the self-understanding of most North American Jews. Social forces, not political theories, underlie the radical transformations in Jewish beliefs and rituals. By now, I suspect no form of Zionism would be able to transform the self-perception of Jews, let alone to reconfigure their social allegiances. At best, some form of Zionism might find support to the extent that it reflects current social patterns in the

Jewish world. Perhaps something like Jacob Neusner's formulation in *Stranger at Home* will gain currency, especially among intellectuals (1981b). But the enduring importance of Israel is based, ultimately, on the simple fact of its compatibility with the idiomatic, social location of most Jews.

## Zionist institutions and the religion of Jewish peoplehood

The idiomatic place of Israel bears implications for understanding the function of mainstream Zionist institutions such as the World Zionist Organization and the Canadian Zionist Federation. These organizations, along with Jewish communal federations and congresses, are important vehicles for the religion of Jewish peoplehood. They furnish both occasions and contexts, especially in connection with public rituals, for a significant level of participation. The explicit focus on Israel makes Zionist organizations all the more effective as outlets for this activity. And, with other organizations, they reward commitment and participation with public recognition, status and power (Waller 1981a)—all of which are important elements in any ethno-cultural system.

In fulfilling these functions, Zionist organizations (among others, to be sure) provide an institutionalized form of Jewish identity, life and community designed not to interfere with individual participation in the larger society of North America. It makes no difference that one of the most important purposes of these organizations, officially endorsed, is the facilitation and encouragement of *aliya*, emigration to Israel. This paradox is explained by the fact that North American Jews, who generally shun *aliya*, participate in Zionist organizations and activities for quite different reasons. The manifest function of these organizations runs counter to the basic commitments of North American Jews, it is true, but the latent function supports them.

## Transcendence and the supernatural

I have spelled out the central symbols, sacred stories and holy rituals of contemporary Canadian Jewry. Still, I would maintain that a silent partner everywhere lurks in the shadows. This has nothing to do with secularity or ethnicity. Words such as "eternal," "miraculous" and "indestructible" modify things of some other world, not this one. And yet the peoplehood of Israel, clearly "in the world," seems endowed with such qualities. Implicitly, at the very least, Israel is the object of processes deemed to be outside this earthly sphere. Israel points to transcendence in this symbolic structure of word and deed. When Jews believe that Israel's existence remains guaranteed in transcendent terms, they point, however obliquely, to a transcendent guarantor—even though they seldom invoke this guarantor by name, either YHWH or anything else. It should come as no surprise that Jews offer no theology for their undeniably religious sense of identity. By not pointing explicitly to a divine hand guiding Israel's destiny, of course, they avoid the need to answer a range of questions that anyone would want to ask about such a God. They can also avoid the possibility of disagreeing over the answers. Whether consciously or unconsciously, a veil has been drawn before the transcendent in this religion of Jewish peoplehood. And it works. Whatever the consensus reached by Jews, God is not part of it. To force God's explicit presence would shake the consensus.

Where have Canadian Jews gone since their immediate ancestors left behind traditional homelands and classical Judaism? Identity-defining stories, symbols and actions have all changed. Continuity with rabbinic Judaism endures, it is true. To what degree, though, is another matter. God and his Torah are central to the rabbinic view of reality. Both have been pushed into the background. Jews have maintained a distinctive group identity yet participate fully in the larger social milieu. That they can do so is due primarily to the particular structure of myths, symbols and rituals that, by consensus, has furnished a new Jewish identity. That Jewish identity, moreover, seems religious in significant ways.

The religion of Jewish peoplehood, then, provides an overarching, coherent and unifying framework for a high proportion of Canada's Jews (see Woocher 1986). It allows them to experience unity despite their diversity. Consequently, it is the shared platform on which groups within the community define their particular modalities of Canadian Judaism. The essays in Part 2 are about these modalities as constructed, in part, by the synagogue rituals of individual congregations.

## Notes

1 Weinfeld (1981) noted that the intermarriage rate is lower among Canadian than American Jews. Within Canada, moreover, the Jews of Quebec have the lowest rate (8%), half that of Ontario (16%) and about one-sixth that of British Columbia (47%). Until the middle or late 1970s, Francophone Jews of Montreal, however, intermarried at a substantially higher rate than Anglophone Jews of the same city. On the other hand, over half of the originally non-Jewish partners in these Sephardi-gentile marriages converted to Judaism, a higher rate of conversion than among non-Jewish spouses of Ashkenazi-gentile couples. More recent essays (Broadbar-Nezer, Cohen, Reitzes, Shahar and Tobin 1993; Brym 1993) confirm the pattern: Canadian Jews intermarry less frequently that American Jews, with Quebec and Ontario having the lower rates in Canada. In the spring of 1994, J. Torczyner (School of Social Work, McGill University) used the most recent figures from Statistics Canada to prepare an initial analysis of the demographic data pertaining to Canadian Jewry. His tentative conclusions were that over the previous decade assimilation had increased among Canada Jews (as it has among American Jews).

2 One indicator of this, ironically, is the increased rate of conversion to Judaism by the originally non-Jewish spouses of third-generation Jews in comparison to spouses of second-generation Jews in the United States. See Goldstein and Goldscheider 1968, 159-61.

3 See above, n. 1.

# PART 2

## Congregational Liturgical Ritual

# 4

## Ritual, Reality and Contemporary Society: The Case of a Reconstructionist Synagogue

### JACK N. LIGHTSTONE

In this chapter, the theoretical issues discussed in chapters 1 and 2 are brought to bear on a specific body of data. I consider here the character and significance of ritual practices at the Sabbath morning liturgy of a Reconstructionist synagogue.[1] To anticipate my conclusions, I argue that the Reconstructionist transformation of this liturgy encodes statements regarding the nature and boundaries of sacred caste, time, space and speech. With respect to all of these realms, one effect is to soften boundaries of what were once clearly differentiated entities. Another effect is to celebrate a mixture of sacred and mundane, special and ordinary, clerical and lay. Congregants believe that the blurring of these particular boundaries fits the social allegiances and proclivities regarding participation in North American culture and society. They experience their liturgical practices as particularly appropriate, in other words, given their social experience; their patterns of social involvement feel emotionally satisfying and cogent in relation to the liturgy. Congregants assert firmly their desire to remain Jews but also to participate in the aesthetic, artistic, cultural, economic and social enterprises of higher-status, educated North Americans. Likewise, they retain, but mix, what were once highly differentiated symbolic realms in their particular variation of the traditional rabbinic liturgy. In this mirroring, both their particular ritual and their ethos are experienced as emotionally satisfying and appropriate.

### Larger problematic

Although there is no point in reviewing what has already been discussed fully in the introductory chapters, some further remarks about the larger problematic of this study are germane to what follows. Too often, the study of religion—contemporary Western religions in particular—fails to document, interpret or explain ritual adequately. Students of religion have tended to concentrate on the effect of modernity on religious belief and theology (Douglas 1982). Social scientists have interested themselves in authority and levels of affiliation among "mainline" religious groups (Wilson 1969). Even those who have concerned themselves in some sustained way with religion in the contemporary Western world (Cohen 1983) have tended to concentrate on the ever-declining level of religious observance among contemporary Western groups as measured against traditional ones.

What scholars have found is hardly news by now. Even so, it continues to be documented as if it defines a major direction of research. Students of religion in the modern Western world have pointed for almost a century to the continued secularization of society. Traditional beliefs and clerical authority impinge ever less on patterns of life and modes of thought. Regular attendance at mainstream churches and synagogues continues to decline. By contrast, moral norms and world-views are increasingly taken from the secular sphere. Psychology and psychodynamics, for example, supply much of the framework by which individuals understand themselves and their relations with others.

All of this is true. For good reason, it is heavily researched. But hardly any attention has been paid to the continuing role of religion, even of established religious institutions, in the lives of undeniably secularized people. Even though traditional belief systems and authority structures are on the wane, people continue to affiliate themselves with established religious denominations and perform their rituals, albeit selectively. Indeed, both Catholicism and Protestantism have experienced so-called revivals of various sorts, even, once again, among relatively secularized people. Judaism, too, has experienced revivals, not only in the *ba'al tshuva* ("returnee-revivalist") movement in Orthodox Judaism but also in the continued reinstatement of traditional rites in Reform Judaism.

This, as Mary Douglas points out (1982), has caught the field of religious studies by surprise and is, indeed, something of an embarrassment to liberal and radical theologians. Witness such ironies as Jacob Petuchowski, a major Reform thinker, calling in 1972 for "limits" to "liberalism" by reintroducing some concept of a normative *halaka* (rabbinic law). For this, he was branded by many colleagues as "neo-Orthodox." His heresy was explained away with references to a more classical rabbinic training received back in Europe. Believing that he had merely reverted to the sins of his youth, critics considered him nothing more than an anomaly. But some 10 to 15 years after Petuchowski's heresy, both male and female (ordained) graduates of the Hebrew Union College-Jewish Institute of Religion wear the traditional *talit* and *kipa* (prayer-shawl and skull-cap) at their graduation ceremonies.

Even this brief example indicates that, with respect to Judaism, terms such as "revivalism" and "neo-conservatism" do not really help in characterizing, interpreting or explaining the phenomenon under discussion; they imply nothing more than a return to the past only, a welcome revival for some and a deplorable anachronism for others. Obviously, male and female rabbis graduating together, each wearing a *talit* and *kipa*, is something other than a return to the past. It is a contemporary integration of tradition and modernity to create something new. It is expressed through ritual, however, not theology.

This example suggests that the inadequate approach to religion in contemporary, secular society is due at least partly to the fact that many scholars are either unwilling or unable to take seriously the continuing, albeit selective, practice of religion. For as Douglas has pointed out (1982a), there exists a bias among contemporary scholars (as among many liberal theologians) in favour of religious belief and theology. Consequently, there is a hiatus in the study of religious practice. Scholars (no less than theologians) attribute an autonomy and primacy to the realm of ideas, mediated in primarily discursive language—an attitude that is tied, no doubt, to their own social context. The result is not only a lack of attention paid to what can be communicated through rituals, but also a dearth of theoretical and methodological tools with which to describe, interpret and "explain" them.

To rectify this situation, the first two chapters of this book have been devoted to conceptual, methodological and theoretical perspectives. In this chapter, I apply them to the study of Sabbath worship at a Reconstructionist synagogue. Before continuing, though, I must add two further methodological points. First, I have adopted a self-imposed limitation. Congregants gave their own interpretations of the liturgy. I have bracketed out such interpretations. It follows from my theoretical stance that a structured variation on the classical liturgy implicitly communicates non-referential knowledge of the world quite *apart from* any interpretations that the participants might offer. For my purposes, their tendency to interpret this way or that is further information *about them* as well as their liturgy.

Second, I must explain how information was collected. Madeleine Mcbrearty attended Sabbath and festival services at the synagogue, on a regular basis, for approximately eight months (see chap. 5). During that time, she documented the liturgical performance, the physical setting, the participation of congregants and the interaction among them. In addition, I attended five or six times. After the service and during the *kidush* (blessing over wine), when informal socializing is encouraged, Mcbrearty had opportunities to chat with congregants about the service. The study had been preceded by some 10 months of interviews, during which time she met with about one dozen families, four times each. This prior phase of the research supplied information about religious observance and belief, occupational and social involvement, attitudes to the synagogue, to the Jewish community and to its institutions. Of particular importance was the use of ritual, broadly defined, in the context of family life. Synagogue officials offered further information about the socio-economic profile of this relatively small congregation. Documents from the local Jewish federation provided demographic information about the Jewish community at large.

## The "setting" of the Reconstructionist liturgy

Performance of the liturgy occurs within a conceptual framework. Common to most members of the synagogue is Reconstructionist philosophy. It is implicit in the community's ritual innovations and is often referred to during the service itself. Using the analogy of drama, the liturgical setting includes both its "staging" (or physical environment) and its "author's notes" to the "actors" (a conceptual framework underlying the "script," which provides a context for deviations from other "scripts"). The setting, in short, is conceptual (the movement and its philosophy), geographical (the synagogue's location), physical (its architecture and interior arrangement), and social (the community and those who attend regularly).

*The movement: Its philosophy and organization*

The Reconstructionist movement differentiated itself from the United Synagogue of America (the Conservative movement) in a number of stages (see Raphael 1984). It originated in the late 1930s as a "left-wing party" within the ranks of both Conservative and, to a lesser extent, Reform rabbis; these rabbis assented to the theology, philosophy and resulting programme of Rabbi Mordecai Kaplan, a Jewish educator and faculty member of the (Conservative) Jewish Theological Seminary. In the last 20-25 years, Reconstructionism has emerged as an independent movement in North America with its own congregational organization and, for its own rabbis, a seminary (the Reconstructionist Rabbinical College in Philadelphia) and professional association. The movement has adopted an institutional structure paralleling that of other mainline Jewish movements in North America, particularly the Conservative movement.

Reconstructionism remains the smallest of these—largely because of its relative "youth" but also, possibly, because of its more pronounced conceptual character. For reasons to be discussed, this appeals to a highly educated stratum of the Jewish population. As in the particular congregation under study, many members of this movement are professionals.

Kaplan conceived of Judaism as the "evolving civilization of the Jews" (1934). He claimed that the canonical texts of Judaism, from the Bible through ancient and medieval rabbinic literature, reflect the various stages of Israelite and Jewish social experience. Heavily influenced by Emile Durkheim, Kaplan saw rabbinic law, doctrine and ritual as collective representations, informing and being informed by the evolving social reality of the Jewish people. Since the God-idea was one aspect of these collective representations, the traditional understanding of God was, first, a reflection of social experience and second, an evolving symbol. Kaplan solved a major problem in modern Jewish thought—how the natural is related to the supernatural—in arguing that the latter was virtually eclipsed by the former.

Kaplan's active program allowed Judaism to serve a social function: enhancing the Jewish social experience and preserving the Jewish people. In addition, he believed that all modern lay people could and should be encouraged, in the spirit of intellectual honesty, to recognize and understand the natural basis of Judaism. Such a program, he hoped, would allow modern Judaism to respond more effectively and change more readily to meet the ethnic-social reality and consciousness of modern, educated Jews in America. A major result, in any case, was the development of the synagogue-community centre, which met the liturgical, religious, educational, social and recreational needs of Jews. Synagogue-community centres are now very popular in all North American Judaic movements.

Reconstructionist congregations can be subdivided into two categories. Some were originally associated with the Conservative (or Reform) movement but had long been served by rabbis of Kaplanesque leanings. Others were founded as Reconstructionist synagogues before the Reconstructionist Rabbinical College opened. The former probably display a more conservative approach to liturgical matters; socio-economic traits of their members will more closely approximate those of "mainline" Conservative (or Reform) congregations. But no systematic study of this has yet been done.

The Reconstructionist rabbinate and movement has issued its own edition of the prayer-book, or *sidur*. It depends heavily on the Conservative one in both substance and form. The latter, in fact, is its point of departure. Hebrew and English are on facing pages, with meditations and other supplementary readings interspersed among traditional elements of the liturgy as well as filling the pages of a substantial appendix. Mediaeval supplementary hymns, which appear in the traditional Hebrew *sidur*, are largely eliminated. The same is true of biblical psalms, which are recited in the traditional liturgy. What remains in the Hebrew focuses on what the ancient rabbis would have called *matbe'a tfilah* ("the basics of prayer"). Even here, though, the text has been modified—especially regarding messianic expectations; the editors have eliminated eschatological references to restoration of the Temple with its cult and the Davidic monarchy. Also eliminated are references to Jewish exclusivity, left largely untouched in the Conservative edition.[2]

## *The congregation: Its building and membership*

The synagogue stands on the northern edge of the central-western part of a residential district. One mile to the south, a mile and a half to the southeast, and for some three miles to the southwest are districts heavily populated by Jews. Major Jewish communal institutions, such as the federation (an umbrella institution for all Jewish communal services), are concentrated less than a mile to the south. Within a mile from the southeast through southwest are some one dozen synagogues, almost all Orthodox. One of the largest Conservative congregations, however, lies only six blocks or so to the south; another is situated about a mile and a half to the southwest.

The Reconstructionist congregation and the major Conservative one define a north-south line separating distinctive socio-economic territories. The neighbourhood immediately to the south and east is middle income and upper-lower income in character. It is ethnically mixed, with some minimal interethnic tension. The area also includes a rather high proportion of elderly Jews. Further to the southeast are upper-middle and upper income enclaves. Immediately to the south and west live some quite wealthy families. Further to the west and southwest are mixed upper-middle and upper income areas.

To the north is a large non-residential area characterized by middle-sized, non-retail business and light manufacturing. About two miles to the north lies the closest northern suburb, which also has a substantial Jewish population in the middle-income range. In all, some 65,000 Jews live within two or three miles of the Reconstructionist synagogue.

The synagogue building is austere compared to the other synagogues in the neighbourhood. It is roughly one and a half stories in height, although it appears even less lofty from the outside. The design is rectangular; even the roof is flat. The sides are faced with normal, household red brick. On the extreme left, facing the street, are the main doors; these are simple doors that might just as easily mark entry into a small commercial or industrial operation. Municipal public works buildings and storage facilities flank the building. It could be mistaken for similar buildings except for a sign on the lawn, the congregation's name over the door and some understated stained-glass windows at the southeastern corner. The building is relatively new, about 20 years old.

The interior is as simple as the exterior—except for an area containing the ark, with its Torah scrolls, behind which are the stained-glass windows. A *bima* (platform) of modest proportions, which rises about ten inches above the floor, occupies this corner of the building; on it are six chairs, the *shulhan* (reader's table) and, of course, the ark itself. Because both its curtain and its doors are transparent, the Torah scrolls are visible at all times. The *ner tamid* (eternal flame) burns immediately above and in front of the ark.

The *shulhan*, from which the liturgy is led and at which the rabbi addresses the congregation, stands in front of the ark. Like the ark, it is of simple design with hardly any decoration. The overall effect in this area is light, open, airy and approachable. It does not seem like a *locus sanctus*, a place set off dramatically from the world outside. Unlike many other synagogues, after all, it is not decorated sumptuously with dark wood panelling, gilded ornaments, rich tapestries and so forth.

The sanctuary contains no permanent pews. Ordinary moveable seats fan outward before and on either side of the corner in which the ark is situated. Normally, seating is provided for about 100-150 congregants. There are no separate areas, of course, for women and men. The rabbi often uses a slightly more decorous chair on the *bima*; on a few Sabbaths, however, he sits in the first row of the congregational seating. This room is not a sanctuary *per se*, then, but it functions as one when the service is in progress. Except for the ark area, it is a large, open, multipurpose room. In the northwestern corner of this room is a mezzanine. Folding partitions can close off the mezzanine and the areas beneath it. One such area is used for the *kidush* (a traditional blessing over wine followed by light refreshments), which takes place at the end of every Sabbath morning service.

Congregants who attend regularly differ in many ways from their counterparts at neighbouring synagogues. They range from about 35-60 years in age; most are in their late 40s. On average, therefore, they are younger than those who go to other synagogues. Nevertheless, no particular accommodation is made for children. There is no nursery or children's service (other than a program held upstairs on the semi-monthly "family Sabbaths"). Many worshippers come as couples. Middle-aged urban professionals are particularly in evidence. Less in evidence than at other synagogues are businessmen and merchants from small or medium-sized concerns. More in evidence, on the other hand, are professional women. Most congregants have undergraduate degrees; many have post-graduate degrees or professional diplomas in addition.

The synagogue has few professional functionaries. The incumbent rabbi arrived some 17 years ago, soon after his ordination. He is its first full-time rabbi. Previously, the congregation considered a lay leader its spiritual mentor and resident expert on Reconstructionism. This man currently enjoys what is essentially the status of rabbi emeritus. One of the more elderly members, he served until recently, on a part-time basis, as a Torah reader. He also instructed those preparing for their bar mitzvah or bat mitzvah ceremonies. His role was roughly that of the *hazan sheni* (assistant cantor) in a traditional setting. There is no professional cantor; the rabbi leads the liturgy.

**Sabbath morning service**

A detailed analysis of the morning service, which follows the Reconstructionist prayer-book, lies beyond the scope of this essay. Here, I focus attention on how the liturgy is *performed* at this synagogue and how the patterns of its performance differ from those of the almost one dozen Orthodox synagogues in its immediate vicinity.

*Typical Orthodox Sabbath*

At most of the large Orthodox synagogues roundabout, the Sabbath morning service begins at approximately 8:30 and ends between 11:00 and 11:45. Men (with sons and younger daughters) straggle in from 8:30 to 9:45. Many women do not arrive with their husbands; they file in (with older daughters) between 9:15 and 10:15. Single young adults arrive any time from 8:30 to 10:15.

At Orthodox synagogues, adults, adolescents and young adults tend to sit in specific areas with others of the same sex. A barrier (*mehitsa*) separates the two sexes. Generally, the women sit further away from the centre of liturgical activity than the men do. Young boys and girls may sit with either of their parents (until, in some synagogues, "junior congregation" begins at 10:00). Children roam about quite freely. Usually off-limits to them, however, are the *bima* (on which the ark and dignitaries' "thrones" are situated) and what amounts to a second *bima* (on which is the reader's table) located more centrally among the men.

The Orthodox (and Conservative) service consists of six main divisions: blessings of the dawn; preliminary psalms; the morning service proper; the

Torah and prophetic readings; the "additional" Sabbath prayer; concluding hymns and psalms. The morning service proper, legally the mainstay requirement of the morning liturgy, consists of two main sections: the *shma* ("Hear O Israel," with attendant blessings and prayers); and the *tfila* or *amida* (the "prayer" said while "standing").

In modern Orthodox synagogues, the rabbi normally delivers a sermon, from 10-20 minutes in length, from a pulpit on the *bima*. This often takes as its point of departure some aspect or passage of the Torah reading and links the latter to rabbinic texts in some skilful manner; both biblical and rabbinic passages are then brought to bear on a contemporary issue.

By the standards of a Reform or Conservative synagogue, the Orthodox service might appear informal to the point of being disrespectful or indecorous. In fact, this informality is more the case at certain junctures in the service than at others. Movement and talking is tolerated (indeed, even permitted under Jewish law) until the beginning of the morning service proper and after the completion of the *kedusha* (the *sanctus*, which is part of the *amida*). What lies between is set off from the rest by proscriptions that have as their alleged aim the maintenance of strict concentration throughout. The same is true (although to a lesser extent) during the "additional" service, again through its *kedusha*. A total proscription on movement is in effect during the *amidot* of both the morning and additional services, again until the *kedusha* is completed. Devotees must stand, feet together, facing the ark (usually located on the eastern wall). So the traditional service can be subdivided according to limitations made on normal activity, movement and mundane speech.

Dress too has a role to play in making the Orthodox service distinctive. Both men and married women must cover their heads. Men normally wear *kipot* (skull-caps); women wear fashionable hats. Women usually dress fashionably, in fact, though "modestly." Men wear *talitot* (prayer-shawls with fringes at each corner)—a requirement for married men—over jackets and ties. The *talit* is an interesting garment. Though it need not be, it is usually white with a black or navy blue trim. The more traditional the congregation, the larger the *talit*. Some men like calling attention to their status or religiosity by using elaborate embroidery along the collar (*atara*); even so, 90 percent of its area usually remains unadorned. In a traditional synagogue, then, the suits worn by men, of normal variety in style and colour, are almost completely hidden by their nearly identical *talitot*. Sitting together, the men form an almost undifferentiated sea of white. The less Orthodox the congregation, the less dramatic the effect. Other aspects of the Orthodox service will be discussed in connection with the Reconstructionist one.

*Traditional and Reconstructionist worship*

The Reconstructionist service commences relatively late on Saturday morning, after 10:00, and ends at around 12:00. As a result, most of those who attend are seated when the service begins or shortly thereafter. Couples arrive together. Husbands and wives sit together. Relatively few unmarried young adults or children are present. Children do come on family Sabbaths, however, and sit with their parents. (Soon-to-be *bene* and *benot mitzva* must attend with their parents at least one service every month.) The rabbi generally sits either on the *bima*, opposite the table, or in the first row of congregational seats.

Men and women are generally well dressed, yet some wear clothing that would be considered too casual at an Orthodox or Conservative synagogue. Not all women wear hats. Of those who do, some wear *kipot* (usually associated with men). A few even don *talitot* (traditionally associated with men). On family Sabbaths, though, fewer women do this sort of thing. All the men wear *kipot* and *talitot*. But many fold their *talitot* so that they look more like scarves than body-wraps. My point here is that the clothing of both men and women (and the hair of women) remains fully visible.

Decorum is evident throughout the service. There is hardly any talking or moving—except, of course, for what is required liturgically (singing and chanting, standing, sitting, moving to and from the table during the Torah reading). No differentiation is made between formal and informal parts of the service; the entire service is marked by politesse. Congregants participate actively, seldom assuming the role of passive auditors.

From the outset, the liturgy is reduced to the Reconstructionist version of rabbinic essentials, the *matbe'a tfila*. After a brief opening hymn, the morning service proper begins (although the Reconstructionist *sidur* does contain the preliminary blessings and psalms). It consists of the *shma* and its blessings, the morning *amida* and readings from the Torah and the Prophets. The service is conducted by the rabbi with a part-time *hazan sheni* to read the Torah and a capable congregant to chant the prophetic text. No effort is made to honour the rabbinic proscription on interruptions during the main part of the service (from the *shma* and its blessings, through the *amida* to the *kedusha*). The rabbi himself, in fact, might interject very short prefatory remarks between passages of the liturgy or even interrupt his own conducting of the liturgy to announce pages for those who cannot follow the Hebrew. The usual congregational response to any use of the divine name in a blessing, "blessed is he, and blessed is his name," is said in violation of the rabbinic proscription—a particular violation, I might add, that is commonly heard even in modern Orthodox and Conservative synagogues. Some parts of the liturgy are read in English or Hebrew by everyone. Other parts are read responsively by the congregants and the rabbi or a designated congregant. The texts recited vary from one week to another. Occasionally, the rabbi replaces a traditional text with a passage by some modern Jewish thinker.

In traditional settings the *amida*, without the *kedusha*, is first recited silently as an act of personal and private devotion. Then, the whole thing is repeated by the cantor, this time with the *kedusha*. Also added is the priestly blessing of Leviticus. (In some synagogues, this is performed by the members of the priestly caste; more often, it is performed by the cantor.) In our Reconstructionist synagogue, the morning *amida* is begun in unison with the rabbi; the *kedusha*, too, is sung in unison. The remainder of the *amida* continues in much the same way as the *shma*: part is chanted by the rabbi and part in unison, part in English and part in Hebrew. The *amida* is not repeated. Silent devotional prayer, in fact, is absent. Interestingly, the priestly blessing has been retained and is said in unison to accompany a kind of family hug: the men wrapping their wives and children in their *talitot*. Everyone understands that the adults are blessing both their spouses and their children. Single adults wrap and bless those next to them. The *kadish* (doxology) concludes the *shma* and *amida*, separating what went before from the scriptural readings.

Following the *kadish*, a Torah scroll (usually one) is removed from the ark while everyone sings standard liturgical hymns. Two congregants, male or female, are honoured with the opening and closing of the ark. The rabbi recites a meditation in English before the open ark (instead of the Zoharic meditation found in Orthodox and Conservative *sidurim*). After the scroll is taken out, the ark is closed. The synagogue president (a woman during our study) holds the Torah, leads a procession among the congregants. Some of them touch the outer covering of the scroll and then kiss their hands (the traditional way to venerate a Torah scroll). At the *shulhan*, the scroll's covering is removed by the reader. This is followed immediately by the reading. As in traditional settings, congregants are called up in turn to recite appropriate blessings over each subsection of the day's Torah portion. This honour is bestowed by a lay officer on men and women alike. These blessings are not, however, those of the traditional liturgy. The latter refer unequivocally to the exclusivity of the Jewish people and to the expectation of eternal life after death. Both have been edited out of the Reconstructionist version in favour of sentiments regarding the Torah's importance as a guide and inspiration for the ongoing life of the Jewish people.

The traditional minimum of seven such "congregant-readers" (excluding one who chants from the Prophets) is not always observed. As a result, the reading of the day's Torah portion (assigned according to the synagogue's triennial cycle of readings) sometimes remains unfinished. A few congregants actually chant the text over which they have recited blessings or do so for other honorees. This is hardly the norm; as in most Canadian (or American) synagogues, even those of Orthodox affiliation, few possess the requisite knowledge; in any event, this must be arranged in advance to allow time for preparation. An ability to read from the Torah (and, to a lesser degree, from a prophetic text) earns high status.

Rabbinic law establishes a protocol concerning the sequence of persons called up to recite blessings over the Torah reading. The first *aliya* ("ascending" to the table) must go to a male member of the priestly caste, the second, to a male Levite. The remainder go to male commoners, or "Israelites." Our congregation has abandoned this protocol, just as it has essentially "democratized" the priestly blessing.

In a traditional synagogue, reading the Torah is a rather lengthy procedure. The reading itself is lengthy, as the weekly portions are defined so as to complete the entire Pentateuch in an annual cycle of Sabbaths. Ancient rabbinic texts indicate that, in second- and third-century Palestine, each cycle took three years (only a third of the Pentateuch being completed in any one year). Our Reconstructionist synagogue has shortened the Torah reading by adopting a triennial cycle (evoking the ancient Palestinian custom as precedent). But this is not the ancient triennial cycle. It is a reorganization of the annual cycle. Only one third of the normal weekly portion (normal, that is, according to the annual cycle) is read each week: in year one, only the first third; in year two, only the second third; and in year three, only the last third. The obvious disadvantage is that the congregation never hears the text in sequence, but only as a curious array of disjointed chapters out of context. The advantage is that they retain the traditional names for individual Sabbaths, each of which is normally referred to by the name of the weekly Torah portion. Furthermore, the synagogue can observe legitimately (from its own point of view) the autumn festival celebrating completion of the annual cycle.

Congregants are attentive throughout the Torah reading, following either the Hebrew text or its English translation. This contrasts with the casual conversations that occur in many Orthodox and Conservative synagogues.

As in traditional congregations of European origin, the scroll is held aloft for all to see when the readings conclude. At this moment, the traditional "catechism" chanted by the congregation specifies that "this is the Torah that Moses placed before Israel, from the mouth of the Lord, by the hand of Moses." Such claims about revelation and Mosaic origins are excluded from the Reconstructionist liturgy.

The prophetic reading in Hebrew follows, chanted by a congregant of either sex with the requisite competence. The Torah service generally continues with prayers for the State of Israel in English and Hebrew (although this prayer is sometimes skipped). These are followed, as in traditional synagogues, by another procession with the Torah, its traditional veneration and its return to the ark. Sometimes, the rabbi recites a meditation in English before the ark is closed.

At this point, in modern Orthodox and Conservative synagogues, the rabbi delivers a sermon. In our congregation, the rabbi leads a sermon-discussion on some topic chosen in advance. He begins by delivering a short discourse, homily or sermonette that introduces the topic and, at the same time, presents his own stance or, more properly, his own "take" on the tradition's stance. The rabbi's discourse-introduction often begins with reference to something in the Torah reading and how it can be related to some contemporary problem, political, social or moral.

During this sermonette, the rabbi plays a role: authoritative teacher and scholar of the tradition. Following the sermonette-introduction, he plays another role: moderator of an open discussion. The social and psychological distance between the rabbi and the congregants is immediately and significantly reduced; he plays this second role much as a professor might in the discussion period following a lecture. No one is particularly reticent about joining the discussion. Congregants disagree freely with one another and with the rabbi. The mode of argument, though it might include appeals to Judaic texts, is primarily discursive and rational. Consequently, congregants can claim the status of pundits (since they cannot claim the status of rabbinic experts on traditional sources). After a reasonable length of time, the rabbi concludes the debate with remarks intended to bring about a harmonious closure. Efforts are made to have guest lecturers on family Sabbaths. After the initial address, once again, the "sermon" evolves into a debate of sorts. One cannot avoid feeling that the sermon-discussion is considered a highlight of the liturgy. When the prayers and even the Torah reading are truncated, it seems, this is done to allow more time for discussion.

The Reconstructionist *sidur* has substantially reduced the concluding additional service, the *musaf*. The latter, in fact, is often eliminated entirely. The liturgy concludes, as Conservative ones do, with three hymns sung in Hebrew (*en kelohenu,* the *alenu*, and *adon olam*). The last hymn is preceded by the *kadish*, recited by mourners.

The congregation retires to its congregational *kidush*. After the wine is blessed, it is time for light refreshments. Congregants greet one another with *shabat shalom* ("May you have a peaceful Sabbath") and engage in casual conversation before departing.

**Meaning**

As I have argued in the opening chapter of this book, the meaning of a contemporary Jewish liturgy is often based, at least partly, on controlled variation from the traditional Orthodox one. This is especially so in the case under study here. Our congregation is located in a sea of modern Orthodox congregations. Many people known to our congregants—friends, relatives and associates—attend these other synagogues, no matter how infrequently. Our Reconstructionists sometimes attend them as well, no doubt, in connection with their social obligations. Most of them, moreover, are "first generation" Reconstructionists. In other words, they have had prior associations with other forms of Judaism, especially Orthodoxy (even if their families were not themselves Orthodox). Many congregants in their fifties and sixties were previously members of more traditional synagogues. Our interviews indicate that many congregants, particularly men, have had extensive religious education in Orthodox settings, often in day schools. Orthodoxy and its liturgical ritual is no distant ancestral memory. Rather, traditional Judaism lies in the past of virtually all congregants and is occasionally experienced even in the present. It is in relation to this traditional environment that they perform and experience their own Reconstructionist Sabbath service.

On the surface, their liturgy intends to provide a meaningful experience of worship for congregants who are highly educated, secular and liberal. The text strives for "intellectual honesty" by reflecting contemporary liberal attitudes and values. The claim of being a "chosen people" is shunned. Allusions to the authority of a revealed tradition are excised. In general, the supernatural is eschewed. Exclusive liturgical roles based on ascribed status, including vestigial ones of the priestly caste, are eliminated. Sexual distinctions are rejected.

Below the surface, though, other things are going on. Translation of the liturgy into an egalitarian, rational and natural idiom indicates discomfort with the older idiom. Basil Bernstein has studied the social factors underlying preferred patterns of speech (1971). Even if his study is ethnocentric, as some critics have maintained, Bernstein's findings are germane to this study. Mary Douglas provides us with an apt summary:

> Professor Bernstein pointed out that humans speak and that it is high time to note that speech is patterned in different ways according to the patterns of social relationships. He likened the control of speech by social factors to a coding system. The difference between fully explicit speech, the elaborated code, and the context-dependent restricted code was obviously going to be crucial to education. For the child of [a] middle-class family is introduced to a set of roles and speech forms which is geared to success in school and the outside world where verbal explicitness counts. The child who can only handle the restricted code and who only knows social roles which are given implicitly, not defined verbally, is at a disadvantage in education (1975, 175).

Douglas goes further elsewhere (1974). She proposes that people who can "handle" restricted codes can "read," in context, the layers of implicit meaning in symbols and symbolic language, the very stuff of liturgy. These people do not feel the need to have such language translated into an elaborated code that explicitly pins down a set of meanings communicating referential knowledge. Those who are more skilled in elaborated codes, on the other hand, require just such a translation. The validity of the resulting referential knowledge is judged by empirical standards. This state of affairs is characteristic of the Reconstructionist congregation, particularly in the overall direction of emendations to the liturgical text.

In Bernstein's view, the character of social relationships is encoded in speech. It is interesting to note that our congregants explicitly reject even vestigial religious authority based on ascribed status—whether by sex, caste or anything else. They value achieved status based on scholarship. This is much more in tune with the values they live by in the larger world. Many, indeed, are rather highly educated professionals. Their socio-economic commitments in everyday life are reflected in the relatively "elaborated code" of their liturgy. Their socio-economic status depends, moreover, on these predilections.

Other aspects of the Reconstructionist service tend to confirm this impression. The sermon-discussion itself effects a transition. It begins with the rabbi playing a relatively traditional role (which is recognized as such by everyone); it highlights the rabbi's traditional expertise and his authority to edify the congregation. But it is complemented and completed with something akin to a discussion or, at times, a debate. Congregants vie with one another (and at times with the rabbi) to display not only their skills at social, moral and philosophical analysis but also their knowledge of Judaic sources (of which the rabbi remains the acknowledged expert).[3] This competition for achieved status based on intellect extends beyond the sermon-debate; congregants compete to display the knowledge required (in ascending order) to read Hebrew, chant the prophetic portion and chant the Torah reading. Each of these talents, which can be compared to academic achievement, wins recognition from fellow congregants.

The structure of a Reconstructionist service, when compared with an Orthodox one, is congruent with this analysis. Just as social distinctions based on ascribed characteristics are explicitly rejected, so the definition of time and space implicitly expresses discomfort with an autonomous and bounded sacred realm. Reconstructionists do not like the idea that particular moments in the liturgy are removed from the realm of normal human activity (such as casual speech and free movement). The Orthodox prohibitions limiting speech and movement of the feet are absent, as I have observed, in the morning service and *kedusha*. No longer is the Torah an inviolate realm, the internal order of which cannot be changed (to which nothing may be added and from which nothing may be removed). According to the triennial cycle adopted by this congregation, portions are read out of order and out of context. Reading the Torah in Hebrew is halted prematurely, moreover, in order to get on with reading it in English; time is thus saved for the sermon-discussion.

The relative lack of distinctively sacred realms is all the more evident in spatial arrangements. Men and women sit together. *Talitot* do not hide the clothing of individuals and thus create an undifferentiated territory of white. The seats are moveable, thus making the room multifunctional. The architecture and internal appointments do not create the atmosphere of a bounded *locus sanctus*. The ark, for example, is transparent. The *shulhan*, moreover, is not always located on the *bima*. When it stands at floor level, the rabbi sits in the first row of seats (thus making him part of the congregation, though never entirely so).

All of this can be interpreted in positive terms as a proclivity toward mixing realms and crossing boundaries. The seating is mixed, with men and women sitting together; some women even wear the liturgical paraphernalia associated traditionally with men. Among the men, normal Western attire is not hidden by traditional religious attire; both liturgical and non-liturgical apparel are fully visible. The perquisites of ancient social castes are not only rejected but also interspersed; anyone in the congregation can do what could otherwise be done only by members of a particular caste. The rabbi, who leads the liturgy, does not even wear liturgical robes. The *shulhan* is often placed in the midst of the congregation; the transparent character of the ark, moreover, allows those outside to see in. The sanctuary is a multifunctional room. The synagogue's exterior resembles that of a secular, medium-sized, business complex.

In this liturgical mixture of realms and groups one finds a collective representation of the congregants' basic social values and proclivities. Among the primary questions facing North American Jews for the last century has been the appropriate degree of assimilation to, appropriation of, and participation in, the non-Jewish world. In what ways can these two realms, Jewish and non-Jewish, be integrated? To what degree would this be desirable? Various groups have responded differently to such questions. Some have expressed the desired degree of mixture in terms of behavioural norms governing social, economic and cultural dealings with the non-Jewish world; this approach is illustrated by contemporary Orthodox legal interpreters such as Rabbi Moses Feinstein. Others have expressed the desired degree symbolically in the style and character of their liturgies; this approach is clearly illustrated by the Reconstructionists under discussion.

The Reconstructionist liturgy of this congregation does not do away with the sacred. But neither does it define the sacred as that which occupies its own homogeneous territory, guarded and differentiated from other realms. The sacred is distributed or dispersed throughout the ordinary. Think of an analogy: material suspended in a liquid. The material does not dissolve; neither does the substance remain a solid block into which the liquid may not penetrate. Relative to a traditional Orthodox service, a Reconstructionist liturgy allows the traditional hierarchy of differentiated realms in social, spatial, and temporal spheres to melt into one another. Thus priestly functions are left to non-priests. The *kedusha, amida, shma* and other prayers do not form a clearly differentiated hierarchy of sacred moments that are defined by proscriptions regarding common speech and movement. In moving toward what Bernstein calls an "elaborated code," the Reconstructionist use of language approaches that of everyday technical and rational society. The architecture of the building and its appointments do not radically distinguish the place of prayer from mundane space; they allow for continuity, on the contrary, between sacred territory and normal territory.

If our Reconstructionists feel comfortable in maintaining any distinctively sacred realm at all, it is in the intellectual realm as expressed in discursive communication and debate about Jewish history, values and sources. If there remains "a people dwelling apart," for our congregants, it exists only in the context of discussion or debate.

In summation, our Reconstructionists' transformation of the traditional Sabbath morning liturgy encodes statements regarding the nature and boundaries of sacred times, space, speech and caste. In all of these realms, its effect is to soften the boundaries of once clearly differentiated entities and to value a mixture of sacred and mundane, special and ordinary, religious professional and amateur. The blurring of these particular boundaries "fits" their social allegiances and values regarding participation in North American culture and society. Their liturgical practice is experienced as particularly appropriate given their social involvements; likewise, their social experience feels emotionally satisfying and cogent in relation to their liturgy. Participating in the intellectual, aesthetic, economic and social enterprises of high-status and relatively well-educated North American society, Reconstructionists still assert the desire to remain Jews. As a result, they feel free to mix once highly differentiated realms.

**Notes**

1  This chapter depends heavily on information collected meticulously by Madeleine Mcbrearty, to whom I express my heartfelt gratitude.

2. The Reconstructionist congregation's prayer-book has since undergone revision. As a result, many of the above issues were matters of debate. To that list one may add gender-specific language.

3  In relation to these points, I note that many congregants refer to their rabbi as Rabbi Jack (not his actual name), but never simply as Jack. By doing so, they simultaneously project on him the image of rabbinic authority (with the attendant social distance) and that of a friend or colleague (with the attendant social familiarity and proximity). They indicate, too, that he can never be only the latter. By contrast, rabbis of other congregations have told me that they suffer from a type of social loneliness. Someone in this situation is always "the rabbi" or Rabbi [Surname]—in other words, denied any personal name and therefore any personal relationships.

# 5

## The Use of Non-vernacular Language in the Sabbath Morning Service of a Reconstructionist Synagogue

### MADELEINE McBREARTY

This chapter's purpose[1] is to address some theoretical issues of the larger project by examining the role and function of a specific element of a religious ritual, non-vernacular language, within the morning Sabbath liturgy of a Reconstructionist synagogue. The data used in this paper were gathered through personal interviews with individual respondents as well as through participation in the weekly and seasonal congregational services.

Clifford Geertz has argued that culture consists in "clusters of significant symbols" that unite to form an organized association providing a society with its unique identity (1973). Using a definition proposed by Susan Langer, he stated that these symbols could be "any object, act, event, quality, or relation which serves" (1973, 91). Not only do individual symbolic structures (such as religions, ideologies or legal systems) constitute patterns of "meaning" that offer clues to the interpretation of culture; they also give meaning to individual experiences and provide legitimacy to human behaviour.

The microcosmic elements of rituals, which for our purposes we will understand with Fred Bird as "any stylized, repeated [and] intrinsically valued act[ions]," serve as the vehicles that express and translate concepts formulated within the larger symbolic structure of religion (Bird 1980; chap. 2 above). Rituals as vehicles of expression, then, can be construed as a language, or as Roy Rappaport suggested, primarily as a mode of communication (1971). Similarly, Edmund Leach proposed that "we engage in rituals in order to transmit collective messages to ourselves" (1976, 45).

If ritual is one language of religion, we must necessarily ask what, in fact, is communicated through the agency of such a performance. Or, given the social and symbolic structures that form the field of our research, what messages, both explicit and implicit, are encoded in the religious ritual performed among intellectual, liberal and highly secular members of a modern Jewish congregation.

Furthermore, the study of religious rituals as communicative language both offers an insight into the nature of a cultural system and contributes to revealing the social identity of its participants. Making use of the work of socio-linguist Basil Bernstein, Mary Douglas attempted to point out the predilections toward distinct modes of communication produced by particular forms of social structures (1973, 40ff.). Without further elaboration, we concur with Douglas that, because of this inclination or bias (as she herself would put it), ritual practices offer a key to the understanding of the larger cultural or symbol system.

In turn, Bernstein affirms that language acts not only as a transmitter of the cultural system but as a guide to the evolution of the social character of the individual. While Bernstein's research was concerned with the speech codes pertaining to families from specific social groups and the implications of such patterns for the educational system, he stated in his larger problematic that "every time the child speaks or listens, the social structure is reinforced in him and his social identity shaped" (Bernstein 1971; Douglas 1970, 44). It will be our purpose forthwith to examine the ways in which the collective messages conveyed through the performance of rituals help shape the social identity of participants.

Contemporary religious rituals are complex amalgamations of composite elements: stylized gestures, factual or symbolic offerings, prayer, reading of sacred scriptures, repetition of shared sacred myths, homilies, music, chanting, singing, dancing and so forth. These constituting factors are fused to produce a complete whole just as semantic units are juxtaposed in the composition of a sentence. Unfortunately, this analogy has often been carried to exaggerated conclusions (as in Lévi-Strauss 1958). But our understanding of ritual as language begs that we should approach the investigation of its meaning in a manner similar to that of the linguist who would undertake a syntactic analysis. While it is true that no single word carries the meaning of a whole sentence, we cannot minimize the importance of single elements within the structure. Furthermore, how better can we ascertain the identity of an author than by examining his choice of words?

In our modern society, no element of ritual action is more pervasive than language. It is through the agency of language that most component parts of ritual find their expression. Silent meditation might form the basis of a ritual in certain instances, but the communal religious rituals that constitute the object of our enquiry require extensive oral communication.

Verbal expression can take several forms and assume diverse functions within ritual performances. While language can serve to convey such practical information as the number of a hymn or the page of a *sidur* (prayer-book), it is also the medium used by believers to express their deepest religious feelings to a Sacred Other construed as most holy. Language can function to express the explicit purpose of a ritual. Or, in conjunction with other elements and in the most oblique fashion, it can operate to suggest an implicit meaning of the same ritual. Oral communication can consist of a few words casually spoken in an ordinary language. Then again, it can involve intricate formularies uttered in a familiar or in a foreign dialect. It is with this form of communication, non-vernacular language as a component of ritual, that we will continue our investigation.

Whatever other characteristics can be assigned to language, its most important feature within a ritual performance is that it is shared by the participants. We turn once more to Douglas, who writes that a "common speech form transmits much more than words; it transmits a hidden baggage of shared assumptions" (1975, 177). If she is right, and she has certainly presented a convincing argument, we must reiterate our previous question and inquire into the meaning of this element of ritual. What collective messages are transmitted through the use of non-vernacular language? What assumptions are shared by a group of people performing a ritual in a formal language perhaps not easily understood? What, for example, is the place of King James English in a contemporary Anglican church service? What are the implications of the use of Hindi or Sanskrit for members of the East Indian community who no longer understand these languages? More precisely, we will seek to understand these questions by focusing our attention upon the Reconstructionist Sabbath morning liturgy in an endeavour to establish the meaning and function of biblical or classical Hebrew for this liberal Jewish congregation.

First, a few notes on the movement and its ideology.[2] The Reconstructionist movement began in North America in the late 1930s as several rabbis from Conservative and Reform Judaism concurred with the ideology proposed by Rabbi Mordecai Emmanuel Kaplan. Although it remains largely parallel to the Conservative Movement, Reconstructionism has become independent in the last several decades, with its own rabbinic association and separate seminary, the Reconstructionist Rabbinical College in Philadelphia.

The particular Reconstructionist synagogue with which we are concerned is composed of a large number of highly educated professionals who give more than a casual assent to the ideology of the movement. In fact, a high concentration of intellectuals seems to be the norm in Reconstructionist synagogues both in North America and in Israel.

A characteristic that seems to attract membership is that within the movement, at least theoretically, the status and role of women is comparable to that of men. Although, in the actual services, the authority structure appears more male dominated, it is undeniably less so than in those of Orthodox synagogues. This equality of sexes has often been stated as the reason why the congregants chose to become members of this particular group.

Mordecai Kaplan construed Judaism as a social experience and, in the words of Jack Lightstone, he was "[h]eavily influenced by Durkheim. . . . Kaplan saw rabbinic law, doctrine and ritual as the collective representations, informing and being informed by the evolving social reality of the Jewish people" (chap. 4 above). Reconstructionism struggles with such theological concepts as the chosenness of the Jewish people, messianic expectations and the domain of the supernatural in general. It was Kaplan's contention that supernatural elements should be dropped in favour of a more natural basis for the religion. A *minhag* ("ritual custom") committee,[3] at least in the synagogue under study, is currently attempting to revise and adapt the liturgy in an endeavour to reflect truly the Kaplanesque ideology. But North American Reconstructionists have retained the supernatural, so far, as part of their myths. This struggle has given rise to striking paradoxes and sharp ambivalences that cannot be minimized. These will become evident through our analysis.

With these all too brief explanatory remarks, the purpose of which is to inform our analysis of Reconstructionist ritual performances, we may return to our problematic. As mentioned previously, the constituents of non-vernacular language used in the Sabbath morning service are biblical and classical Hebrew, as well as Aramaic (the latter, primarily in the mourners' *kadish*, to a much lesser extent).

Reconstructionists have made, and continue to make, a conscious effort to "reconstruct" Judaism. To accomplish this, they have extensively revised the Orthodox, rabbinic liturgy. While a thorough comparison of Orthodox, Conservative and Reconstructionist *sidurim* would prove enlightening, the task cannot be performed at this time. It will suffice to point out that only a core of traditional prayers remains in the latter.

The service always begins and ends with Hebrew psalms or prayers. Although English might be interjected, the *shma* as well as the repetitions of the *amida* are always sung in unison in Hebrew. The Torah reading is conducted in Hebrew, although English might be used to complete the reading of an unusually long portion. The *haftara* and its accompanying blessings are invariably recited in Hebrew.

Hebrew, therefore, appears as the language of prayer as well as the language used to recount the sacred myths. As a non-vernacular language, it functions within the liturgy to define boundaries between the sacred and the profane as well as between members of the group and those perceived as non-members.

Perhaps the greatest dichotomy that exists between the rational assent given to an ideology and the implicit meaning derived from the analysis of ritual is to be found at the level of this distinction between the sacred and the profane, which is effected in the performance of the ritual. Reconstructionists do not appear to impute an intrinsic and permanent quality of sacredness to a being or to a material object that would then be construed as possessing this attribute ontologically. Rather, it is the quality of impermanence that best describes the sacred. This impermanence is certainly reflected in the concept of space.

The building in which congregants meet for their weekly services is very unostentatious. Viewed from the outside, as noted in chapter 4, it could easily be mistaken for a structure belonging to the city's public works department, because such buildings occupy the immediately adjacent area. Unlike the interiors of Orthodox or Conservative synagogues, that of the Reconstructionist synagogue is not divided into several rooms; the main sanctuary is housed in the central core of a large hall that is almost directly accessible from the outside. During the morning liturgy, folding partitions are drawn across the room with the effect of reducing its size. Simple metal chairs that can be rearranged easily allow the room to function as a reception hall. This hall can then be used for a congregational meal (*kidush*), either on a regular Sabbath or following a bar mitzvah or bat mitzvah. The *shulhan* itself is often moved off the *bima*, depending on the desired formality of the Sabbath service. Finally, even the ark in which the Torah scrolls are stored does not stand in a prominent place, nor does it constitute the focal point of the room during times when the liturgy is not performed. The result of this spatial arrangement is that the synagogue is considered not a permanent sacred space but a multipurpose, functional centre. This, I might add, is in keeping with Kaplan's program.

As congregants arrive on Sabbath, they greet each other informally and stand around the periphery of the auditorium. But as soon as the rabbi intones the first words of the Hebrew psalms, which constitute the first portion of the liturgy, attention becomes focused on the performance of the ritual. Non-vernacular language acts not only to demarcate the beginning of the ritual, therefore, it also serves to distinguish between ordinary time and sacred time. It allows profane space to take on a sacred character. On the whole, it operates to give an aura of factuality to the otherwise elusive concept of the sacred. Through the use of Hebrew, participants are able to recreate sacrality every time the ritual is performed.

As mentioned previously, we remain unable to apprehend fully the constituents of this sacred realm, but this is an ambivalence that Reconstructionists themselves experience. Whatever this non-ordinary domain is perceived to be, it is a domain that is not approached casually. Non-vernacular language facilitates and regulates this intercourse with the sacred. Through their assent to a Kaplanesque ideology, the supernatural is eschewed. Through the liturgy, however, Reconstructionists address the deity as "God, king of the Universe." Hebrew, then, allows congregants to gloss over concepts that would require much elucidation if uttered in the language of rational discourse.[4]

A further role played by non-vernacular language is to delineate boundaries between members and non-members of the Jewish community. Although Reconstructionists have made more than a few alterations to the traditional prayer-book, as we have mentioned previously, they have preserved Hebrew as the language of the liturgy. This has the effect that, on Sabbath mornings, Reconstructionist congregants retain a sense of belonging to the larger Jewish community; its adherents have in the past, and are now, rehearsing the same liturgy, however truncated it might appear in its present setting. In a society made up mainly of people who do not identify themselves as Jews, the use of Hebrew in the liturgy reinforces the collective identity of the participants as members of a distinct group.

Certainly, ambivalence toward the concept of chosenness plays an important role in the setting of guidelines for the acceptance of non-Jews within the congregation. I have been informed repeatedly that non-Jewish partners in mixed marriages are neither required nor urged to convert to Judaism. At least theoretically, the borders of the community appear wide open. Yet the same people who so graciously accept these non-Jewish spouses are emphatic in their refusal to allow their own sons or daughters to marry non-Jews. Furthermore, members of the Reconstructionist movement, through their disregard of *halaka* (though not more than many Orthodox or Conservative Jews), manifest behaviour attesting to their complete integration, if not assimilation, into the larger society. When the same people assemble for the Sabbath morning service, however, conversations almost invariably turn to the fact that anti-Semitism is a real threat to the members of the Jewish community. The use of Hebrew would appear to strengthen the sense of belonging to this community, then, a community not permanently or inherently chosen but one set apart from the larger society of which Reconstructionists are also citizens.

Apart from its role in establishing and strengthening boundaries, there are two other functions of non-vernacular language. I would like to address these briefly: affording status to individuals who demonstrate their competence in Hebrew; and producing immediately efficacious results.

It might seem strange to those who are accustomed to Orthodox or Conservative modes of worship that Reconstructionist services are held with considerable decorum and with a high degree of participation by the congregation. Even those who cannot read Hebrew hold up their *sidurim* as if they were, in fact, reading the text. And they join the chanting during the better-known prayers (such as the *shma*, the *amida* and *adon olam*), which they obviously know from memory. Unlike other synagogues, the Reconstructionist one does not retain the services of a cantor. Rather, a volunteer from the congregation reads Torah portions. Except in the case of bar mitzvah or bat mitzvah, the Torah reader is a particular individual. This man, however, is now in the process of training other members to replace him. The *haftara* is performed, and I use that word carefully, by a different person every week. Upon the completion of the *haftara*, a reader is warmly embraced and enthusiastically congratulated by other congregants who comment generously on his or her performance.

Although Torah or *haftara* readers gain instant status and recognition, congregants readily identify themselves with these competent performers and vicariously assume their proficiency. More than once, I have heard members of the congregation boast of the fact that many among them are competent to perform the tasks at hand. The use of Hebrew presents itself as a reminder and reinforcer, therefore, of the socio-economic consciousness of upper-middle class, highly educated, intellectual congregants who have proved themselves competent and successful in other areas of their lives.

Finally, a word on the propensity imputed to non-vernacular language to effect immediately efficacious results. To illustrate this point, I must relate the details of a short encounter I had with a Reconstructionist congregant, a woman with whom I had previously become acquainted when I conducted personal interviews on the role of rituals in family life. Our chance meeting took place on the street one day. The woman informed me that she and her husband were planning to take a trip to Europe the following week. She then told me that she had not attended *shul* (Yiddish for "synagogue") for quite some time but that she certainly would be there on the coming Sabbath. Aware of the fact that this woman did not feel the need to attend synagogue every week, and quite surprised that she would choose to go at such a busy time, I inquired as to the reason she was so adamant about not missing the Sabbath morning service. Her reply was simply, "We're going on a trip; we must go and get our blessing."

This woman's answer immediately reminded me of the many times I had witnessed the conferment of such blessings by the rabbi during the Torah reading. Usually, seven *aliyot* are given (often to a couple but also to single people, either men or women) during the time when the appointed reader recites the weekly portion of Torah. Although the *aliyot* appear to the observer to be distributed at random by the *parnas* of the synagogue, they are understood by congregants as a means of conferring honour or marking a special occasion. For a birthday, an anniversary, an impending trip, the birth of a child, vicariously for a sick member of the family or any event that is considered outside the realm of the ordinary, one becomes eligible to be "called up" to the *bima*.[5] On most occasions, those who have received an *aliya* recite only the customary blessings that accompany the reading of Torah; on certain occasions, the rabbi, who usually sits aside during this time, approaches the *shulhan* and announces to the congregation that he will read a particular blessing for a special event that has occurred or is about to occur in the individual's life. The rabbi's announcements are done in English, but the blessings are recited in Hebrew. Even if the congregant does not understand Hebrew, there is a sense that these Hebrew blessings act as magical formula apprehended as effective to ensure blessings such as the welfare of the individual, recovery from illness, safety while on a trip or good fortune for the coming year. The Hebrew blessing, in its language and highly formulaic style, is considered efficacious. It does appear to be a welcome element of the ritual, because it allows the summoning of benevolent forces that will keep the destiny of the individual on the right course, a summoning, however, that remains effected outside the realm of rational discourse. Again, the use of Hebrew frees the congregant from having to give conscious intellectual assent to that toward which she or he is ambivalent.

## Notes

1. This article was written during the tenure of a doctoral fellowship provided by the Social Sciences and Humanities Research Council of Canada. I wish to express my appreciation to the Council for its generous financial support. An earlier version of this paper was given at the annual meeting of the Canadian Society for the Study of Religion, Hamilton, Ontario, June 1987.

2. For a thumbnail account of the development and ideology of the Reconstructionist Movement, see Jack Lightstone's account in the previous chapter.

3. One task of this committee is to determine the proper manner of performing the liturgy.

4   I do not wish to imply that Hebrew is not readily understood. As with the language of formal prayer, however, and through its formulaic style, non-vernacular language allows assent to theological concepts outside the realm of rational discourse.

5   There are certainly other times when *aliyot* are given for no specific reason other than recognizing or conferring honour upon an individual.

# 6

# Ritual Performance in a Reform Sabbath Service

## MARC P. LALONDE, LOUISE MAYER and JACK N. LIGHTSTONE

**Introduction**

The community described in this paper is a Reform congregation. The data were assembled over a year and a half between the fall of 1987 and the spring of 1989. During this period, one of the authors regularly attended the Friday evening Sabbath service; another attended on a less frequent basis. (There was no substantial service on Saturday mornings.) The observers freely took notes during the service itself, with the knowledge and consent of the rabbi. Members of the congregation were fully aware that we were present to study their ritual expressions. Similarly, we participated in the *oneg shabat* (a reception in honour of the Sabbath) after each service, seeking information in a less restricted atmosphere. This activity resulted in a number of insightful statements offered by those who attend regularly, allowing us to familiarize ourselves with this particular group and to glimpse the disposition, tone and temperament that inform it. Finally, the rabbi was interviewed about the history and evolution of the service and about the nature of the congregation. In this way, it is hoped, we are moving toward what Clifford Geertz called a "thick description." That is, we have tried to gain access, however modestly, to the "conceptual world in which our subjects live so that we can, in some extended sense of the term, converse with them" (Geertz 1973, 24).

This essay, though, attempts an introductory analysis of how a well-orchestrated service, together with the controlled ritual changes, represents a model of "reality" as well as a model for social interaction and "mapping." Within a socio-anthropological framework, we examine the temple setting, the main actors and their roles and the liturgical script.

We contend that one significant meaning of this religious "drama" is tied to its implicit communication. Communicated through the service are two things: shared perceptions concerning the locus of, and the modalities of access to, the sacred; and relations between the latter and the social allegiances of our congregants in their lives beyond the synagogue. Most immediately, the liturgical drama observed appears to convey the sense of being part of an audience before, and drawing from, a sacred Judaic realm. This realm is revealed and mediated by others, mainly religious professionals. The sacred is not experienced as a Judaic realm effected by the ritual activities of the congregation as whole, in other words, for it appears that the congregants do not, even during the service, come to experience themselves as inhabitants of that realm. This way of mapping the locus of, and their relation to, the sacred (that is, Judaism) accords with the ethos of this particular community. But we hope this analysis does not find merely "correlations between specific ritual acts and specific secular ties." We hope it sheds some light on how people's "notions . . . of the 'really real' and the dispositions these notions induce in them, color their sense of the reasonable, the practical, the humane, and the moral" (Geertz 1973, 124). In this case, the "really real" seems to manifest qualities that are inherently tied to modernity. As such, the ontological vision of this Reform congregation not only reflects the tenets of the modern, secularized world but also values them.

## Theoretical considerations

The introductory chapters of this volume discuss in detail the specific methodological and theoretical framework that informed this study as one among an ensemble of coordinated studies. Beyond that specific frame of reference, and as already noted, the more general formulations of Geertz have guided what follows. In particular, his discussion of ritual as a model both "of" and "for" reality allows us to understand how the information we gathered communicates the way a world-view is functionally related to its symbolic expression and its resulting ethos. According to Geertz, a "model of" reality involves the "manipulation of symbolic structures so as to bring them ... into parallel with the pre-established" world-view (1973, 93). By "world-view," he refers to people's "picture of the way things in sheer actuality are, their concept of nature, of self, of society. It contains their most comprehensive ideas of order" (1973, 127). In effect, a model of reality *articulates*, in an alternative medium, the relations embodied by their conception of ultimate reality. A model for reality, on the other hand, involves the "manipulation of the . . . [world-view] in terms of the relationships expressed in the symbolic [realm]. . . . Here, the theory is a model under whose guidance physical relationships are *organized* . . ." (1973, 93; emphasis added).

Together, according to Geertz, models "of" and "for" reality participate in those cultural patterns that "give meaning, that is, objective conceptual form, to social and psychological reality both by shaping themselves to it and by shaping it to themselves" (1973, 93). What this implicit Durkheimian thrust suggests is that our psycho-social reality is formed by cultural patterns and, at the same time, that we try to mould these cultural patterns according to our psycho-social propensities. Thus, models "of" and "for" reality are related to psycho-social reality itself, both passively and actively.

In terms of our particular study, a pre-established world-view incorporates both Reform ideology (understood in the non-pejorative sense of that term) and the idiosyncrasies of our Reform community. At this point, it must be stressed that we are not identifying Judaism *in abstracto* as the matrix of this pre-established world-view. One reason for abandoning this identification is that it leads inevitably to a coalescence between "Judaism" and its Orthodox interpretation. When Orthodoxy is established as the norm for Jewish belief and practice, analyses of Reform, Reconstructionist or Conservative expressions tend to be one-sided. If our goal is to converse with the "conceptual world in which our subjects live" (Geertz 1973, 24), we must be aware of the elements that constitute it. Undoubtedly, aspects of Orthodox Judaism are part of the Reform world-view. Indeed, at many junctures in its ongoing process of self-definition, Reform articulates its world-view both explicitly and implicitly in relation to traditional rabbinic Judaism and its contemporary Orthodox interpretation. But this does not mean that a direct comparison should be our point of departure. We want to understand the Reform service in its own right, as something that communicates a "conceptual world" with an "ethos" that informs it and is informed by it.

A community's ethos, writes Geertz, is the "tone, character, and quality of their life, its moral and aesthetic style and mood; it is the underlying attitude toward themselves and their world that life reflects" (1973, 127). Ethos and world-view, moreover, validate each other. That is, the "ethos is made intellectually reasonable by being shown to represent a way of life implied by the actual state of affairs which the world-view describes, and the world-view is made emotionally acceptable by being presented as an image of an actual state of affairs which such a way of life is an authentic expression" (1973, 127).

What our theoretical considerations ultimately suggest, is that the models "of" and "for" reality observed in our Reform synagogue communicate a world-view associated with both Reform Judaism in general and the specific ethos of this Reform congregation in particular. This can reveal some useful insights about the nature and character of the latter's particular appropriation of the former. Before examining the symbolic structures of this complex, we must introduce the community in question by commenting on its history, economic foundation and political constitution.

In assessing the information we collected, it is crucial to understand that this study took place in what now seems to have been a decade or so of significant transition. During the entire post-war period, the character of this synagogue, or "temple," had been aptly and intimately represented by the style of its rabbi, a man who had served the community for many decades. (We shall call him Rabbi Cohen.) He had retired to the position of rabbi emeritus. His physical strength and vitality diminished, Rabbi Cohen withdrew slowly from temple affairs. During this period, the congregation sought an adequate replacement. This proved to be a difficult task, for he had uniquely embodied the explicitly and implicitly shared perceptions of at least the most influential members. These perceptions were challenged by successive "replacements," of course, but also defended by the "old guard." A brief account of the history, constitution and economic organization of this temple will provide some of the most basic facts that form the background of, and correlate with, this transitional state of affairs.

## The temple's history

The Reform community under study is one of the two in the immediate area. Reform Jews are few in this city; most Jews consider themselves either Orthodox or Conservative (in that order). Of the two Reform temples, this one is the older (having been established as the first of its kind in Canada around 1882) and the larger (claiming about nine hundred families). The other temple was founded in the mid-1960s. It is about a tenth of the size of the older temple. The Reform community described here, then, holds a unique position in relation to both the larger Jewish community and the larger Reform community.

The synagogue building is located near the city's downtown core but on the edge of an old and wealthy neighbourhood. Unlike many other synagogues, it is not located in a Jewish district.

As it now exists, the congregation is the result of a merger. During the 1950s, some dissatisfied members of the original congregation (which we shall call Temple A) broke away to form a more conservative or traditional kind of Reform community (Temple B). But due to financial circumstances, the two joined forces once more in 1980-81—after the retirement of Temple A's rabbi. Another important period in the history of this community involves the temple's venerated Rabbi Cohen. Arriving in 1927, he "put the temple on the social and religious map," as the saying goes. His "progressive" views on intermarriage and Jewish-Christian dialogue, along with his intense preaching style, became famous. In fact, he quickly became a major figure in both the Reform world and the Christian one. His accomplishments include attracting such celebrated speakers as Martin Luther King, associating with such important political figures as David Ben-Gurion, Menachem Begin, John Diefenbaker and Queen Elizabeth II and forming friendships with eminent Catholic and Protestant leaders. In short, it was no exaggeration to say that Rabbi Cohen "dines with Royalty." Because of his activities, our community was considered by many to be among the most prestigious in Canada. At any rate, it attracted many important and wealthy people.

After serving the temple community for 45 years, Rabbi Cohen retired in 1972. Until his death, he served as "rabbi emeritus." To this very day, however, the auspicious memory of this celebrated man looms large in the minds of most members. Many sermons, official speeches and even casual conversations still refer to Rabbi Cohen and the glory he represented. His sayings are quoted alongside those of the biblical prophets. Many people still dream of returning to this "mythological era" before the advent of ordinary time.

During the years following Rabbi Cohen's retirement, multiple search committees were unable to generate an adequate long-term replacement. In fact, many rabbis have occupied the pulpit over the past 10 years. In each case, the incumbent either resigned or was dismissed in an atmosphere of grave disappointment and bitterness. When we began our project, yet another rabbi had been hired on a one-year contract (with the possibility of renewal). He was forced to leave before the end of his contract, however, and a series of visiting rabbis occupied the pulpit while the synagogue, once again, sought an incumbent. Someone was named in March of 1989, which coincided with the end of our presence at the temple. He took up the position several months later.

## Economic foundations

On one level, the temple is a kind of business, an institution that provides a service to interested parties. Whatever might be said about its religious function, in other words, the temple community requires a financial base in order to sustain itself. We knew that, over a 10-month period in 1987, the capital assets of this community totalled around $2,120,000. Of this amount, $405,000 represented the contribution of Temple B upon returning to the mother congregation in 1980. The principal assets of our temple included the land, the building and its equipment; these were valued at $1,350,000. As for outstanding debts, the temple had accrued a long-term deficit of $37,000. Nevertheless, the temple generated income. It earned $560,000 during the same 10-month period. Of this sum, $436,000 was attributed to membership fees. On the other hand, expenditures came to $602,000. In short, the community's excess of expenditures over income was around $43,000.

Although it is impossible to provide financial details for such an institution, it is reasonable to surmise from these figures that the community is in a relatively secure financial position. In our judgment, the temple's assets are described rather conservatively. For instance, the temple structure, land, and equipment were valued at cost in the fall of 1987 and took into consideration neither the appreciation nor depreciation in value. The temple is located on the edge of the city's core and just within a very wealthy residential area. The building, moreover, occupies most of a city block. A more accurate value might have been $7,000,000 or $8,000,000, if not more, during the fall of 1987. Furthermore, the community did not have a mortgage; aside from a debt of $37,000, it was free of debt. If this temple were a business in the ordinary sense, it would be a safe investment.

The primary financial difficulty facing the community was its cash flow. The $43,000 excess in expenditures indicates that this congregation was unable to generate fresh income and had to rely, therefore, on its capital assets to cover expenses. Consequently, its executives and directors were preoccupied with membership numbers and fees. Their reasoning ran as follows: the total budget was around $760,000; they had about one thousand families; therefore, an average annual fee of about $800 would have covered the budget. But the synagogue used a graduated scale to determine membership fees. Some members, 56 to be exact, paid between $1,200 and

$3,500 annually. But 386 members paid less than $400. Of these, moreover, 61 paid only $100. The goal at this time was to encourage those paying between $400 and $800 to increase their fees. As one temple document stated the matter: "We have a big heart for those unable to pay more, but it means that those who can, must and should pay more. This is the only way to ensure the survival of our Temple in particular and Reform Judaism in general. . . ."

**Institutional constitution**

The sense of urgency in that statement might be somewhat exaggerated in view of a relatively healthy financial situation. But it might have been motivated by a desire to hide more serious and pressing problems. One of these was surely the desire to attract new and enthusiastic members. The temple community was aging; not enough young people were available for leadership roles. According to one estimate, 80 percent of those on the temple's board were over 50. On the other hand, there was more to this sense of urgency than demography. It was caused partly by a power struggle. As one document notes, "the younger generation, those of thirty to forty-five years of age . . . may be overwhelmed by the presence of a larger number of trustees from another generation." Indeed, as one informant told us, "it takes a very long time to become a part of the temple 'higher-ups,' and it discourages the young people from joining in the temple life."

These statements pointed clearly to a struggle occurring within the congregation. Apart from anything else, this struggle was caused by animosity between the two congregations that had merged. One informant told us that Temple B "lords their $400,000 . . . over our heads, as if it's some big deal. Because of this, they don't feel they have to dip into their pockets to help out the community. Well you just can't do things that way." The division between Temple A and Temple B seemed to have an impact on many concerns. Consider the search committee established to find a new rabbi. Some members considered it autocratic; it did not heed the concerns, they said, of ordinary members. Similar comments were made about the ritual committee (involving the rabbi, the cantor and selected lay members), which organizes the liturgy and thus sets the tone for each service. The committee's members comment on the sermon, for example, and select the music to be performed. But the fact is that, for all intents and purposes, both of these committees serve only the 60-75 people who show up every Friday evening (as distinct from those who show up for holidays, weddings and other special events). As is so often the case in contemporary Canadian synagogues, the people who have power, use power and argue about power are seldom among those who actually attend.

Let us turn now to the Sabbath service held every Friday evening, its physical setting and its participants.

## The temple setting

The temple was built in the 1950s, just after a fire destroyed the old building that had stood on the same property. The service takes place in the main sanctuary. This room could easily be identified as a large concert hall, one that could seat a thousand people. The seats themselves are exactly like those found in a concert hall. The front half of this sanctuary is the most elaborate. Most dramatic of all is its ceiling. The "dome" rises to a point in the centre, like a huge tent with "creases" or "folds" that run from the centre to the walls. Embedded in these "folds" are small round spotlights that create the illusion of stars. The effect is one of openness and immensity. Looking up to the ceiling is like looking up into the heavens.

Facing the sanctuary seats, on a stage, is an ark containing the Torah scrolls. It is placed against the western wall, not the eastern one (or the one facing Jerusalem, as it would be in most other synagogues). The ark is also shaped like a dome. Unlike the ceiling dome, which is angular, this one is rounded. It is perfectly white and gives the appearance of solid stone. On each side of its doors hang dark velvet curtains. These are pulled open, making it difficult to read the embroidered words in Hebrew. Covering the doorway itself are sheer curtains that can be opened and closed by pulling cords hanging nearby. These sheers allow the inside of the ark to be seen at all times. During the service, therefore, the numerous Torah scrolls (dressed in blue velvet with silver breast plates and resting on white fabric) are permanently visible features of the stage setting. The Torah scrolls are surrounded by splendour. Just above the ark's door hangs an eternal flame, a lantern of red glass suspended from three long metal rods.

To the left of the ark is a lectern. It holds the cantor's sheet music, a gold reading lamp and, discreetly placed, a water pitcher and glass. On a small table beside the lectern sit the sabbath candles and the cantor's silver *kidush* cup. In front of this ensemble are some plants and flowers. To the right of the ark, is the rabbi's table (*shulhan*). About four feet long, it is placed at a slight angle in order to face the centre of the sanctuary. It is made of a dark, rich wood; on the front panel is an engraved design. This table holds a gold reading lamp and a silver *kidush* cup. Like the lectern, it is surrounded by plants and flowers.

Behind the lectern and the table are eight high-backed armchairs; each is covered in orange velvet and has a dark, wood trim. These chairs are reserved for the rabbi, the cantor, the temple president and special guests. Officials enter the stage directly through a concealed door in the wood-panelled wall.

The temple's electronic equipment includes three microphones. One is for the rabbi and another for the cantor. The third, placed inside the ark, is for anyone speaking or singing in front of it. Use of the microphone is interrupted, therefore, only when the rabbi and cantor parade around the temple with the Torah scrolls. Another piece of electronic equipment is the video camera. This is placed strategically on the wall behind the cantor. It allows the professional choir and organist, who are hidden behind the centre wall in a loft, to see the cantor and thus avoid the risk of an uncoordinated performance. An appropriate motto of the performers, in fact, would be: "we will not risk an uncoordinated performance." This attitude is indicated not only by the careful placing and use of electronic devices but also by the grand architecture and elegant décor. It communicates comfort, simple but refined and gracious.

### The principal actors, their roles and the service's script

Contributing to this sense of tasteful balance are the main actors of this religious drama and their respective roles. The performers include a male rabbi, a female cantor (in the congregation's parlance, a "soloist"), a paid choir and organist, "honoured guests" and, of course, members of the congregation. The latter, though, are more like members of an audience attending a performance. This last point will be discussed later in more detail.

At this temple, the Sabbath service is on Friday evening, not Saturday morning. This state of affairs was once common in the Reform world but, over the past few decades, has become less common. Because there is no service on Saturday morning, elements of that liturgy (such as reading the Torah) and items of the regalia (such as the prayer-shawl) have migrated, as it were, to Friday evening. The Reform prayer-book has long accommodated this situation. In addition, some of the rituals performed at home on Friday evening (in more traditional communities), such as lighting the Sabbath candles and blessing the Sabbath wine, have migrated to the temple.

The rabbi's role is to lead the service. His status at our temple is expressed in several ways. For one thing, he wears a long black robe and a prayer-shawl (*talit*). The latter has migrated from the traditional service on Saturday morning. Our rabbi wears it about the neck like a scarf, however, not over the shoulders like a shawl. And he does not wear a skull-cap (*kipa*). The cantor, a woman, is dressed in precisely the same way. This places her on a parallel plane of authority. The honoured guests are neatly dressed in suits or dresses. Whether male or female, they wear their prayer-shawls as scarves. Aside from the clergy, no participants wear prayer-shawls and only a very few (men) even wear skull-caps. What this suggests is that a strict separation exists between the audience and the *viri religiosi*. The rabbi, the cantor-soloist, the president and the honoured guests all enter from a door at the right side of the stage. They all sit, facing the congregation, in distinctive chairs. And they all wear prayer-shawls. This strongly suggests that ordinary people come as spectators to watch officials perform the liturgy for them (and, literally, before them).

This interpretation is supported by the roles of each performer. The rabbi's role, once again, is that of an official leader. His responsibilities include telling the congregation where to find prayers and hymns in their books, asking them to stand up or sit down, parading the Torah around the

Temple, reading the Torah and giving the sermon. The last two, in particular, establish his religious and intellectual authority.

Although the Torah portion is relatively brief (not more than around 10 verses of a chapter), it presents an opportunity for the rabbi to demonstrate his mastery of biblical Hebrew and of the unpunctuated, unvocalized script of the Torah scroll. This is an important and differentiating virtue. Most congregants cannot read (even vocalized) Hebrew. For obvious reasons, they consider this ability an essential attribute of their religious leader. Interestingly, reading the Torah is not assigned to the rabbi in other, especially more traditional, synagogues; that is the cantor's job. Reading the Torah, our rabbi alternates between Hebrew and English; he translates the passage line by line. Interrupting the flow of Hebrew text in this way would be unthinkable in more traditional settings. It is worth noting, moreover, that the rabbi translates even though every pew is equipped with a translation of the Bible. The relative ease with which he translates, however, underscores his competence. For instance, one visiting rabbi translated the verses as if he were telling a story, using plain, everyday English expressions to communicate its message. Many congregants were quite impressed by this display.

The rabbi's other major responsibility is to preach. The sermon is considered a highlight of the service. One informant commented that the sermon is her sole motivation for attending the service. The sermon, after all, is what clarifies the relation between religion and modernity. The rabbi must be able to shed some religious light on a variety of pressing demands that arise in the secular world. For this reason, to explain Judaism, he must demonstrate his mastery of secular learning. Not only must he account for the nature and character of modernity, but he must also display a critical awareness of his own religion in relation to modernity. During the sermon, therefore, he often mentions Jewish contributions to the "secular city." References to prominent Jewish authors—Primo Levi, Philip Roth, Mordecai Richler, Benjamin Disraeli or George Steiner, to name but a few—are particularly popular. In demonstrating his Jewish expertise, moreover, the rabbi often provides brief overviews of theologians or philosophers such as Abraham Joshua Heschel and Emil Fackenheim.

On the other hand, he might offer his own thoughts on the "essence" of Judaism. What this often amounts to is a comment on the relation between Reform Judaism and Orthodox Judaism. It is commonplace for Reform (as for Conservative) Jews to define themselves in relation to Orthodox Judaism (or their perception of it). Our congregation is extremely sensitive to the Orthodox belief that Reform Jews are not "real" Jews. This belief is combatted in a variety of ways. One sermon suggested that Judaism is like a tree with many branches, each moving out in a different direction; when one limb denies the existence of another, the whole tree dies. The rabbi went on to assert that the Reform interpretation has played an essential role in the salvation of this "tree." He argued that Reform's acceptance of modernity—both aesthetically and intellectually—has halted the trend toward assimilation. Modern Jews oriented toward the values and benefits of a contemporary lifestyle need not leave Judaism in order to fulfill their ambitions; they need only embrace the Reform expression of Judaism. The bottom line throughout these discussions, though, is the oneness of the Jewish people. As one (visiting) rabbi stated, "Orthodox, Reform, Ashkenazim, Sephardim—we are, above all, Israel."

Being attuned to modernity and demonstrating a critical awareness of Judaism is ultimately supported by the rabbi's practical experience. This is confirmed by the tendency of many (visiting) rabbis to mention their contribution to some kind of task force concerned with the future direction of Reform Judaism. This demonstrates that they are struggling with the different challenges facing their religious movement. Another way to affirm the value of practical experience is for the rabbi to mention his involvement with teaching, especially at the university level—especially if some of his students are Christians. One visiting rabbi, in particular, constantly reminded the congregation that he taught at a Catholic university. To illustrate the importance of both scholarly expertise in Jewish culture and active participation in the majority culture, he told the following story: "A Roman Catholic girl, who was an anti-Semite, took my class at . . . College. She didn't know anything about Judaism. After taking my class, she was transformed. . . . No longer was she an anti-Semite, at least that's what she said. But I said to her, 'that's not good enough. Be my ambassador.'" The real ambassador for Reform Judaism, of course, is the Reform rabbi. Through modern education, both religious and secular, he has entered the Christian world (dispelling ignorance) while remaining with the Jewish world (stimulating progress).

The other major religious figure in our temple is the cantor. Her primary role, shared by the organist and choir, is of great significance. Their performances give the service an intense impact that it would otherwise lack. With an absent cantor, organist or choir, the service disintegrates into a muddle of flat notes, a confused recitation of the liturgical program. Even the "layman's service," a 50-year-old institution at the temple, employs a soloist and organist during the summer months while the official staff vacations. For the remainder of the year, congregants enjoy an excellent level of musical professionalism, one that is always carefully orchestrated. A typical service begins with an organ prelude, for example, while people take their places and exchange pleasantries. This prelude is often a complicated classical piece performed with great skill. It continues until the officiants and honoured guests take the stage. During the service itself, the cantor and the choir sing a selection of hymns (mostly in Hebrew); both are given opportunities to "shine." Sometimes, the cantor introduces a new song or a new musical arrangement of a familiar one. At other times, she calls attention to a particular musical style. This generally occurs after the sermon. It is her moment to demonstrate special expertise. Her operatic voice fills the sanctuary with flair and drama. Were it not for the context, a synagogue service, one might expect those present to applaud such a polished musical performance. When the choir is in the spotlight, the cantor usually sits down. Rich harmonies mysteriously, almost magically, filter down from the hidden choir loft. Quite often, the choir sings English hymns. The organist's accompaniment (prohibited on the Sabbath in most Conservative or Reconstructionist synagogues and all Orthodox ones) is constant, excluding the odd *a cappella* piece. He gently supports reflective moments in the service. He provides appropriate background music as congregants read silent meditations or as the rabbi recites the names of those who have died and those who are being remembered on the anniversaries of their deaths. Finally, the organist concludes the service with a "postlude."

Every week, four honoured guests are chosen in advance from the community. One of them is always a woman. Her main task is to recite a blessing over the Sabbath candles at the beginning of the service. This ritual has migrated from the home (including many Reform homes); that is where Sabbath candles have traditionally been lit by the "woman of the house" to inaugurate the Sabbath. The other honoured guests share the task of saying prayers before and after each reading from the Torah or the Prophets; one of them also reads the latter, the *haftara*, in English. At our temple, the *haftara* is usually around 16 verses—that is, longer than the Torah portion. One person is always an honoured guest: the temple's president (or a replacement in his absence); he always sits in the same chair. His role is to remind the congregation of special occasions, to offer thanks or congratulations as the circumstances dictate and to announce the sponsor of the *oneg shabat*. Following the service, all performers gather at the front of the stage to form a receiving line: the rabbi first, then the cantor, followed by the president and other honoured guests. Many congregants wait in line to shake hands and exchange the customary salutation "good Shabbos." Finally everyone gathers in the community hall for the *oneg shabat*: light refreshments enjoyed in an atmosphere of casual conversation.

Up to this point in our presentation, we have said relatively little about the role of congregants. This does not mean that they are unimportant in connection with this study. The ethos of our temple could not be understood without considering their response to this religious performance.

Congregants wear what one would expect of any middle-class people at their place of worship. Women wear conservative dresses or skirts. Men wear ties and jackets. The dress code is neither ultra-formal nor ultra-fashionable. People are expected to look neat, respectful and restrained. Women seldom wear hats of any kind. Because men (apart from those on the stage) wear neither *kipa* nor *talit*, nothing mitigates the appearance of variety and individuality, the natural result of personal choice in clothing. There is no "sea" of white, for example, as there would be in an Orthodox synagogue (where men, sitting apart from the women, wrap themselves in large, white prayer-shawls).

Most of those who attend regularly are over 45 years old. The modal age, in fact, probably exceeds 55. Two of the regulars are not Jewish. One is a local Protestant clergyman. The other is the sister of another regular who has married a Jew. These two, along with any visiting non-Jews, are warmly accepted by everyone.

This is a very orderly group consisting of 60-75 people. They conduct their interactions with the utmost politeness and decorum. Conversation during the service is kept to a minimum and seldom rises above a whisper. The seating pattern is fairly regular. Once seated, moreover, people stay put until the service ends. This formality corresponds to, even generates, a considerable degree of passivity when it comes to congregational participation in the service.

For example, the audience is highly dependent on what happens at the "altar." People neither stand up nor sit down without a cue from the rabbi. This is so even when instructions are explicitly stated in the prayer-book. No matter how familiar people are with the service, after years of regular attendance, very few of them would take the initiative for themselves. Some people begin to stand up or sit down of their own accord; if they notice others waiting for the rabbi's cue, though, they hesitate or even abort the act.

Congregational singing is quite hesitant, even inhibited. Here is the basic pattern: for a familiar hymn, the cantor invites everyone to sing along (which is not the case when she introduces a new hymn). Many people respond at first. Inevitably, though, they come to difficult parts that can be sung effectively only by the cantor. Participation wanes. By the end of a hymn, only the cantor and choir remain singing. The only exception we found was during the stay of a particularly enthusiastic and humorous rabbi. When audience involvement began to fade, he would encourage their rejuvenation by exclaiming; "Come on! Get with it!" or "One more time, let's really sing out!" This informal approach seemed to ignite a spark in the congregation, at least temporarily. But soon after the rabbi's encouragement, the audience slid back into lethargy. Apparently trying to emulate the rabbi, the cantor motioned vigorously with her arms, calling for a demonstration of the same spirited response. When no one responded, she was visibly disappointed.

Everything said so far suggests that this service is like a theatrical production. There is a clear distinction between the actors (paid performers) and the audience. The "show" itself is tightly organized to ensure a smooth presentation. The relatively passive behaviour of the congregation suggests that they come to watch their religious rituals performed for them. It is true that both the rabbi and the cantor encouraged people to participate more actively. This would seem to indicate that congregational passivity is not desired by those who lead the service. But inherent in the nature of this liturgy, as will be made clear later on, is something that encourages people merely to "take things in."

In describing the primary actors and their roles, we have said much already about the flow of the service. We turn now, in a more systematic way, to the order of worship itself.

## A Reform Sabbath Service

As noted by Fred Bird in chapter 2, this service, like any public ritual, has a script. The service is divided into three parts. These can be identified as act 1, act 2 and act 3. (For a chronological list of all the rituals that could be included in each, see Appendix 1.) These three acts correspond to the divisions found in any Reform prayer-book. Into this structure are inserted readings from the Torah and Prophets (which are, as already noted, imported from the service on Saturday morning in more traditional synagogues). The prayer-book used in our temple presents a menu; the ritual committee can choose any one of several services. Each is oriented in a slightly different way. The aim is to satisfy a variety of religious moods. In addition to this choice of set "scripts," though, the temple introduces its own variations (see appendix 2). On any one Friday evening, therefore, the service as performed adheres strictly to none of the set scripts of the prayer-book. Of great significance here is the fact that variations are not spontaneous. They are chosen carefully by a committee.

On a Friday evening just after Remembrance Day, the reading of the *haftara* was deleted so as to allow time for a memorial celebration. The flags of Canada, Quebec, Israel, the United States and the Hirsch's Legion were displayed on both sides of the stage. Military outfits and medals were worn with obvious pride. Military funeral music (with the "Garde-à-vous" posture) replaced, at some points, the cantor's sophisticated performance. The list of those *morts au champ d'honneur* preceded the regular list of the dead. The closing song was "O Canada."

Six months later, on a Friday evening chosen to celebrate Israel's Independence Day, the variation was even more radical. Not only was the *haftara* not read, but the Torah itself was not read. The scroll was not even taken out of the ark. Nor did the rabbi deliver a sermon. In its place was a march of children dressed in long white gowns and holding candles. They read poems written by children in the Nazi death camps and sang typical Israeli songs. Although this special performance was led by the cantor and the Sunday-school teacher, it lacked the lustre of a regular service due to the unprofessional skills of young children.

But liturgical variation was not restricted to special calendar dates. Though some tunes recurred from week to week, new melodies were introduced every week by the cantor. In some cases the congregation was expected to learn the new melody "on the spot." At other times, a different melody was expressly meant to preclude congregational participation—that is, to provide the cantor with an opportunity to act as a soloist. The same holds true for the organist and choir. Their contribution at times encompassed the familiar but was expected to proffer the new as well. Finally, the rabbi's contribution went far beyond the selection of one service or another from the prayer-book. In an interview, the (newly arrived) rabbi expressed his personal dissatisfaction with the degree of constant variation. We got the impression that he had inherited a sad state of affairs, wanted to change it, but had encountered, or expected to encounter, resistance.

Ultimately, these changes led us to consider the invariable rituals that occur in each service (see Appendix 2). Some permanent features of the service are thematically associated with either family rituals or the family itself. These include blessing the candles (imported from the home), reciting the *kidush* and drinking the wine (traditionally done both at home and at synagogue), and reciting the *kadish* (a doxology for mourners or those marking the anniversary of a death). Other invariables are reciting the *shma* ("Hear, O Israel...") and the *alenu* in front of the ark. Both communicate an identification with the Jewish people as a whole—which is to say, the extended family. (Our appendices note in detail variable and invariable components of our temple's service; references are to the opening words or standard titles of liturgical passages.)

**Preliminary analysis of some significant features and conclusion**

According to Geertz, "What all sacred symbols assert is that the good for man is to live realistically; where they differ is in the vision of reality they construct" (1973, 130). At this stage, we want to pursue the vision of reality communicated by the symbolic structures of our Reform service and to outline relations between the world-view and the ethos of our Reform congregation. We want to bring out the cultural patterns expressed through ritual, in other words, by showing how they come to shape psycho-social reality and how this reality, in turn, influences ritual.

An appropriate place to begin is with some statements from the Central Conference of American Rabbis, which is the official organ of Reform Judaism in America. These passages are from its pamphlet, *Reform Judaism: A Centenary Perspective*:

> It now seems self-evident to most Jews: that our tradition should interact with modern culture; that its forms ought to reflect a contemporary aesthetic; that its scholarship needs to be conducted by modern, critical methods; and that change has been and must continue to be a fundamental reality in Jewish life (Borowitz 1976, item xix).

> Reform Jews respond to change in various ways according to the Reform principle of the autonomy of the individual (Borowitz 1976, item xix).

> Reform Jews are called upon to confront the claims of Jewish tradition, however differently perceived, and to exercise their individual autonomy, choosing and creating on the basis of commitment and knowledge (Borowitz 1976, item xxiii).

It is evident that our Reform community strongly endorses the overarching attitude toward modernity expressed in these statements. Of course, the exact nature of any interaction with modernity works itself out in specific ways. In our case, this fundamental affirmation of the contemporary, modern scholarship and critical exegesis is expressed largely within the sermon. This, in fact, is what establishes the rabbi's credibility. Also contributing to the community's affirmation of modernity is its history while under the leadership of Rabbi Cohen. In those days, the community embraced modernity through his activities. So the "model of" reality expresses an essential relation to the modern situation, while the "model for" reality has its roots in the practical experience of Rabbi Cohen.

The first statements just quoted indicate the concern that Reform Judaism "ought to reflect a contemporary aesthetic." In the context of our temple, this idea is communicated brilliantly through architectural splendour and liturgical professionalism. Very much in keeping with the contemporary aesthetic is the cantor-soloist. Her performance suggests that the model for reality here is an expert or professional who performs a service both for and before clients. This conclusion is supported by the socio-economic status of this community: middle and upper middle class.

In regard to confronting "the claims of the Jewish tradition," our community has reacted to this by carefully selecting certain rituals that remain constant from one service to the next. Their criterion seems to be very simple: selected rituals are those that affirm the family. The idea of family, however, extends to the Jewish people. Congregants consider themselves to be in essential continuity with the larger Jewish tradition *in abstracto*. They take exception, therefore, to Orthodox attacks. Safeguarding at least some traditional expressions of faith reflects their cautious relation to tradition. This is why they insist on the rabbi's mastery of biblical Hebrew. The fact that he must translate each line into English, of course, suggests that there are limits as to how far the relation to tradition can go.

Recognizing the limits to tradition signals our temple's fundamental affirmation of change as an inherent part of reality. This is clearly illustrated by ritual changes occurring not only on Remembrance Day and Israel's Independence Day but also in the number of seemingly spontaneous liturgical novelties turning up every week. But the community's approach is based on an implicit paradox: congregants affirm their self-understanding as people who have fully accepted the majority culture; at the same time, they affirm their self-understanding as a significant segment of the Jewish people. In the final analysis, this ambivalence could be tied to Reform's concern for the "autonomy of the individual," who is able to transcend "nationalism even as [he or she] affirms it, thereby setting an example for humanity which remains largely concerned with dangerous parochial goals" (Borowitz 1978, item xxiv). Thus the ritual changes associated with the observance of both Remembrance Day *and* Israel's Independence Day mediate a basic belief in both universal humanity *and* the democratic right to personal autonomy and self-definition.

We suggest, therefore, that the service every Friday evening implicitly affirms two things: universalism (which allows congregants to feel part of a larger world); and personal autonomy (which allows them to select whatever they want from the tradition). This hypothesis explains the apparently passive role of congregants. To the degree that the service makes of them individual auditors or spectators of a liturgy performed by others, they are free to take whatever "bits" of meaning speak authentically to them. Individuals are not subsumed into a "congregation," as would be case if they were performing the liturgy together, with the clergy as "first among equals."

This situation seems further reinforced by the rules governing space in the sanctuary. Members of the audience sit in an area that is visibly separate from the stage. Significantly, all those who take part in the service, whether professional performers or honoured guests, enter the sanctuary from a door at stage level; no one is "called up" from the audience to be honoured with a ritual role (which is the norm in most North American congregations). Performers mingle with members of the audience only twice: when they come down during the service to parade around with the Torah scrolls; and when they come down after the service to form a receiving line. Sacred space is confined to the stage; only there are individuals subsumed in some sacred (and exclusive) social unit, which is indicated by the fact that both professionals and guests wear prayer-shawls.

Another telling observation is consistent with this interpretation. As we said earlier, the service is open to both Jews and non-Jews. In fact, the Jews feel very comfortable in the presence of non-Jews. On one occasion, a non-Jewish clergyman carried a Torah scroll in the procession that wended its way through the congregation. Remember that Rabbi Cohen had invested much time and effort in creating occasions to welcome non-Jews. In the face of fierce criticism from rabbinic colleagues, moreover, he officiated at mixed marriages (in which the non-Jewish spouse did not convert to Judaism even according to Reform protocols). So valued was his policy that its continuation was originally a selection criterion for his successor. In the audience, at any rate, individuals sit as individuals, whatever their origins or persuasions. This area is symbolically analogous to the culturally differentiated and religiously pluralistic world in which our Reform congregants claim total participation as individuals.

What, then, can be said about the vision of reality communicated implicitly by this community's symbolic structures? In other words, what is their world-view or, more properly, their "mapping" of the world? We suggest the following: members of the community experience the sacred, ultimate reality, as a realm that somehow informs, supports and legitimates modernity. They locate themselves both as individuals and as individual Jews in that highly differentiated, universalistic and pluralistic realm. The hall (below and in front of the stage) is a symbolic recreation of it. No wonder non-Jews are welcomed there so warmly. They provide living evidence of pluralism, a major feature of modernity. What probably interests our congregants more than modernity as such, however, is modernity as an indicator of social class, or cultural attainment. This is represented by the calibre of performance expected from the soloist, say, or the organist and choir. Because Reform Jews embrace the majority culture as free and equal citizens, they expect access to the best modernity has to offer. And this includes not only democracy and scholarship but the arts as well. Being free and equal citizens, of course, means that they can identify themselves with Jewish tradition from a secure position as modern individuals. The centennial booklet proclaims: "To be faithful to the eternal spirit of Judaism is our principle; to recognize the stream of contemporarity is our purpose; and to be relevant to the age we live in and the society we serve is our goal."

The community's state of affairs is at odds with its optimistic worldview. Judging from our earlier consideration of its economic and political troubles, the community is not as secure as it once was. The urgency expressed over membership fees and, more significantly, the lack of an enthusiastic younger generation suggest that the temple is unable to attract as many people as it did in the days of Rabbi Cohen. Since his departure, continuing power struggles have created rifts in the community. Unfairly, perhaps, these structural problems have been blamed on a rapid turnover in rabbis.

This pattern, transient relationships with a succession of rabbis, might also be symbolically expressed. Most specifically, the controlled changes in ritual might indicate at one and the same time both the kind of change associated with modernity and the kind of change associated with power. Even structural instability, then, might be a model "of" and "for" the world as perceived by our congregants. If so, what would be the long-term effect of this internal instability? If new rabbinic and lay leadership were to generate stability, on the other hand, would it be reflected in the way liturgy is conducted? Would it modify the way congregants map their places in the world? In both cases, the answer could be "yes," especially if changes in liturgy and leadership attract new members with different perceptions of Judaism and its relation to the larger culture.

# Appendix 1
## Outline of a regular Friday evening service

**Act One**

Blessing over the candles
*Leka dodi*
Meditation
Responsive reading
Reader's *Kadish*
*Barku*
Responsive reading
Responsive reading
*Shma*
Responsive reading
*Mi kamoka*
Responsive reading
*Veshamru bene israel*
Meditation
*Tfila*
*Yismehu*
Responsive reading
*Retze*
Responsive reading
Responsive reading
*Shalom rav*
Meditation

**Act Two**

Responsive reading
*Se'u she'arim*
*Shma*
*Leka adonai hagedula* (parade)
Undressing Torah
Blessing before reading Torah
Reading Torah in Hebrew & English
Blessing after reading Torah
Dressing the Torah
Blessing before reading *haftara*
Reading of *haftara* in English
Blessing after reading *haftara*
Returning Torah to ark

Responsive reading
*Ki lekah tov*
*Hashivenu*

**Sermon**

**Cantorial Solo**

**Act Three**

*Alenu*
Meditation
Naming the dead
*Kadish*
Announcements
Cantorial
Banns
*Kidush*
Closing hymn

**Receiving Line**

*Oneg Shabat*

# Appendix 2
# Liturgical Elements

**Invariable**

Time
Place
Guests on stage

**Variable**

Location of *kidush* cup
Service number
Rabbi

## Act One

Blessing candles
*Barku*
*Shma*
Responsive reading
*Mi kamoka*
Responsive reading
*Tfila*
*Veshamru bene israel*

*Leka dodi*
Reader's *kadish*
*Retze*
*Shalom rav*
Meditation
Responsive reading
Some tunes

## Act Two

Torah parade

Reading the Torah
Reading the *haftara*
*Se'u she'arim*
*Shma*
*Ki lekah tov*
Responsive reading at ark

Number of scrolls
Persons in parade
Torah portion
*Haftara* portion
Person undressing Torah
Person dressing Torah
Person returning Torah
*Hashivenu*

## Act Three

**Invariable**                          **Variable**

*Alenu*                                 Meditation
Naming the dead                         Names
*Kadish*
Announcements                           Content
*Kidush*
Closing hymn                            Content
Blessings

7

# The Synagogue as a Symbol of Ethnic Identity: The Case of a Sephardi Congregation

## MADELEINE McBREARTY

We protest against the idea that we are merely a religious sect and maintain that we are a nation. —1898 Jewish Orthodox Platform

**Introduction**

Some historians of religion have argued that, with the advent of modernity, religion has undergone a major transformation. In pre-modern society, religious affiliations were governed by the group of which the individual was an integral part; this was nearly always through the accident of birth. With modernity, one's religion became a voluntary and private affair (Cohen 1983). No longer is one's secular or religious life as intricately dependent upon the larger community as it was in the villages and *kehilot* of eastern or western Europe (see Zborowski and Herzog 1952).[1] Unlike the period prior to the Enlightenment, characterized by the secularization process that occurred in both Judaism and Christianity, religious excommunication (in the rare instances when it still occurs) no longer bears severe socio-economic consequences or complete ostracism from the community. In fact, it is generally agreed that the prerogative of modern individuals is to choose their religious affiliations as well as their modes of praxis, without undue concern for the constraints imposed by religious communities and the dogmas of particular religious traditions.[2]

Some social scientists, however, have maintained that due to this transformation, at least in the modern Western world, the importance of religion is unquestionably decreasing to the point where even major religious traditions, such as Catholicism and Judaism, will eventually be "eroded by acculturation and assimilation" within the greater melting pot of American culture. This theory of the decline in prominence and significance of religion is derived from the evidence of diminishing attendance at religious services (Gans 1979, 15) and of dwindling enrolment in religious institutions. In fact, surveys of the Boston Jewish community in 1965 and 1975 (see Cohen 1983) indicate a rise in synagogue membership and attendance among Jewish Orthodox groups.[3] Although religious observance has decreased in the overall population, it would be erroneous to conclude that the phenomenon of religion has diminished in importance for those individuals who consider themselves religious.

Hans Mol acquiesces to this transformation of religion from an obligatory function necessary for survival within the community to a more personally selected pursuit. He submits that this transformation resulted in a possible redefinition of the source of the constituent elements in the formation of the modern individual's basic identity. In modern societies, Mol suggests, religion plays a role in the self-definition of individuals, affecting their concept of identity at the level of the "transient, changeable self as persons move from one social encounter to another, offering a somewhat different identity, as it were, in each place" rather than in the "immutable or slowly changing core of personality that shows up in all of a person's encounters" (see Hammond 1988, 2). Mol attributes this change not only to religion but also to ethnicity and its role in the definition of one's identity.[4] In our pluralistic society, this thesis would entail that members of religious or ethnic groups proceed from one situation to another, from one encounter to another, divesting themselves at will of their religious or ethnic identity.

This statement might appear dubious, and we must ask not only what constitutes and influences the "immutable . . . core of personality" but also why, in the face of evidence for the personalization and decline of religion, there is a renewed emphasis on religious observance, albeit not in the traditional fashion (Glazer and Moynihan 1970; Lightstone in chapters 3 and 4 above)?[5] Why, furthermore, "in the face of modernity and disenchantment with traditional ways (including disenchantment with primary group obligations), are many people turning to creeds that reassert traditional doctrines" (Hammond 1988) or, I might add, to rituals that reinforce their differences with majority groups?

Confronted with the assertions of those (such as the proponents of the straight-line sociological theory of ethnicity) who predict that acculturation and assimilation are "secular trends that culminate in the eventual absorption of the ethnic group into the larger culture and general population" (Sandberg in Gans 1979, 2), it is imperative not only to question whether there really is a resurgence in ethnic group identifications but also to determine the role of this phenomenon in self-definition.[6] We must ask why there are those (such as ultra-Orthodox Jews, American blacks or French Canadians) who not only continue to identify themselves strongly as members of religious or ethnic minority groups but do so with renewed fervour.

In their comprehensive study of the different ethnic groups that constitute the population of New York City, Nathan Glazer and Daniel Moynihan have suggested that questions concerning the recrudescence of ethnic identification can be answered partially in connection with the decline of other elements, such as religion and occupational or social status, that have traditionally contributed to the individual's sense of self-identity (1970, xxi-xliii). It is their contention, however, that the unique dimension of the contemporary renewal in ethnic identification is that members of modern ethnic groups do not necessarily identify with their counterparts in the country of origin; they often identify instead with other immigrants, similarly coloured by entrenchment within the larger North American society. My research will not only corroborate Glazer and Moynihan's findings, but also, because of the nature of the group under study, offer one of the possible explanations for the increase in religious observance.

**Methodological considerations**

The data for this study were gathered through personal interviews with individual respondents as well as by observation of the Sabbath morning ritual in a modern, Orthodox, Canadian, Sephardi synagogue.

I have argued in chapter 5 that the analysis of religious rituals, which are understood to imply "any stylized, repeated, [and] intrinsically valued act[ions]" (Bird 1986; chap. 2 above), offers a key to the mapping out of the social configuration of the group under study. Clifford Geertz has alluded to the dual nature of religious rituals (1973). Not only do rituals reflect the religious beliefs of the congregants, according to him, but they act to provide a legitimate pattern for daily behaviour. The communal re-enactments of those religious rituals, construed as representing tangible manifestations of the sacred, express and reinforce individual convictions concerning the very nature of the sacred realm. Furthermore, these re-enactments strengthen the identity of the individual as part of a community with commonly held beliefs and thus afford a paradigm for daily living. I must concur with Emile Durkheim that religion can never be divorced from its social nexus. Religion, to borrow the words of Saussure concerning language, "exists perfectly only within a collectivity." For Durkheim, the sacred is borne out of the "collective conscience." If individuals gather during a religious ritual to experience and reinforce their "collective conscience," it is appropriate to assume that their own identity as members of the group performing such a ritual is thereby reinforced.

Congregational rituals, by their very definition, take place in environments that offer physical settings for social interaction. Through the ages, particular symbols have come to be identified with distinct religious traditions. The cross, the *magen david* and the crescent are easily recognized symbols attributed to specific religions. The modern structures that are designated to house religious gatherings almost always exhibit the monothetic symbols attached to their traditions. If we agree with Mary Douglas that not only language but also myths and symbols offer pre-coded messages imbued with implicit meanings (1975, 249-75), we must endeavour to decipher the meanings that are offered by the material symbols surrounding the performance of religious ritual. For example, the interior of a particular Reform synagogue in Canada is decorated with very few "Jewish" symbols. Were it not for the Hebrew words that adorn the ark, the large auditorium could easily be mistaken for a concert hall or the interior of a Protestant church. In fact, it is very much in keeping with Reform ideology to project an image that compares with such reference groups as the Protestant segment of Christianity.

A further consideration must necessarily arise when we endeavour to study a group of people with a distinctly Jewish ethnic character. Harold Abramson (1980, 870) has defined an ethnic religion as one that is not "a pan-national, ecumenical force larger than society." He has argued that "ethnicity equals religion" for groups such as the Amish, Hutterites, Mormons and Jews (1980, 869). We can question his assertions in light of the multitude of Jews who are religiously non-observant, but we must remember the citation quoted at the very beginning of this chapter: "we protest against the idea that we are merely a religious sect and maintain that we are a nation." This declaration was made to counteract one made by the Reform movement. It stipulated that Judaism should be construed, like any voluntary associations, as no more than the religion practised by a group of citizens from a particular country. Today, however, even those identified with Reform and Reconstructionism have accepted the concept of peoplehood as a fundamental element of Judaism (although they often struggle with the question of "chosenness"). When we proceed to study the mode of ethnic experience among Canadian Jewish immigrants, therefore, it is with an understanding of the dual nature of their ethnicity. First, Jewish ethnicity arises from the fact that Judaism, which offers a notion of peoplehood comparable to that afforded by a nationality, is apprehended as an ethnic religion in every country of the world with the sole exception of Israel. Second, Jewish ethnicity arises from the fact that Jews, through immigration, have become members of an ethnic (quasi-national) minority.

It is in the light of these methodological considerations that I present my analysis of a modern, Orthodox, Sephardi congregation. First, I examine the physical setting of the synagogue. Then, I turn to the participants and the range of social behaviour through which their ethnicity is communicated (Abramson 1980). Finally, I discuss my findings.

## The liturgical performance

### The setting

Charles Liebman has identified four different types of contemporary Orthodoxy: modern, ultra-traditionalist, traditionalist and non-observant (in Neusner 1975, 131-53). The congregation under study can be classified as modern Orthodox, a classification based on the architectural design and interior arrangement of a synagogue, the form of its services, the dress code that prevails and the degree of halakic observance of the congregants.

The synagogue, which moved to its present location approximately 50 years ago, is situated in a district of the city that consists largely of immigrants. Although many blacks and Vietnamese live in the area, many of the residents are Jewish, some of whom are among the 15-20,000 Moroccans who came to the metropolitan area in the late 1960s and early 1970s. Many other Jewish communities, such as the Lubavitcher Hasidim, have their headquarters in the district. At close proximity to the synagogue are a Jewish library, a large Jewish community centre and a branch of the YM-YWHA. Adjacent to the synagogue is a Jewish day-school that shares some of its office space; it is not unusual to see students in the hallways of the synagogue during the week. A large Jewish population either lives in the immediate vicinity of the synagogue, therefore, or regularly visits the neighbourhood.

The synagogue is a three-storey building. Both its basement and third floor contain the offices of the adjacent day-school. On the second floor are located the offices of the rabbi, the *hazanim*, the sisterhood and so forth. The main floor of the building houses the large sanctuary where Sabbath and holiday services are held, a small chapel that accommodates the daily services, two sizeable reception halls, a reception area and a cloakroom.

The main sanctuary is extensively decorated with what I have alluded to previously as "purely Jewish symbols." The eastern wall, behind the *hekal* (an ark containing Torah scrolls, called the *aron hakodesh* in Ashkenazi synagogues) is decorated entirely with *magen david* motifs. A huge chandelier hangs over the middle of the auditorium from a structure designed with the same motif. Two large *menorot* stand on either side of the ark. A representation of the tablets, upon which the first few words of the Ten Commandments are written in Hebrew, stands directly above the Torah niche. In front of the ark is the *ner tamid*, or perpetual flame.

The sanctuary is divided into five sections. The women's sections, accessed through separate doors, are located on either side of the sanctuary. These are elevated and divided from the larger men's section by a *mehitza*, the height of which would be unacceptable according to certain rabbinic authorities.[7] The men's section forms a semicircle around the *bima*, a platform. The weekly Torah portion is read here from a table, the *shulhan*. When male congregants are called to the Torah for an *aliya*, they come here. The rabbi and the assistant *hazan* sit here, moreover, while the head *hazan* conducts the liturgy. This *bima*, one of two, is located directly in front of the ark but does not form an extension of the platform upon which the ark is positioned. That platform is another *bima*. Dignitaries of the synagogue sit there during services. It is from that *bima*, moreover, that the rabbi delivers both his sermon and other announcements pertaining to weekly services or other events organized by the synagogue. Choir members sit between the two *bimot*; they are not easily seen, therefore, by the entire congregation.

## *The participants*

*The clergy and synagogue dignitaries*: The current rabbi is an American of remote eastern European origin, an Ashkenazi Jew who came to the synagogue in 1970. Under his leadership, the paid membership of the synagogue escalated from 300 to 700 families. A radical change has also occurred during his tenure. The percentage of Ashkenazi members, which in 1970 was estimated at 85 percent, has been reduced to a low of 25 percent. Sephardim, mainly French-speaking Jews from North Africa, Spain, France and the Middle East, now account for 75 percent of the total membership. The rabbi's role during the service is to ensure that the congregation follows the liturgy. From time to time, he announces the page of the *sidur*, the prayer-book from which the liturgy is read. He informs congregants as to the portion of Torah or the *haftara*[8] to be read that day. The rabbi will also confer with the *shamash*, or sexton, as to who will be called to the Torah for an *aliya*. These *aliyot* are determined from a list of special events or anniversaries in the lives of male participants. Unless there is a special occasion for an invited guest to address the congregation, the rabbi delivers the sermon. Finally, the rabbi offers a benediction at the beginning of the *kidush*,[9] which immediately follows the service.

Second in importance to the rabbi are the *hazanim*, cantors, who conduct the morning liturgy. In fact, the head *hazan* holds an extremely important office; in this synagogue, at any rate, it is impossible to have a proper liturgy without him. He and his assistant are Sephardi Jews from Morocco; both were hired four years earlier as replacements for a Moroccan cantor and his Ashkenazi assistant. Although the head *hazan* sings the prayers and recites the blessings after each *aliya*, it is the assistant *hazan* who sings the weekly Torah portion. He also leads the choir, which is composed of approximately 20 boys running in age from four or five to the late teens.[10] All boys in the choir are dressed uniformly in pale blue gowns with matching *kipot*, or skull-caps.

The *shamash* is also a member of the clergy. He is also a Sephardi Jew from Morocco. I have been told that he is in charge of decorum. Throughout the service, he walks up and down the aisles to ensure that congregants behave properly. His task is made easier by the fact that this synagogue is quite remarkable for the degree of attention paid to the liturgy, for its overall decorum throughout the service. On an ordinary Sabbath, when there is no bar mitzvah, almost everyone follows the prayers and Bible readings; there is no excessive talking among congregants. The *shamash* might offer assistance to someone who cannot find the right page in the *sidur*, but his main function is to choose those who will be called for an *aliya* as well as those who will open the *hekal* and carry the Torah scrolls around the synagogue.

The *shamash*, the *hazanim* and the rabbi are dressed in long black robes.[11] Their shoulders are enwrapped in large *talitot*, prayer-shawls. Instead of wearing the usual *kipa*, however, they wear three-cornered black hats.

The dignitaries, four to six men who sit on either side of the ark during the service, are chosen from among the members of the synagogue's executive committee. Some are dressed with top hats and tails. All are dressed very formally. All wear very large *talitot*. If a male speaker is invited to address the congregation, he is asked to sit on the *bima* with these dignitaries. Among them, only two play an active role during the service.[12]

These *parnasim*, according to Orthodox custom, stand on either side of the Torah while the weekly portion is read. Between *aliyot*, a *parnas* covers the Torah scroll with a square piece of cloth. In this synagogue, one of them is Ashkenazi and the other Sephardi. Those who stand on the *bima*, where the *hekal* is located, must bow quite formally to both the *hekal* and the dignitaries.

*The congregants*: Most of the participants are regulars. Due to the number of young boys in the choir, the average age of the male participants is approximately 40 years. Though very few young girls attend the service,[13] the average age of female participants is more or less the same. A peculiarity of this synagogue is that the regulars are ethnically or nationally different from both their leaders and the other members.

Prior to my interview with the rabbi, I assumed that Moroccan Jews constituted 80 percent of the membership; after all, they constitute 80 percent of those who attend the service every Sabbath and 80 percent of those who lead the service. But there is a discrepancy. Among the members, 40 could be classified as Iraqi; 25 percent as Ashkenazi; 15 percent as Moroccan; 15 percent as Egyptian or Lebanese; and 5 percent as other (Greek, Turkish, Algerian). Of 20 people on the board, only two are Moroccans. Only one is on the executive committee. I was told by both Moroccans and non-Moroccans that Moroccans are very "religious," that "they love to pray," but that they do not like to be involved in the administration of a synagogue. This would account for the fact that Moroccans outnumber all others at the Sabbath service. I was also told that synagogue membership was not customary in Morocco; therefore, Moroccans do not necessarily even join synagogues on a formal basis. Another factor might be involved: Lebanese and Egyptian Jews hold their own services separately in a small chapel intended for daily prayers.[14] The fact remains, in any case, that most of those present are Moroccans.[15] In my discussion of the ritual, I maintain that it is possible to discern the identity of the participants by their actions during the service. At this point, it is enough to say that the seating of the male congregants tends to be segregated along lines of ethnicity.[16]

Finally, I must point out that most male participants wear dark suits. All wear white *talitot* and *kipot*.[17] Strictly speaking, only married men over the age of bar mitzvah must wear a *talit* during the Sabbath service. Even so, I witnessed one scene in which the guest at a bar mitzvah (perhaps not a Jew) failed to wear a *talit*. Immediately, the *shamash* brought him one and told him with unequivocal gestures that wearing it was required. The women wear dresses or skirts. All married women cover their heads with either a hat or a circular piece of lace. As in other Orthodox synagogues and most Conservative ones, the women (with one exception) do not wear *talitot*.

*The ritual*

Although liturgies for the High Holy Days at Sephardi synagogues are quite different from those at Ashkenazi synagogues, the same is not true of liturgies for the Sabbath.

What makes the Sephardi ritual so distinctive is its formality, or decorum. This is due primarily to the melodies used for praying and for chanting passages from the Torah. Until four or five years prior to my study, the Sephardi style was used for praying and the Ashkenazi for chanting. This was changed by the current *hazanim*, who introduced the Moroccan (Sephardi) style for chanting as well. In this style, each word of almost every prayer is enunciated clearly. The entire liturgy is sung responsively; one line is sung by the cantor and choir, in other words, and the next by everyone together (cantor and choir along with male and female congregants).[18] If the *hazan* makes even a slight mistake in pronunciation during the Torah reading, or if a congregant honoured with an *aliya* errs in chanting the *haftara*, male congregants raise their voices to correct him. When queried about this, a *hazan* said that both the words and the melodies are divinely ordained and, therefore, unchangeable.

The *amida* is not repeated aloud by the cantor in either the *shaharit* or *musaf* services. In both cases, it is begun with the cantor and congregation chanting aloud together until the *kedusha*; after that, the cantor continues aloud while the congregants do so in silence. Unlike an Ashkenazi service, this one seldom encourages personal meditation or silent prayers. Exceptions, in this respect, are brief periods when the *hekal* is opened or closed and the Torah scrolls displayed to the congregation. At these times, the men simply bow. But the women, especially the Moroccans, extend both their hands towards the Torah (in a gesture similar to that of a photographer trying to imagine the frame for a snapshot); after this, they touch their closed eyes and mouths with the tips of their fingers and murmur almost inaudibly. When I questioned someone about this, she told me that the women use these moments to make personal requests from God (in view of the fact that he gave the Torah to his people, Israel).

It was reiterated to me by both the clergy and the congregants that the Torah is unequivocally sacred; promises or pledges made in front of it must not be dismissed summarily or neglected. Unlike Reform Jews (who might curtail or even eliminate a Torah reading for the sake of time) and Reconstructionists (whose weekly portions are a third of those read in Orthodox synagogues), those in our synagogue attach extreme importance to the Torah and its reading. In this, these Orthodox Jews do not differ from their Ashkenazi counterparts. They do differ, however, in connection with some of the rituals that surround the reading.

As in other Orthodox synagogues, the first three *aliyot* are given, respectively, to a priest (*kohen*), a Levite and a common Israelite. In this synagogue, an additional and "final" *aliya* may be given to the priest or the Levite. It may also be reserved for someone recently bereaved or for someone marking the anniversary of a death. After the concluding blessings, he—not the cantor or a professional reader as would be the case in an Ashkenazi synagogue—recites the "half-*kadish*" (a truncated version of the doxology associated with bereavement).

A peculiarity of the *aliya* ritual in Sephardi synagogues has been all but eliminated in most Ashkenazi synagogues. Someone so honoured is called up by his Hebrew name. The man comes onto the *bima*, kisses the Torah scroll with the fringes of his *talit*, recites a customary blessing and stands beside the *hazan* while the latter chants the Torah portion. When the reading is finished, the *hazan* recites a blessing over the man, who might also require that the names of his wife and children be mentioned at this time. The blessing is recited in Hebrew. The ritual ends with a declaration that this particular man will give a specific amount of money to the synagogue. The amount varies from one man to the next, of course, but the most common is $18.00. This amount is auspicious, because the Hebrew letters that signify 18 are read as *hai*, which means "life." Higher donations are not only chanted but translated into English, presumably for the benefit of those who do not understand Hebrew.[19]

Immediately following this announcement, the man honoured with an *aliya* shakes hands with everyone on the *bima* and with others as well. Unlike many religious traditions, this one allows participants to "own" a very elaborate ritual, complete with its own rules of etiquette.[20] Although all male congregants, both young and old, shake hands as they enter and leave the synagogue, it is following an *aliya* that Moroccans are most easily distinguished from the others. Most Moroccans kiss the male members of their families on both cheeks. They also kiss their close friends. They do not kiss distant acquaintances or non-Moroccans. Instead, they shake hands with them and kiss the index fingers of their own right hands, which they have formed into fists. The rabbi, like all other Ashkenazim, never gets kissed. Ashkenazim shake hands with those seated on the *bima*, after an *aliya*, and those seated nearby in the congregation. When the service ends, participants greet each other with the traditional *shabat shalom*, but few of the men or women shake hands at this time.

The last portion of the ritual is the *kidush*. This custom is not indispensable in the fulfillment of the ritual. It is not unique to our synagogue, for it forms part of the Sabbath morning ritual in almost all other North American synagogues. What is unique, however, is the type of food served and the manner in which it is eaten. The *kidush* is organized by the members of a special committee and is often sponsored by those who are celebrating a special event. In the latter instance, it might be served by an Ashkenazi caterer, but the clear intention is to offer Sephardi food; many of the dishes are, therefore, of either Moroccan or Middle Eastern origin. The *kidush* is served in a large hall where several tables, arranged as an open-ended rectangle, are set with small glasses of wine and several different dishes. The great majority of those in attendance at the service can be found at the *kidush* table. The rabbi and other members of the clergy, along with special guests or a bar mitzvah family, stand at the head of the table. Over a silver goblet of wine, the rabbi says one blessing for the Sabbath day and one for wine. Other members (men, women and children) gather around the table. It is not unusual in the wintertime to see people standing in their outdoor clothing while drinking wine and eating from plates set before them. The rules of proper etiquette, which would ordinarily prevail at a party, are not in effect around the *kidush* table. People start heaping food on their plates even before the rabbi finishes reciting the blessing. Although the *kidush* is always referred to by the congregants as a time to socialize with friends, only perfunctory conversation takes place. It would seem that people come to eat and then, promptly, to leave. After several attempts at making sense of the seemingly absent sense of decorum during the *kidush*, I can surmise only that congregants allow themselves to partake of the food as they would in a place where they are totally at ease and where they are not required to exhibit forms of behaviour that are prevalent when eating among total strangers. At some level, then, partaking of this food might symbolize the closeness of the community, even if little social interaction occurs.

## Discussion

On the basis of the data adduced, I now address some of the theoretical questions that I formulated at the beginning of this paper: specifically, the effect of synagogue attendance on the maintenance and reinforcement of one's sense of self-identity both as a Jew and as member of a particular ethnic community. Via its ritual performance, how might the group under study symbolically represent and reinforce certain social boundaries?

The mere act of entering the synagogue and attending services creates a demarcation between the group and the non-Jewish world. However, it also establishes a definite link of peoplehood with other Jews. The synagogue is replete with monothetic material symbols that reflect a strong Jewish tradition. Throughout the sermon, the identity of the participants as Jews, members of the people of Israel, is not only presumed but reinforced through constant repetition.[21] The use of a common non-vernacular language, Hebrew, which presumably would be familiar only to Jews, strengthens the sense of religious and ethnic identity.[22] The presence of a non-Jew who could demonstrate an ability to read Hebrew, to follow the liturgy and to sing the prayers, would be considered both anomalous and a threat to the classificatory system innate to the members of the group.[23]

Attendance at synagogue services, therefore, reinforces one's identity as a Jew. It also contributes to the sense that one is not only a Jew but a member of the Jewish community. While this identification certainly can proceed from a variety of sources—even negative ones such as anti-Semitism—synagogue attendance allows those present to experience and reinforce within themselves the Jewish "collective conscience." In our synagogue, however, one's consciousness is not only that of being a Jew but also, emphatically, being a Sephardi Jew.[24]

One would expect the ritual to reflect the reality of the Ashkenazi presence, which preceded that of the Sephardi Jews and which persists as a minority element within the congregation. On the contrary, the ritual is almost entirely Sephardi and primarily derived from Moroccan traditions. The melodies as well as the manner of pronouncing the Hebrew words are unquestionably Sephardi. Most of the clergy, who bring leadership and mediate the sacred, are also Moroccan Sephardim. While the rabbi is not Sephardi, he neither openly advertises nor denies his Ashkenazi origins and has adopted Sephardi litugical custom. Other members of the clergy have even offered a redefinition of his ethnic background. They admit that the rabbi was born Ashkenazi, but they argue that he has now become Sephardi through his behaviour. Some adduce that the rabbi has some Sephardi ancestors in his remote past. Whether justifiably so or not, members of the clergy are perceived as Sephardi.

Those elements of the ritual that are essentially associated with the sacred, therefore, reflect the ethnic identity of the majority of those present at the Sabbath morning service but not of the leadership or membership. One could surmise that services are allowed to display a predominantly Sephardi character because Moroccans attend services; their presence allows the institution to be perceived as thriving. While I have been told repeatedly that a newly arrived Moroccan immigrant would not find in our synagogue a replica of the services as performed in the home country,[25] the reality is that the Sabbath morning service offers an opportunity for Sephardim to assemble and participate in a ceremony that is undeniably Sephardi and even Moroccan.

Even though the leadership of the synagogue endeavours to attenuate the differences between the members of different ethnic backgrounds, it remains true that these are differentiated. And the difference is reflected in ritual. Although the sense of wider group identification is constantly reinforced through the responsive chanting of the prayers and the habit of extensive hand shaking, divisions are clearly evident within the sanctuary. The boundaries are not easily crossed.

First, the demarcation between the congregants and the clergy, officials of the synagogue, is determined by both mode of dress and location during the service. The clergy and the choir are dressed, with uniformity, in robes. The dignitaries are dressed, also with uniformity, in formal attire. The men present a semblance of uniformity with their large white *talitot*. The women bear very little similarity to each other, aside from the fact that they cover their heads. It would seem that clothing becomes increasingly formal and uniform as one approaches that which is construed as the locus of the sacred.

As mentioned previously, the seating in the men's section clusters according to ethnic groups whose behaviour is governed by specific rules of etiquette. The men's and women's sections are clearly divided by the *mehitza*. The men's sections and the *bimot*, the domain of the sacred, are again separated by a similar partition. The divisions between each section are not easily breached. While men may pass through the women's section, it is extremely rare that a man will be found in this section. Certainly, none would sit there during the service.[26] No one may come onto the *bimot* uninvited, and those who do must follow exact rules of behaviour such as extensive bowing to the *hekal* and to the dignitaries. Even the rabbi, who freely ascends the *bima* where the *hekal* is located, invariably finishes his sermon with a bow to the synagogue officials seated on both sides of the ark.

In accordance with my theoretical framework, then, I submit that ritual, which suggests a pattern for daily living, also offers a metaphor for the social configuration of those engaged in its repetition. Because they are Sephardi Jews, congregants choose to attend a synagogue that will exhibit and reinforce this aspect of their identity. This also helps maintain their ethnic identity across generations. The clear boundaries evident in the formality of the service, in the specific functions of those engaged in the ritual, as well as in the arrangement of the sanctuary reflect the social reality of Sephardi Jews whether Iraqi or Moroccan. This social reality encompasses a multiplicity of boundaries that have to be maintained in order to preserve the ethnic character of a group that faces the external threat of acculturation.

Like other Jews living in a pluralistic society, Sephardim must maintain the usual demarcation between Jews and gentiles in order to avoid assimilation. Moreover, because they have been ritualistic traditionally, it would appear that Sephardim must minimize the appeal of other Jewish groups such as Conservative, Reconstructionist, or Reform Jews. Finally, most Sephardim are francophones. In order to preserve their culture, they must oppose their absorption into the greater Jewish population, which is primarily Ashkenazi and anglophone. Whether the threats of assimilation and acculturation are real or imaginary, the fact remains that boundary maintenance is imperative to those who perceive these threats as potentially dangerous for their religion and culture.

The synagogue, therefore, serves as a place where the Sephardi religious tradition and culture is maintained for the older generation and transmitted to the younger one.[27] Some of the congregants, who came to Canada during the first wave of Moroccan immigration 20 years earlier, still consider themselves Moroccan Jews first and foremost, while their Canadian citizenship assumes only a secondary role in their self-identification. We cannot presume that synagogue attendance is the sole reason for the fact that Moroccan, or Sephardi, identity is sustained over an extended period of time. We can surmise that the synagogue offers an opportunity to maintain contact with the Sephardi community, however, and that the form of the ritual (which is perceived as traditional) not only reflects but also nurtures, perhaps implicitly at times, the sense of one's self-identity as a Sephardi Jew.[28]

## Notes

1. This assertion is made despite the resurgence of fundamentalism in countries such as Iran, where freedom of religion has been severely curtailed in the past several years.
2. I submit that this degree of freedom varies immensely from group to group and is largely influenced by the mode of primary socialization of the individual (see Berger and Luckmann 1966).
3. Evangelical Protestant churches have noted similar increases.
4. In this paper, we will understand ascription by both the member of an ethnic community and the recognition of that fact by outsiders to be the necessary criterion of membership in an ethnic group (see Barth 1969, 9).
5. Again, we must emphasize that this renewal has occurred mainly among those who were already considered more religiously observant than the general population.
6. Herbert Gans denies that this is a real phenomenon; he believes that symbolic ethnicity is emphasized by modern America.
7. See responsa by Moshe Feinstein in his *Igrot Moshe*.
8. If there is a bar mitzvah, the boy reads this portion of scripture. Otherwise, a congregant or an invited guest reads it.
9. The *kidush* is not an indispensable element of the service.
10. The two cantors have many other functions—preparing boys for their bar mitzvahs, singing at weddings and so forth—but these have no direct bearing on the topic under discussion.
11. The rabbi and cantors wear white robes during the High Holy Days.
12. The others, like all other male participants, merely follow the service.
13. The boy/girl ratio is at least 10 to one. This might be explained by the fact that many boys are preparing for their bar mitzvahs; they are recruited by the *hazan* as members of the choir. Bat mitzvahs are not emphasized at this synagogue. I have not witnessed one. Nevertheless, I know that they have occurred in the past.
14. The way in which this separate service came into being is not directly relevant here. It should be pointed out, however, that Lebanese and Egyptian Jews join the larger congregation on minor holidays. On major ones, four different *minyanim* are held. One is for the Iraqis, one for the Lebanese and Egyptians, one for the Moroccans, and one for all other members (those who choose to remain in the main sanctuary or those who do not identify with these ethnic groups).
15. The number of Ashkenazim who attend services at this Sephardi synagogue is in proportion to those who attend services at Ashkenazi synagogues (see Cohen 1983). Do Iraqi Jews show a similar pattern?
16. This statement must be qualified, and it must be said that although groups seem quite clearly demarcated there is a certain amount of intermixing among the congregants. Also, it must be pointed out that people tend to sit in regular seats although this is not a fast rule.
17. It is interesting to note that *kipot* are used to identify guests in the synagogue for a specific event—a bar mitzvah, say, or the *aliya* of someone about to be married. A

family might distribute blue or red *kipot*, for example, inscribed with a boy's name and the date of his bar mitzvah.

18  A very high proportion of the male congregants can read Hebrew. Some of the women do as well; even those who do not know Hebrew, however, can usually sing or chant with everyone else.

19  These donations are far more modest than annual membership fees. Even so, they add up to a significant source of revenue for the synagogue. Members of the clergy are uncomfortable with this custom of announcing the amount of money given by an individual. In interviews, they all tried to minimize its importance. I was told of an attempt by the administration to eliminate it, an attempt that was prevented by members of the congregation.

20  Handshaking could be the object of a study in itself. Hindus would never shake hands with fellow worshippers at a temple, for example, while Catholics and Protestants do so during religious services only at predetermined times.

21  Not only is the affinity with biblical or historical Jewish people reaffirmed, but the ties with Israel are maintained. During the service that remembered Israel's fortieth anniversary, the Israeli national anthem, *Hatikvah*, was sung. All the participants knew the song, which they sang with fervour.

22  On special occasions, such as a bar mitzvah, there might be some non-Jewish guests, but their lack of familiarity with the prayers and the service make them conspicuous. At any rate, we are concerned with the regular Sabbath service, where practically no non-Jews are in attendance.

23  This last statement is borne out by personal experience. When participants discovered I was not Jewish, they became confused and some even refused to continue a conversation. There seemed to be no place in their taxonomic system for a non-Jew to exhibit behaviour usually associated with members of the group.

24  Most Moroccans equate the two adjectives Moroccan and Sephardi. I hesitate, at this time, to make mention of the Moroccan component since some of the congregants are non-Moroccans. It remains, however, that it is the intention of both the clergy and the congregants to give a Sephardi character to the synagogue if not to convert it to a totally Sephardi place. For non-Moroccans, the service affords a means of identification as Sephardi Jews.

25  This could be explained by the fact that traditions differ even from one Moroccan city to another. What one would find in this synagogue, therefore, is a uniformity of tradition that has taken shape after it issued from a mixture of Ashkenazi and Sephardi modes of worship.

26  I have seen a man in the women's section only once. He was appointed to guard the doors while an invited guest delivered her homily.

27  The primary socialization of young boys starts with synagogue attendance and participation in the choir; it culminates with the rites of bar mitzvah. See Simcha Fishbane's essay in chapter 10 and works by Schoenfeld (1988; 1990; 1992). Maintenance of identity across several generations must form the subject of a further study.

28  Indeed, most of the congregants retain several identities: Jews, Sephardi Jews, and Jews with specific national backgrounds. These identities are muturally reinforcing, not mutually exclusive.

# 8

# Back to the *Yeshiva*: The Social Dynamics of an Orthodox Sabbath Morning Service

## SIMCHA FISHBANE

My intent in this study is to address several theoretical issues by examining a Sabbath morning service at a *shtibl*, a small sanctuary located in a private home or store-front. More precisely, I will examine what is encoded in the religious ritual performed among modern Orthodox members of a small independent synagogue. Furthermore, I will argue that this style of religious orientation attempts to imitate the rituals as performed in the *yeshiva* (rabbinic academy) prayer service. The *shtibl* participant, through his attendance at this synagogue service, is thereby identifying with the *yeshiva Weltanschauung*. This religious behaviour can conceivably carry important associations for an increasingly right-wing modern Orthodoxy.

The synagogue to be examined is located in an area of a major Canadian metropolis that is densely populated with Orthodox Jews. The data were gathered through both personal interviews with individual respondents and participation in the weekly and seasonal congregational services.

The theoretical and methodological issues bearing on this paper are extensively dealt with in other essays in this volume.

### Modern Orthodoxy, a new trend

During the holiday of Sukot (Booths, or "Tabernacles"), I visited a synagogue that had recently been acquired by a group of "right-wing" Orthodox Jews. The front half of the sanctuary, a large auditorium, is a facsimile of a *yeshiva* study hall. On either side of the ark, situated on the eastern wall, is a podium (*shtand*) at or behind which the rabbinic leaders of the congregation sit. Congregants sit at folding wooden tables. Along the wall stand bookcases filled with traditional rabbinic texts. The other half of this auditorium retains signs of its former "life" and was lined with theatre-style seats. To allow for room to dance during the Simhat Torah holiday, which falls at the conclusion of Sukot, the theatre seats had been unscrewed from the floor and removed from the sanctuary. I returned to this synagogue on the Sabbath following Sukot, expecting to find the room returned to its former state. However, instead of the theatre seats, the entire sanctuary was now lined with *yeshiva*-style study-tables.

Furthermore, other rituals and behaviour in this synagogue resembled the world of the *yeshiva*. The men's dress is conservative, usually a dark suit, dark leather shoes, a white shirt and tie. During the prayer service, all adult men wear dark hats perched on the head at an angle. At other times, they wear large black skull-caps (not knitted ones). The language spoken is a *yeshiva* dialect, an amalgam of English, Yiddish, Hebrew and Aramaic. Samuel Heilman terms this dialect *"gemoreloshn,"* a language that transforms and recasts ideas from one Jewish culture into another (1983, 167). William Helmreich cites an example of this pattern:

> When it comes to going to movies I *take* [really] hold [feel] that there's a *sakanah* [danger] that something there could be *mashpia* [influence] on you in the way that could undermine your whole *hashkofo* [belief system]. Therefore, it's not *kedai* [worthwhile] to go and put yourself in such a *matzav* [position]. Do you *hap* [grasp] what I'm saying (1982, 148)?

The liturgy in this visited synagogue is recited slowly, but with few cantorial insertions. Specific prayers, such as the *shma* (Hear O Israel), are emphasized vocally and in unison. The *amida* is recited with emphasized body movement. This prayer is recited in a whisper and very slowly. Following the *shma* and the *amida*, prayers commence according to the cue of the rabbinic authority, a local *rosh yeshiva*. The synagogue and the behaviour of its participants have become a facsimile of the *yeshiva* study hall and liturgy.

Menachem Friedman sees this behaviour as symbolic of a trend amongst western Orthodox Jews (1987). Friedman notes that others identify the phenomenon described above as "Bne Brakism." Friedman terms it *haredut*. Both describe this scenario as a search by the observant Jew for a more stringent *halaka*. The *haredi* Jew opens a book of *halaka* that might proffer alternative views and rulings regarding a specific case. This student will then extract the view of the more stringent adjudicator, especially if the latter is a popular rabbinic authority. For example, there are different views regarding the quantity of *matza* to be eaten at the Passover *seder*, or the length of time after sunset before the Sabbath is terminated. The *haredi* Jew seeks the maximum requirement: eating almost a complete *matza*, for example, or waiting at least 72 minutes after sunset (the longest period required by most halakically observant Jews.

Friedman attributes the *haredi* behaviour among the western Jews to the influence of the nineteenth-century, eastern-European *yeshiva Zeitgeist*. This argument might hold for the behaviour of first- and second- generation Jewish immigrants, but the contemporary *haredi* Jew does not consciously or subconsciously identify with the eastern European *Zeitgeist*. Rather, objectively and subjectively (to borrow Peter Berger's and Thomas Luckmann's phraseology) he manifests the Israeli and North American *yeshiva Weltanschauung*. The eastern European religious and cultural drama has become part of the constructed, historical, rabbinic universe that began with the Hebrew Bible and continued until nineteenth- and early twentieth-century rabbinic leaders such as Rabbi Israel Meyer Hacohen Kagan (the Hafetz Haim).

The subsequent sections of this essay will explore a specific synagogue, its participants, and their identification with the *yeshiva* world. For the purpose of comparison, these are the props and roles of a modern Orthodox synagogue:

1. The position of the rabbi is highly managerial as well as spiritual.

2. The cantor leads the Sabbath services in an operatic style.

3. Little emphasis is placed on any one section of the liturgy.

4. The rabbi, cantor and lay leaders sit on throne-type theatre seats facing the congregation. These seats are placed on a raised platform alongside the ark.

5. Women sit in the same sanctuary behind a partition, which is usually no higher than four feet.

6. Only prayer-books and Bibles with an English translation are found in the sanctuary. They are often placed in pockets adjacent to the participants' seats.

7. A sermon is delivered during the Sabbath prayer service. It is given in English. When Hebrew words are employed, an English translation is immediately offered. The theme of the sermon is a contemporary Jewish issue.

8. The behavioural components and setting are similar to a modern Protestant church. These include stained-glass windows, ushers to greet the participants, a choir and sanctioned dress. Furthermore, the "members" are mere observers while the rabbi and cantor serve as intermediaries between the divine and the mundane on behalf of the congregation. In addition to his spiritual role, moreover, the rabbi is perceived as an organizational leader.

9. The *bima* is raised and placed in the centre of the synagogue.

10. Prayer-shawls are offered only to male participants. The shawls cover the upper part of the back and are often made of silk, not the traditional wool.

11. English is the language of conversation, but Hebrew is the language of the service.

12. Membership is acquired by paying dues.

### The setting of the observed *shtibl*

The synagogue under examination is located on the bottom level of a two-storey house. Its rabbi/owner resides on the top floor. The first-floor apartment serves as the *shtibl*. This lower apartment is partitioned into four rooms and a kitchen. The largest of these rooms, the sanctuary, is situated in the front of the apartment. It is approximately 12 feet wide and 24 feet long.

In the sanctuary, against the eastern wall, stands the ark. Built as a permanent structure, it rises from floor to ceiling and covers a large portion of the wall. On the curtain covering the ark appears the name of its donor. There is also a small picture of Jerusalem suspended from the front of the ark. Adjacent to the ark hangs a "synagogue" calendar. It provides dates, times and rituals related to the synagogue and Jewish celebrations.

On the northern flank of the ark sits the *shtibl*'s charismatic leader, the rabbi. His thronelike chair is placed at the head of a long wooden table (in the style of the *yeshiva* study-table). This table extends the length of the northern wall, and participants sit on both sides. A large memorial board covers a major section of the northern wall.

On the southern flank of the ark sits the rabbi's assistant, who is also his primary student and apprentice. The organization of the southern sector is similar to the northern. A long wooden table extends the length of the wall, or, in this case, a window facing the street. The assistant sits at its head and the participants on either side. Each table can seat 10 adults comfortably. An additional 10 chairs are placed against the western wall.

In the centre of the sanctuary stands the *shulhan*, the traditional table employed for Torah readings and often for leading the prayers. Due to the lack of space, prayer-books, Bibles and prayer-shawls are placed in a small case that stands in the hallway. Shelves of traditional rabbinic texts (including those published by the rabbi) cover the walls of an adjacent room, the library.

Because men and women must be separated during the Orthodox Jewish prayer service, the library serves also as the women's section for all religious and social functions. For example, the two or three women (only) who join the Sabbath prayer services are directed to the library. In addition to the books, two wooden study-tables fill the room. The remaining facilities, a kitchen and two rooms, are used infrequently. In rare instances, refreshments are served after the prayer service in one of these rooms to the male participants. The women who prepare the refreshments eat separately in the library.

### The rabbi

The rabbi, who is also the owner of the *shtibl*, serves as the charismatic and spiritual leader of the congregation. He was born, educated and ordained in eastern Europe. His education consisted only of rabbinic studies. The rabbi, now in his sixties, has been living in North America for 40 years. He prefers to speak Yiddish but will not hesitate to converse in English when required. His fluent English carries a heavy European accent. The rabbi dresses in the traditional *rosh yeshiva* garb. This includes a black suit and either a hat or a large skull-cap made of cloth. On *shabbos*, his black suit jacket is replaced by a long black coat. The rabbi has a full beard, which is always trimmed and well kept.

In 1948, two years after his arrival in North America, the rabbi moved to this city, where he was hired by the local rabbinic academy to serve as one of its *rashe yeshivot* (leaders of, and teachers in, a rabbinic academy). In 1974, due to personality conflicts, he was compelled to leave the institution. Because he did not wish to leave the city or change professions, the rabbi established his own *yeshiva*. Although the academy never developed into a classical-style *yeshiva* with a full-time student body, it was nevertheless identified as such by the Jewish community. This recognition can be attributed to the rabbi's personality. He continues to conduct himself as a *rosh yeshiva*. This persona is expressed through such actions as the classes he teaches both in his academy and in other institutions throughout the city, his behaviour in the *shtibl*, his dress and his conversation. In general, the Jewish community continues to recognize him as a *rosh yeshiva* and hires those whom he ordains as rabbis.

Due to his ambiguous situation, a *rosh yeshiva* without a *yeshiva*, the rabbi was compelled to establish a Sabbath *minyan* at his institution. To attend another synagogue as a member would undermine his role as *rosh yeshiva*; he would not have the spiritual and administrative leadership that emanates from such a role. A *minyan* (the quorum of the men required for public worship) at his institution, moreover, further legitimates his *yeshiva*. The prayer group also offers greater interaction with members of the Jewish community, thereby perpetuating his status as a *rosh yeshiva*.

Although the rabbi projects the role and image of a *rosh yeshiva*, he is considered to be "modern." People do not hesitate to discuss with him issues and problems that they would hesitate to present to the traditional *rosh yeshiva*. Thus the "clientele" attracted to the *shtibl* and classes includes former *yeshiva* students who currently do not attend a *yeshiva*.

## The male participants

I have classified three groups of actors in the *shtibl*. They can be identified according to their seating arrangement. One group sits at the rabbi's table. The age of these people ranges from 50-65, and they were born in either Canada or eastern Europe. The language spoken is either "*yeshiva* English" or Yiddish. This group belongs to the managerial and entrepreneurial sector of society. Its members wear dark suits, hats and large black felt skull-caps. Their Jewish education has included some type of *yeshiva* experience, but none of these members has been ordained. Their secular education does not extend beyond high school. Except for one participant, all are clean-shaven.

The appointed lay president of the *shtibl*, who is part of this group, sits opposite the rabbi.

The participants who sit at the southern table are between the ages of 35-50. They were born in North America, Israel or French-speaking countries. The language spoken at their table is English, Hebrew or French. All three languages are interspersed with *yeshiva* jargon. For example, words such as, *davening* (praying), *toire* (the Yiddish pronunciation of Torah), *shul* (synagogue), *ye'ush* (despair), *lihora* (it would seem to say), *avedeh* (certainly), *memanafshak* (in any event), and *pashtes* (simple) are repeatedly employed. These actors have studied in post-secondary institutions and Hebrew (Jewish) day-schools. They have also had some *yeshiva* experience. They belong to the professional and academic world. Only one of them is directly involved in the field of Judaism. Although these participants dress conservatively, they wear sport-jackets and knitted skull-caps.

The chairs along the western wall are used by participants below the age of 35. (At times, they gravitate to the southern table.) They are Canadian-born and have a day-school or *yeshiva* education. They speak English and dress in a fashion similar to the members at the southern table. This area includes the children of the synagogue participants. All three groups include "*yeshiva* language," along with their mother tongues, in conversation.

Two reasons were offered by the actors of all three areas for their membership in the *shtibl*. They attributed it either to their loyalty to the rabbi or to the possibility for prayer with greater *kavana* (concentration). I will discuss these responses later.

Of all the Sabbath morning male participants, not more than five are the rabbi's students. The others have no interaction with the rabbi other than at the Saturday morning services. Furthermore, no financial payment is required of them in the form of either dues or donations. The institution is supported by outside contributors who do not necessarily attend the prayer meetings. Participants receive "services" without monetary payment, but they offer the rabbi, through participation in the prayer services, recognition and legitimation as a *rosh yeshiva*.

Two additional categories of participant that should be noted are guests and women. Guests, or infrequent participants, are directed towards the areas they would be associated with if they were regular actors. Women, as I have observed, pray in a separate room. On an ordinary Sabbath, when there is no bar mitzvah, there will be a maximum of four female participants. The inaccessibility of the women's section to me, as well as the low number of women, makes it difficult to classify them. Therefore I will be concerned only with the male participants.

## The Sabbath morning service

As the congregants arrive on Sabbath morning, they are greeted informally by the rabbi. Fearful that there will be an insufficient number of participants to form the *minyan*, the rabbi waits with anticipation at the window for potential members and welcomes them at the entrance. During this period, prior to the commencement of the liturgy, the attending participants congregate around the rabbi at his table adjacent to the window. The rabbi either initiates a discussion concerning the Jewish community or responds to a halakic problem posed by one of the congregants.

Although the service is scheduled to commence at nine o'clock, it does not begin before 9:15. The rabbi appoints a participant to lead the first section of the morning liturgy (*psuke dezimra*), sending him to lead the *davening* (praying). At the initiation of the service, the men wrap themselves in *talitot* (prayer-shawls). These ritual objects are wool and cover most of the body. The rabbi and several congregants place the *talit* over their heads. The *psuke dezimra* section is read at a "steady pace" with very few cantorial flourishes; the tunes are those traditionally used at rabbinic academies.

The second section of the morning liturgy, *shaharit*, is led, in most instances, by the rabbi's assistant. As before, cantorial singing is hardly ever introduced. The *shaliah tzibur* (prayer leader, sometimes the *hazan* but usually a lay person) does not initiate a new prayer prior to the rabbi's completion of the invocation. Thus the rabbi, not the *shaliah tzibur*, sets the pace. This is emphasized during two prayers, the *shma* and the *amida*, or *shmone esre* (a silent prayer). Only when the rabbi begins to chant the *shma* does everyone join him. The *shaliah tzibur* does not continue until the rabbi has completed the recitation of the last paragraph of the *shma* out loud. By the same token, the repetition of the *amida* is not initiated until the rabbi gives the cue at the completion of the invocation. This process, similar to the behaviour of most rabbinic authorities, is very long. The rabbi is usually the last to complete the reciting of the *amida*. During the repetition of the *amida*, congregants, especially those at the "younger table," examine biblical and rabbinic texts.

The third section of the liturgy is the Torah reading. The dearth of steady "torah readers" requires volunteers, thus encouraging the congregants' participation in the liturgy. Those called to the Torah for the *aliyot*, are designated by the rabbi. These honours are dispersed according to political and financial considerations or the desire to honour rabbinic scholars. This point is emphasized in the specific *aliyah* assigned to the scholar. The two *aliyot* considered most important are the third and sixth; priority for these is given to the rabbinic representatives.

The *musaf* service (a concluding, or "additional" section) follows the same pattern as *shaharit*. In contrast to the modern Orthodox synagogue, and in accordance with the *yeshiva* service, no sermon or lesson is delivered during or at the conclusion of the service. Moreover, "announcements" are made only when imperative.

Following the service, participants approach the rabbi and wish him "*gut shabos.*" To guarantee a *minyan* for *minha* (the afternoon service), the rabbi reaffirms the participation of congregants by asking them if they intend to come. Members with halakic or "religious" questions remain behind to discuss these, briefly, with the rabbi.

An examination of the Sabbath prayer service and study-hall sanctuary in most rabbinic academies (Helmreich 1982; Heilman 1983) reveals a striking similarity to the service and synagogue I have described. Due to this similarity between the *yeshiva* and *shtibl* services, I find it unnecessary to burden the reader with a separate description of the former.

**Discussion**

Ritual behaviour communicates a message. What is the message communicated in the ritual process I have reported?. This is the central question raised here.

In *The Social Construction of Reality*, Peter Berger and Thomas Luckmann discuss the entrance of individuals into society or the "group" with which they identify. The process "begins with 'taking over' the world in which others already live" (1966, 150). This milieu then becomes the world of "inductees." By this, new members understand, share and reciprocally define situations, actions, and language with the other individuals of the group. There develops "an ongoing mutual identification" between new and integrated members (1966, 150) . When this degree of interaction is reached, Berger and Luckmann argue, the inductees can be considered members of the society. This ontogenetic process, by which incorporation is brought about, is called "socialization." The process of socialization entails two principal stages: primary and secondary. Additional types as "alterations" are contingent upon the two principal categories (1966, 176). Primary socialization is defined as the "first socialization an individual undergoes in childhood by which he becomes a member of society" (1966, 150). In this first stage of socialization, initiates undergo a process of cognitive learning and emotional change. They learn to identify consciously and subconsciously with objects and persons. They adopt the roles and attitudes of the group and its world.

Secondary socialization occurs later and replicates this process at the adult level. The process of socialization into the *yeshiva* world is one of secondary socialization and is analogous to aspects of the primary stage. The *yeshiva* society consciously seeks to incorporate students into its world. These young men, and we are dealing with a specifically masculine institution, are taught a new language, or dialect, with which to identify (what has been referred previously as *yeshiva* language). Their previous societal identifications, if inconsistent with those of the *yeshiva* world, are expurgated. Students enter not only a new and objective social structure but also an objective social world. This new reality is where they seek their primary group relationships. For *yeshiva* novices, as for children, new attributes (such as cognitive learning, emotional attachment and adoption of attitudes) are internalized and become their own. They then dress in the costume of the *yeshiva* milieu and speak its dialect. Students enter into a world that lacks doubt. The latter is perceived as a nomic structure that is almost perfect. "It implies the internalization of society as such and of the objective reality establishment of a coherent and continuous identity. Society, identity, and reality are subjectively crystallized in the same process of internalization" (Berger and Luckmann 1966, 153). The dichotomy between subjective and objective reality is eliminated. Each is equally real. Only now do students identify themselves, only now are they identified by others, as part of the *yeshiva* society.

Because Berger and Luckmann have assigned primary socialization to childhood, they classify the primary process of transformation of older individuals as "alteration." This re-socialization, as in *yeshiva* students, replicates the process, attributes and characteristics of primary socialization. These are different from primary socialization because initiates must "cope with a problem of dismantling and disintegrating the preceding nomic structure of subjective reality" (Berger and Luckmann 1966, 177). The *yeshiva* milieu and its members offer ideal social conditions for an effective transformation. There is an intense concentration, in a closed society, of all the significant attributes of the internalization prerequisites for socialization.

"Primary socialization ends when the concept of the generalized other has been established in the consciousness of the individual" (Berger and Luckmann 1966, 157). In the case of *yeshiva* students, this "rite of passage" from the alteration stage occurs when they terminate their formal status as students. In most instances, the "graduates" embark on careers that have no official relation to the *yeshiva*. At this point, secondary socialization commences. However, my interest in this study is not the process of secondary socialization but how the reality internalized in primary socialization is maintained in the consciousness of individuals.

Berger and Luckmann argue that this reiteration is acquired through "the explicit and emotionally charged confirmation that his significant others bestow on him." The primary "others" that maintain and confirm his subjective reality can be family or reference groups. Furthermore, the reinforcement of these significant others is dependent upon a specific social base, such as the *shtibl*. The social base works best if it is similar to that of the primary socialization. For individuals to maintain and confirm their subjective as well as objective reality, they must interact in a milieu that confirms their identity. The observed *shtibl*'s Sabbath morning prayer service, a facsimile of the *yeshiva Weltanschauung*, maintains this reinforcement. The objectivity of *one* reality, as in the *shtibl*, within the total of the individual's social world is imperative for his implicit reaffirmation. Furthermore, the earlier socialization period is projected by many things practised in the social base of this one reality—language, conversation, objects, dress, ritual behaviour and techniques, collective rituals and rabbinic leadership—and thus help maintain the subjective reality.

Berger and Luckmann emphasize the component of language and conversation in the process of reality maintenance. They conclude: "Thus the fundamental reality-maintaining fact is the continuing use of the same language [as in primary socialization] to objectify unfolding biographical experience" (Berger and Luckmann 1966, 173). This maintenance is accented through the "group-idiosyncratic language" of the primary stage. The individual returns to his reality when he returns to the few individuals who understand his in-group allusions. Furthermore, as Heilman correctly argues in his examination of Talmudic study groups, language reflects the group's collective existence (Heilman 1983, 173). At times, the reflection is lexical. At other times, it is syntactic or morphological. At still other times, it is intonational. Whatever the sign, the fact remains that language use cannot help but demonstrate social and cultural identification.

An additional factor required for the success of reality maintenance is that one's experiences with the "reality" be continual and consistent. In their discussion of the frequency of conversation as an example of reality-generating potency, Berger and Luckmann add that the lack of frequency can sometimes be compensated for by the intensity of the conversation when it does take place (Berger and Luckmann 1966, 174).

The observed *shtibl* and its Sabbath morning ritual conform to this theoretical construct. The *shtibl*, its leadership and rituals are modelled after the *yeshiva*. The "one" reality for the individual is his "intensive," or focused, participation on Sabbath morning in the *shtibl* service. Although members duplicate only the *yeshiva*'s prayer service, not its academic studies, they are able to reaffirm their own reality, the reality of their previous socialization. By attending a facsimile of the *yeshiva* prayer service in the *shtibl*, they effectively maintain their alteration stage.

This theoretical model helps explain as well the presence of the participant who did not receive formal *yeshiva* schooling. As I have observed, Friedman (1987) has shown that modern Orthodoxy has become "right wing" and is interconnected with the *yeshiva Weltanschauung*. The power of the Orthodox movement, both financially and politically, is in the hands of this group. The number of *yeshiva* graduates has grown. This has a strong impact upon modern Orthodox Jewish communities. Halakically observant Jews prefer to identify with this group. They now want their reference group to be identified with the *yeshiva* milieu. This behaviour is also manifested in the choice of schools; at this *shtibl*, even those who do not themselves have a *yeshiva* education send their children to rabbinic academies or Orthodox day-schools.

The participants in the *shtibl* I studied have chosen this synagogue as they do not completely desire to socialize into the *yeshiva Weltanschauung*. They seek, however, to mix "their" world and that of the *yeshiva*. The *shtibl* thereby permits Jews who have not been educated at a *yeshiva* to be identified with *yeshiva,* or "right-wing," Orthodoxy, and it does not "alter" completely their behaviour. Participation in the *shtibl* liturgy is what Heilman terms "ritual conformity" in contrast to "ritual rebellion" (1983, 73). These people continue to wear sports jackets and knitted skull-caps, but they are identified by the "right-wing" community as halakically observant Jews.

A possible consideration that follows from the above observation is that the behaviour described can be pronounced in the larger Orthodox community. The modern Orthodox synagogue of the 60s now attracts non-halakically observant Jews. Observant Jews of traditional "modern" Orthodoxy have converted their synagogues, whether large or small, to accommodate *shtibl*-style services. They have modelled their Sabbath morning prayer services and rituals on the *yeshiva*. Through the liturgy and "public" rituals practised in the *shtibl*, participants reflect, communicate, perpetuate and develop the pattern of meaning and inherited conceptions that the *yeshiva* world defines as its culture. These shared involvements of *shtibl* participants confirm and perpetuate the reality of this world.

# 9

# Sabbath Morning Services in a Traditional Conservative Synagogue

## VICTOR LEVIN

### Introduction

This essay derives from my study of a Conservative synagogue in a large eastern city. Like the other essays of this volume, mine interprets Jewish Sabbath morning services as symbolic expression that communicates participants' mapping of their world and of their place within it.

The data selectively presented in this paper resulted from participant observation and interviews. For seven months between 1988 and 1989, I participated in services, talked with congregants and interviewed leaders. What follows concentrates on the service, the participation of congregants and on common patterns or variations. In addition, my attempt to interpret the observed patterns in evidence in the Sabbath morning service encompassed the consideration of "official" and scholarly interpretations of the Conservative movement and statements by Conservative spokespersons. The latter culminated, in 1988, in the first unified statement of principles by Conservative leaders, *Emet ve'emuna* (Truth and Faith).

### Subjects—the service and congregants

Our subject is twofold: the service and the participants at a Sabbath morning service in a Conservative congregation in a large urban Canadian setting. Patterns of participation are complex. People arrive at different times and participate in various ways, suggesting varied types of participant with various orientations toward the service and its meanings. Prima facie, the service is twofold, both ritual and event. For some congregants, it is significant primarily as a religious *ritual*, repeated regularly. For others, it is significant primarily as the bar mitzvah or bat mitzvah of a friend or relative, a transitional ceremony and a social and ethnic event experienced episodically. On many Sabbath mornings, both groups are well represented. As the service progresses throughout the morning, its character changes in ways that parallel changes in the participating groups. Thus the service unfolds like a drama with a succession of acts.

The service also reflects historical developments, not only in the Conservative movement and its rabbinic leadership, but in the congregation itself as a result of decisions by active members to modify the service. Such changes can help us to understand its present significance, for they express the intentions of people who make these changes—or consent to them.

Participants in the service include synagogue officials, lay congregants and guests. Synagogue officials include the rabbi, the *hazan* (cantor), *hazan sheni* (assistant cantor), the president and vice presidents, along with the *parnas* (administrator) and the *gabai* (co-ordinator). Lay congregants can be classified as core, regular and occasional. The core group comprises 10-12 men who attend from the beginning of the Sabbath service, and form the *minyan* (quorum of 10 men required for public worship) during the week as well. Most are immigrants from central or eastern Europe (who arrived in Canada after either World War I or World War II) and over 70. Regular attendees, more than half of them men, number 40-70, depending on the time of year. Most are over 60. Occasional attendees bring the total number to somewhere between 60-200—or even more when bar mitzvahs, bat mitzvahs and major holidays are celebrated. In general, then, the participating congregation is elderly. It represents a small fraction of a far larger congregation of about 650 families, mostly younger people, who are seen only at special events or on major holidays.

### General theoretical and conceptual issues

The service embraces, or at least reflects, a variety of cultural forms: from traditional rabbinic authoritarianism to contemporary secular liberalism; from right-wing Conservative traditionalism (near Orthodoxy) to left-wing Conservative progressivism (near Reform). It moves, within minutes, from prayers to restore ancient sacrificial practices to announcements of the kind of cultural events that enliven modern synagogues. Congregants display a similar variety.

Not all reasons for congregant attendance and participation can be reduced to the conscious design of people who have modified the service in recent generations or to the conscious thoughts of congregants. Many reasons are deeply rooted in the continuities of congregational and Jewish history and in characteristics that congregants share with greater or wider socio-cultural streams. A Conservative congregation such as the one we are studying has a strong interest in keeping the service traditional. Thus, to understand the service, we should not confine our attention to modifications but seek to understand the continuing force of older institutional, socio-cultural, moral and religious orientations and meanings. In view of Conservative ideology, espousing a combination of the best in Judaism and modernity, we might expect a balance between factors specifically Jewish and factors common in wider socio-cultural streams and movements.

We could hypothesize that developments in the service reflect a continuing need to increase intelligibility by reducing incoherence and conflict between the various cultures represented by both the congregants and the service. We can expect heightened emphasis on those ritual forms and values that are least dissonant—that is, most compatible with the primary cultural systems represented. We can hypothesize that the direction of the service reflects an interest in mediating and harmonizing differences between varied identifications and associations, thus avoiding the experience of conflict between different orientations. We might predict, therefore, that the service will emphasize meanings and values common to various types of congregant as well as to the cultures they represent.

### The setting of the Sabbath morning service

Built in 1940, about three miles from the centre of a major eastern city, the synagogue is located in a semi-suburban, largely residential area. The city is primarily Catholic, but the neighbourhood is primarily Protestant. The Jewish community is served primarily by Orthodox synagogues, several of which are located in the same neighbourhood as our Conservative congregation. There is a Reconstructionist synagogue one mile north and a Reform synagogue two miles east. There are also three other Conservative synagogues. One, well known, is nominally Conservative with Orthodox services.

The synagogue is a rectangular brick structure, simple in basic structure and lines. Tall windows, rounded at the top, recall the stone tablets of the Decalogue. Functional architecture is combined, in other words, with Jewish symbolism. The building houses a large main sanctuary. Used for Sabbath services for most of the year, it is enhanced by extensive ornamental and symbolic decoration. This sanctuary has seating for approximately 1,200 people. (A balcony must be used, nevertheless, on High Holidays.) The raised *bima* (stage) is at the front of the sanctuary. A marble ark, containing the Torah scrolls, stands against one wall of the *bima*, in the centre, and is flanked by high-backed armchairs for the rabbi, rabbi emeritus (when he is in town), cantor, assistant cantor and several synagogue officials. These chairs are behind a low, elaborately carved, wooden balustrade. The latter is broken by elaborate wooden pillars rising some 10 feet to an overhanging choir loft (although the choir itself cannot be seen). On each side of the *bima*, toward the front, is a table for the Torah reader and the *hazan*; on the other side is a pulpit for the rabbi. Pews, in four sections, extend for some distance from the foot of the *bima* to the entrance (under the balcony); these sections are separated by an aisle in the centre and two on the sides. The sanctuary is much longer than it is wide, and the distance to the *bima* from the entrance is considerable. Consequently, where one sits in the sanctuary significantly affects one's experience of the service.

The synagogue building also houses administrative offices and reception halls. It serves as a community centre, not only as a house of worship. Adjacent and attached to the synagogue is a Jewish day-school (primary grades only) associated with the Conservative Movement; it is administratively independent, however, of our synagogue.

### The service: Overview and outline

The service is Conservative, like the synagogue, though this was not inevitable; it could have been Orthodox, as it is in a well-known Conservative synagogue nearby. In numerous ways the service is atypical, representing the traditional wing of the Conservative movement. The Sabbath prayerbook is Orthodox. All prayers but one are read in Hebrew. The Torah reading is complete. There is no organ, no Friday evening service, and women are not given *aliyot* (asked to read from the Torah or to recite blessings before and after someone else does).

In other respects the service is modern, though, and reflects the Conservative mainstream. Men all wear prayer-shawls (*talitot*) and skullcaps (*kipot*). The congregation has held both bar mitzvahs and bat mitzvahs for several decades. The rabbi's sermon is a highlight of the service, and its orientation is contemporary. Mixed seating was introduced about six years ago. For most of the year, there is a mixed choir with female soloists. And women participate in several rituals on the *bima*: opening and closing the ark, conducting modern prayers in English and, due to a recent innovation, removing Torah scrolls from the ark.

The liturgy followed is primarily Orthodox. Thus the service begins with blessings, psalms and hymns of praise leading to the morning service proper, or *shaharit*. This includes the *shma* (proclaiming God's unity), accompanying benedictions, the *shmone esre* or *amida* (also known as the congregational prayer) and the Torah service. The latter, in turn, includes prayers and processions, readings from the Torah and *haftara* (the Prophets) and two brief talks by the rabbi. Sometimes the Torah service includes a bar mitzvah or bat mitzvah ceremony, with a brief address by the rabbi to the young initiate. The Torah service is followed by the rabbi's sermon and an additional service, or *musaf*, with a repetition of the *musaf amida* followed by prayers, announcements and a concluding hymn.

The service runs from three to three and a half hours, beginning at eight forty-five or nine o'clock (depending on the time of year). To be more specific, that means about 45 minutes for *shaharit*, 75 for the Torah service, 20 for the rabbi's sermon and 40 for the *musaf* and concluding announcements.

**The beginning: Early morning prayers**

One by one, members of the core group arrive and sit quietly or in quiet conversation. At the appropriate time, they check to see if they have a *minyan*. Other men arrive within a few minutes. If necessary, though, more can be found. A reader, either the *hazan sheni* or a congregant, leads the assembled congregants in "davening" the early morning service, reading quickly through prayers together in a traditional manner. "Davening" requires marked skill in reading; this distinguishes members of the "core group" from most other congregants. Coming at the beginning of a three-hour service, it also suggests unusual devotion. The role of reader is honoured, espececially when performed by a congregant. Yet custom does not call for a trained voice and cantorial expertise. The "reader" (and leader) is more like an honoured congregant, a *primus inter pares*. Early morning prayers—morning blessings (*birkot hashahar*) and hymns (*psuke dezimra*)—are indistinguishable from what would be found in an Orthodox congregation of eastern European immigrants (except for the physical setting provided by this contemporary Conservative sanctuary with its mixed seating).

For *shaharit*, the morning service proper, the congregation is joined and led by the highly trained and expert cantor. The rabbi announces page numbers of prayers from time to time.

The congregation grows gradually. In contrast to members of the core group, the new arrivals are more equally divided by sex; between one third and one half of them are women. Congregants arrive in no easily generalized pattern. Some arrive alone. Others arrive with two or three others, friends or relatives. Most, by far, are over 50. But several young professionals, most of them between 30-45, attend more or less regularly. And one young family, visiting from Israel, attends regularly.

Among those seen less often, some attend to perform rituals related to the death of a close relative, either in the period (week or year) after the death or for a *yortsait*, or annual remembrance. At this synagogue, departing from custom, a *yortsait* is marked on the Sabbath before the anniversary so as to maximize observance of the custom. Occasional congregants may attend on happier occasions—to bless an imminent wedding, for example, to name a child, receive an honour or, most frequently, to attend a bar mitzvah or bat mitzvah.

People begin to arrive for a bar mitzvah or bat mitzvah shortly after nine o'clock. Friends and relatives of the young initiate sit at the front of the sanctuary, near the *bima* (where the Torah is read). Between 50-200 people are involved, varying widely in age. They continue to arrive until well into the Torah reading.

## Modes of participation

Congregational participation becomes much more varied after the early morning prayers. Congregants can be seen praying, conversing, studying or sitting quietly and attentively. All these activities are part of the communal event. They represent different degrees of involvement in prayer. Generally speaking, regular congregants are more active than occasional congregants in prayer. Many people move back and forth from active prayer to quiet conversation or even silence. Some remain silently passive throughout. Others are active throughout. The presence of a professional choir guarantees that passivity on the part of some congregants never results in silence, or near silence, at moments requiring congregational response and participation. Thus the style of the service, coupled with the control an attendee may exercise in regulating his or her distance from the bima, the centre of action, permits, in effect, the accommodation in the same sanctuary of persons comfortable with and seeking quite different modes of participation in the service. Those proficient in reading Hebrew exercise artistry and independence, especially in responsive prayers that involve both the cantor and congregation. Their spontaneity contrasts with the predetermined conformity of much congregational prayer. It is probably more common in Conservative synagogues than Reform synagogues but much less than in Orthodox synagogues.

Despite individual differences and marked variations between prayers, there is a succession of key prayers, especially the *shma* and *amida*, in which virtually all congregants are either actively involved or respectfully silent and attentive. There is a general trend toward heightened attention and concentration, which reaches a climax during the Torah service.

Some congregants, having arrived late, read through some or all of the prayers that they have missed; this is more or less in keeping with traditional Orthodox practice. Most people, however, do not observe this custom.

Percentages of congregants singing vary widely from one part of the service to another. At any one time, the rate could be anywhere from 10 percent to 90 percent. Such variation can be explained in several ways. Congregants display different levels of competence in reading Hebrew, for example. Then, too, most people are familiar with some prayers but not others; even those less than fluent in Hebrew might be familiar with some well-known prayers. Melodies, too, are either more or less familiar; some of them vary from one week to the next.

Prayers reserved for only part of the congregation include: prayers of sanctification by mourners (the *kadish*); prayers of remembrance; prayers honouring participants in the Torah service and their families; and prayers for the sick. These prayers are led by the rabbi, sometimes with English translations. This seems to signify a special effort on the rabbi's part to engage people in prayers that might be personally meaningful to them. Occasional congregants often attend specifically to recite prayers of this kind.

Conversation is common during services. Normally subdued, however, words are usually inaudible to all but the person addressed. Discussions extend to a wide range of topics. The most common topics are personal and family welfare; the performance of people in the service; issues in the synagogue and Jewish community; news of others in the community or congregation; important events in public life; plans to travel or receive visitors; and business contacts. It is customary to make observations, usually complimentary, about those from the congregation who make major contributions to the service. Several of the older and more traditional members examine prayers and weekly readings in a more studious or analytical manner, their aim being to make comments on them and perhaps to discern new meanings. It is not unusual to hear discussions of themes raised by the rabbi.

### The Torah service

The Torah service, which is the central event, brings a change in the overall pattern. From this point on, the ceremony involves a larger number of actors in distinctive roles. The choir of 11 men and women, some of them volunteers and some paid professionals, joins the congregation for the beginning of the Torah service. Some melodies are traditional and well known, so many members of the congregation feel free to join the choir in song. Other melodies are not well known; because these involve more complex harmonies, counterpoints and rhythms, most members of the congregation can join the choir only with difficulty. As a result, they are passive and receptive. Later, during a "show-piece," congregants are expected *not* to sing.

Beginning with the Torah service, the liturgy takes on the quality of a dramatic performance presented before the congregation—even though congregants remain active and even though a few of them are asked to perform special parts. With this in mind, the *gabai* approaches several people: women to open the ark; men to receive *aliyot* (reciting prayers over the Torah, which the *hazan sheni* reads "by proxy" on behalf of those honoured); and men to raise, guard, undress and dress the Torah.

The rabbi talks briefly about the Torah reading, focusing on an event or a theme that has moral implications. He might refer to rabbinic commentaries, but he does not present them as authoritative and binding. He often points out variant commentaries or adds his own.

By tradition, the Torah service involves the most sacred object in Judaism, the scroll containing God's revelation to Israel. With great ceremony, it is brought down in a procession from the *bima* to the congregational level; there, it is greeted by some congregants with customary kisses.

On completion of the procession, selected male congregants are called for *aliyot* (anglicized by many congregants to "*aliyas*"). They go up to the *bima*, recite blessings over the Torah and then receive a blessing from the reader. These roles are seen as honours, and are given out with due consideration of traditional priorities. These are modified, however, during a bar mitzvah or bat mitzvah. Close relatives of the initiate are given highest priority for most *aliyot*, and the number of *aliyot* is increased from seven to ten or even twelve (thus involving the relatives more than they would be otherwise). The final *aliya* is given to the bar mitzvah (boy) himself; he reads the *haftara*. In the case of a bat mitzvah, however, the girl attends her father while he reads it. This congregation does not yet give *aliyot* to women, but the possibility is being discussed and a change might well occur within a year or two.

The Torah portion itself is normally read by the *hazan sheni*. At a bar mitzvah, though, a capable boy might read one portion. If so, he earns more respect from both officials and congregants. The reading by the *hazan sheni* is normally done very quickly, often without precise attention to details of melody or enunciation. This is due to several factors. For one thing, there is a tension between the expectation of some congregants that the entire Torah portion will be read each Sabbath and the intolerance (or disinterest) of other congregants in sitting through a long, slow, but more carefully enunciated, reading. The reading is already long, often close to half an hour. Most congregants understand hardly any Hebrew. Many, judging by their behaviour during the reading, are not very interested in the text, even in translation. The reading, which roughly follows a traditional *trop* (melody), is not distinguished by musical qualities suited to sustain the aesthetic interest of a modern audience.

Despite such factors, there is a significant lack of conversation during the Torah reading. A few people go in and out; half a dozen converse quietly; most remain seated and respectfully silent. Some people, probably fewer than 25 percent and mostly regulars, attend to details of the Torah reading. They follow it line by line and comment on the quality of the reader's performance. Some study the Hebrew or the English translation with interest in the content. Some read rabbinic commentaries in the text. A few even provide their own.

Reasons for the respectful attention or silence are varied. The Torah is regarded by many, conceivably most, as sacred in some sense. Congregants might respect the right of others to approach the reading with solemn reverence. Silence being customary, it is supported by the example of most congregants rather than active enforcement. The performance is more interesting than it might otherwise be due to the elaborate ceremony that surrounds it and the fact that congregants or guests participate.

When a bar mitzvah (boy) reads the Torah, all congregants are respectfully silent and attentive; the sanctity of the Torah is complemented by the importance of the ceremony in the life of the young man, his family, their guests and the community at large. On such days, this is the primary ceremony for which many have come. Many comment on the quality of the young man's reading, especially when he does it well. Upon conclusion of the Torah reading, all rise as one congregant holds the Torah aloft, accoutrements are returned to the scroll and an honoured congregant is left to guard it.

The rabbi provides a brief introduction to the *haftara* reading. It is similar to the comments he made before the Torah reading. In fact, he usually links the two readings. The *hazan sheni* sings the *haftara* using a distinctive *trop* (although a congregant, guest or bar mitzvah receives more attention for doing so). Everyone is respectfully silent during this reading, if not attentive. There is no evidence to suggest that the content of the reading accounts for the greater respect and attention it receives. Rather, these seem related to the special honour associated with a congregant or guest doing a difficult reading.

The Torah scroll is returned to the ark much as it was brought out, with much ceremony and considerable congregational participation. During bar mitzvahs, before returning the Torah, the choir normally sings the final prayer, *ets hayim hi*, in a melody from the movie *Exodus*. This melody, marking the greatest departure from tradition, arouses strong positive feelings; these are probably associated with Zionism, the creation of Israel and the renewal of Jewish life after the Holocaust. Although the melody is new, the arrangement preserves the proper accents of Hebrew words.

For a bar mitzvah or bat mitzvah, the rabbi talks to the initiate before the assembled congregation. By tradition, this ceremony marks a young person's entry into adulthood, becoming subject to the laws of Israel. These days, however, it often marks the culmination and completion of a young person's Jewish education. Despite the apparent loss of much of its traditional meaning, the ceremony has remained an important and popular part of the ritual, and might even have gained in significance (see Fishbane, chapter 10 of this volume; Schoenfeld 1988; 1990; 1992). Many people, the occasional congregants, come to the synagogue for no other reason. The attention given by both members and invited guests suggests that its significance, for many people, surpasses that of prayer, Torah, rabbinic teaching and the musical accomplishments of cantor and choir.

The rabbi now personally addresses the bar mitzvah or bat mitzvah. His address recalls a recent meeting with the initiate. It speaks of the young person's character, past record, interests or goals. On this basis, the rabbi usually develops an analogy with some aspect of Jewish life, usually a moral one, and encourages the initiate to lead a meaningfully and vitally Jewish life. For example, a girl oriented toward designing might hear about the effect of our designs on our world and on the people around us. Or, a boy interested in ecology might hear about the importance of living in harmony with our immediate environment and with the people closest to us. The rabbi always refers to traditional Jewish values, usually honour and humility. He combines appreciation for the initiate with admonitions. In any event, the talk speaks personally about the initiate and to the initiate, connecting personal facts with Jewish moral and cultural values.

What is omitted in the talk is also significant. There is no talk of authority—biblical, rabbinic or divine. (In one exception, the rabbi approvingly quoted a bar mitzvah boy who equated being Jewish with doing what rabbis say. But the words came from the boy.) All congregants are respectfully attentive during this talk; its general meanings, pro-moral and pro-Jewish, are not likely to be lost on them.

## Musaf

After the Torah service, there is an additional service, the *musaf*, with a second *amida*. This contains a prayer for the restoration of ancient sacrificial rites. This prompted a former official to comment that we are fortunate to read these prayers in Hebrew (that is, without understanding them). There is also an extended performance of one portion. This is designed to show the cantor and choir at their best. It offers an ideal opportunity for congregants, by now passive, to rest during a service that has already lasted well over two hours. The performance incorporates classical and romantic motifs, while conveying a distinctively Jewish spirit. Yet even the comments of the most religious are about its artistic qualities, its performance, rather than its spiritual qualities.

The rabbi normally delivers a talk or sermon during this part of the service. This talk is a highlight, normally sustaining the respect, attention and interest of most congregants. There is sometimes conversation but far less than during the Torah reading. The talk often begins with a brief reference to the Torah or *haftara* reading but moves quickly to more general or contemporary themes and interests. Thus the rabbi might speak of problems that people face in their personal lives, or challenges that Jewish people and communities now face either at home or in Israel. In general, he encourages or challenges people to respond personally to moral challenges and the possibility of a more meaningful Jewish life.

Again, he rarely claims authority for rabbis, Torah or God. He refers on occasion to rabbinic commentaries, not to appeal to past authority, but to raise questions for intelligent, contemporary Jews. He presents a world in which Jews are connected with other people (especially with other Jews), in which Jews have values and interests that make life meaningful in the face of current challenges. When introducing a guest speaker or recalling a recently deceased leader from the congregation, he gives praise to people, usually Jewish, whose virtues, achievements and contributions are worthy of emulation.

The rabbi also mentions principles and developments associated with the Conservative movement in Judaism, sometimes in clear opposition to Orthodoxy. For example, he expounds a Conservative commitment to democratic principles, opposing the threat of theocracy in Israel. And he represents a growing willingness among Conservatives to challenge Israel toward a more morally committed policy.

The rabbi's talk evokes associations with many features of Jewish life: the synagogue and its history; Conservatism Judaism; Zionism and Israel. Sometimes, though, it expresses a sense of connection with the wider, non-Jewish, world. He speaks of the value of idealism for a better life. His interest in advancing the role of women in Judaism reflects changing conditions in the larger society (in the face of a congregation mostly content to preserve tradition in this area). At times, such as on the anniversary of *Kristallnacht*, he expresses interests and concerns shared with Christian neighbours and churches.

Differences with congregants are implicit in much of what the rabbi says. He represents Jewish, moral and humane values to a congregation mostly less religious than he is. Privately, he noted that congregational involvement tends to be more ethnic than religious. This suggests a fundamental difference in priorities.

The attention, respect and interest given to the rabbi's talk reflects not only his status as religious leader of the congregation but also his lifelong immersion in Jewish culture and community life, concern with Jewish history and issues, rhetorical art, moral commitment, humanism, intelligence, learning, ability to reflect congregational concerns and ability to express values, attitudes and identifications that congregants share or appreciate.

## Conclusion of the service

The period of the service following the rabbi's talk and the musical performance of the cantor and the choir includes closing prayers, hymns and announcements by the rabbi. He reads a long list of past members of the congregation who died at this time of year. This reading can evoke a sense of connection with those who were personally close, with the history of the synagogue and its memory of those who have been lost and with truths that might be best expressed within a religious context. The rabbi also reads a list of announcements of upcoming services, community and cultural events, mostly in the synagogue. These represent ways that people can be more actively involved in Jewish life.

The final announcement is about the *kidush* (communal meal) to be held in one of the halls following the service. It has been sponsored by a congregant. This gift bestows honour on the giver and is the final highlight of the congregational event (even though it is not, strictly speaking, part of the service). The meal gives congregants personal access to their leaders and represents the Sabbath event at its most sociable and communal. Most congregants who attend services remain for the meal.

## Interpretation: The challenge of unification

Congregants share in a common service yet display diversity in religious behaviour. There is clear evidence, especially in attention and participation, that many congregants are interested less in prayer and more in other features of the service. Somehow, the rabbi must unite everyone. He faces this challenge most directly in his daily life.

We have considered how he addresses congregants to engage them in his talk and unite them around common themes and interests. A difficulty the rabbi faces is to keep diverse identifications compatible, to give them expression while conveying a unified focus and conveying a clear and definite message. One way to preserve compatibility is to emphasize what is common and avoid areas of serious controversy or differences, especially in matters of religion and politics. For example, the rabbi tends to refrain from expressing personal religious commitments that could alienate many congregants.

On the other hand, the rabbi is more than willing to present congregants with *moral* challenges implicit or explicit in their tradition, to confront them with ideals that they share or come to share. Moral challenges represent a respected and acceptable way of confronting and challenging the limits of conventional attitudes or habits. And they derive strength and respectability from values that are, in some sense, common to religious traditionalists and religious liberals, to the religious and the non-religious, to Jewish and more highly secularized, humanistic cultural streams.

The rabbi represents, attracts and appeals to a diverse and heterogeneous congregation. He inherits the role of representing Judaism, Jewish life and Jewish history before his congregation. His job is to guide congregants in their association with a tradition that is itself nothing if not protean.

A prominent Conservative rabbi, Max Routtenberg, wrote of the comprehensive unification of roles that the rabbi is called upon to perform as "preacher, teacher, pastor-counsellor and social engineer." Recent discussions at the synagogue, aimed at finding a new rabbi to replace the present one after his retirement, reflect congregational interests and values in this area. In general, officials and leading congregants hope that the new rabbi will present the qualities of a gifted scholar, speaker and pastor. This would not only satisfy members but, in addition, bring in new members. There are differences among congregants and leaders about the relative importance of the rabbi's roles. But there is general agreement that all these roles have some importance and must be embodied in a single person.

Unification also depends on the activity of members. Upon the advice and consent of provincial legislative bodies, the congregation was created, by a group of 20 merchants and advocates, in the name of "His Majesty." As an ecclesiastical corporation under provincial law, it is empowered to own property and make by-laws.

Formal decisions regarding ritual are made by a religion committee, which is composed of members; highly important decisions pass to higher bodies, including the executive committee and the board of trustees. One such decision, made around 10 years earlier, was on the introduction of mixed seating. This matter, being the most dramatic and visible departure from traditional custom, was highly sensitive and controversial, and there was a long period of discussion and education, involving all congregants, to prepare for a smooth transition. Ultimately, all members voted on the issue. As a result, very few members left. As expected, the change led to a substantial increase in the number of younger families affiliating with the synagogue, even though most of them are seen only several times a year.

At present, the committee is concerned with issues pertaining to the role of women in the service, especially the possibility of *aliyot*. It is also concerned with the choice of a new Conservative prayer-book to replace the old Orthodox book in use on Saturdays.

The committee is formed by voluntary participation of members, all of whom receive a list of committees once each year and choose which, if any, they wish to work on. Decisions, made by discussion and voting, are intended to establish a broad consensus. The committee is headed by a traditionalist of Orthodox background. But members form a cross-section, which broadly represents different interests and orientations in the synagogue.

The rabbi is approached, in a consultative capacity, as a specialist and authority on Conservative Jewish law. He represents expert knowledge of what is permitted and required in Conservative Judaism. His authority remains but with diminished scope. The committee apparently respects this and will do nothing explicitly forbidden. However, there remains considerable scope for choice within these limits. Thus the committee, and through it the congregation, functions much like a constitutional democracy. The requirements of Conservative Judaism, together with the laws and by-laws pertaining to the congregation, form the constitution. Committee members, self-chosen rather than elected, but representative both of the congregation and of its interests, form its "parliament." It is democratic in that all members of the congregation are eligible to participate. Of course, the committee, and through it the congregation, is responsive primarily to those most actively involved, and to others only as they are represented.

Within the range of available choices, the rabbi's views carry a certain moral weight but are not binding on congregants. For example, he favours much greater participation of women in the service. Many congregants, including women, want to preserve a more "traditional" service and are not eager to introduce *aliyot* for women.

At the synagogue under study, traditionalists remain strong among congregational leaders. There could be several reasons for this traditionalism. Some congregants believe in the moral authority of rabbinic traditions; they might even consider themselves neo-Orthodox—or, as one put it, Conservadox. Some argue that (what they believe to be) two-thousand-year-old practices should be respected. Others defend the historic practices of the synagogue, thus trying to preserve continuity with more than half a century of congregational life. Others still are sensitive to the orthodoxy of practices at a nearby Conservative synagogue and do not wish to diverge too much from its example.

To some extent, such traditionalism reflects the Jewish tradition that custom acquires a moral force akin to law. It recalls the orientations of leaders—certainly unknown to the congregants in anything other than name—who gave impetus to the emergence of the Conservative movement. Zacharias Frankel believed that a positive value should be placed on Jewish history as it has developed,[1] for instance, and Solomon Schechter believed that "The norm as well as the sanction of Judaism is the practice actually in vogue" (Schechter 1945). Then, too, traditionalism reflects as well the predominance of Orthodox Judaism in the surrounding urban Jewish community. Moreover, it expresses nostalgia for the Jewish familial or communal experiences of another time; traditionalism is a way to restore the link with one's youth, one's earliest contacts, one's origins, one's past. Overall these reasons suggest a Conservative respect for history, pride in history or attachment to history. This must be distinguished from respect for rabbinic or divine authority, which makes traditionalism increasingly a cultural style and not a matter of detailed religious obligations.

One key to developing unity is acknowledging plurality and co-ordinating diverse appeals or orientations. But this was slow in coming at the level of the movement. For a long time there was a significant lacuna with regard to Conservative belief. This left the movement at a disadvantage, at least in this respect, in comparison with Reform and Orthodoxy, which were more systematically articulate.

Conservative leaders finally met this problem with the publication in 1988 of *Emet ve'emuna*, a document presented as a statement of principles by leading rabbis, scholars and lay people. Kassel Abelson, president of the Rabbinical Assembly, calls it "official" in contrast with the personal views previously set forth by scholars and rabbis. But that declaration is in his personal Foreword, not within the "official" document.

The word "official" suggests a certain authoritativeness, expressing a consensus among scholars and leaders, both religious and lay. Indeed, there was a degree of consensus surprising to many in the movement. But the term "official" can also suggest a *contrast* between the professional establishment and the laity. Sociologists might wish to consider how representative the "official view" is of Conservative Jewish views generally. Let us focus on religious services as times for prayer.

The official account makes several statements about prayer. For example, prayer is: an act of petition, acknowledgement, praise, thanksgiving, confession or return to God; structured and fixed according to requirements of Jewish law; said, ideally, with the appropriate *kavana* (intention and feeling); promoted by modern revisions of the prayer-book; and encouraged at any time.

The document goes on to describe ways in which prayer makes it possible to gain spiritual meaning: (1) by appreciating values, above all God's holiness, from a perspective beyond ourselves; (2) by creating ties that transcend loneliness; (3) by teaching the tradition and renewing attachment to its heart and mind; (4) by expressing and feeling emotions in a beautiful service; (5) by reminding and stimulating us to be more moral; (6) by obliging us to keep a discipline that may lead to the proper *kavana*; (7) by having an efficacy that is understood in various ways, such as linking the worshipper to God and to other Jews or transforming the person who prays by "its ability to give voice to our yearnings and aspirations, to refine our natures, and to create a strong link to God" (*Emet ve'emuna*, 50-52).

This is an enlightened interpretation of prayer. But it is more concentrated in its ultimate focus and more spiritually oriented than most Conservative Jews would want. They understand the prayer in terms of its human significance—as an expression of personal, social and cultural life. This interpretation is preferable not only for social scientists but also for many congregants. Yet for a sociologist of religion, studying members of a religious movement, to neglect the movement's own most articulate self-interpretation would be a serious omission.

A generation ago, Louis Finkelstein, a leader of Conservative Judaism, gave another interpretation of Jewish religious services. It was closer in both terminology and spirit to the language of the social sciences. He saw Judaism as "a symbolic system, expressing basic ideas, primarily in the form of commanded behavior . . . which must be acted out as in a pageant, not articulated as verbal assertions" (in Siegel 1977, 202). He associated this with the belief "that existence, as a whole, has a theme and is essentially a symbol" (1977, 206). So, there is *one* theme symbolized by both nature and Torah, or shared by both human process and divine ones (1977, 207).

Finkelstein understood that the symbolic expression of basic truths about the moral and spiritual realms "is necessarily as relative to the life of the community as any other means of communicating ideas" (Siegel 1977, 210). He was reserved about formulating basic truths. But he observed that the Pharisaic schools of Hillel and Shammai, though opposed regarding human worth, shared a "common approach to life as a pageant, in which the basic theme of existence . . . had to be enacted" (1977, 212-13). They shared one purpose, "the raising of the standards of human conduct, in which the glory of God becomes most clearly manifest on earth" (1977, 211). Life, conceived as having meaning and purpose, "could become a liturgical drama . . . conveying ideas and thus serving a purpose beyond itself" (1977, 212-13). But the leading schools in the rabbinic movement remained divided as to human worth. The school of Hillel, based in a lay, urban, democratic environment, was anthropocentric; it stressed the likeness of the immortal human spirit to God. The school of Shammai, deriving from a priestly, rural, aristocratic and provincial culture, was theocentric; it stressed the human capacity for temporal service to God, to be holy in service rather than in a spiritual nature similar to God's. Finkelstein was concerned about the lack of clear purpose that has resulted from the continuing difference between the schools.

The rabbi at the synagogue being studied presents congregants with a focus: the moral challenge to live a better life. The Sabbath service is a central ritual in such a life, expressing much of Judaism's meaning and historical vision, involving people and orienting them toward a better, more Jewish life. The service is a model for this life.

Congregants seem to appreciate much that services offer. One elderly man viewed the congregation as a place where "I know everyone, or everyone knows me." Another remarked that this was home for him. Much of what we have seen suggests a shift in emphasis and meaning from traditional religious significance toward more human, social and cultural significance. Most of the comments that I heard expressed a response to social or cultural aspects of the service—honours to congregants, initiation ceremonies, musical performances and stimulating or provocative rabbinic talks.

However fundamental the spiritual and specifically religious aspects might be for understanding the behaviour of congregants, these aspects are expressed far less than the social and cultural ones—even by the most religious. This fact might reflect current avoidance of *talk* about religious topics (considered personal and sensitive, important yet uncertain) more than a decline in religious belief. It might reflect the fact that religious phenomena, such as services, have always been multifaceted (comprising social and moral, aesthetic and intellectual aspects); casual comments can be expected to focus on relatively uncontroversial aspects. Finally, it might reflect changing ways of understanding religiosity—being more oriented toward meaningful identification, association and involvement with a developing religious culture but less oriented toward obedience to centuries-old and authoritative interpretations of divine requirements.

It is not only congregants who represent a movement away from traditional religious emphases. Even the leaders who wrote *Emet ve'emuna* represent an increasing orientation toward spiritual meaning beyond the terms of traditional religious belief and obligation. In this sense, the spiritual orientations expressed by religious leaders and the cultural or ethnic orientations emphasized by lay people are complementary developments. They share an orientation beyond the perceived limitations of traditional religion.

A religious dimension clearly remains and is important. Congregants identify themselves as Jews not only in an ethnic sense but also in a religious sense. They attend religious services at a Conservative synagogue considered traditional.

The service under discussion embodies traditional forms of religious practice that are modified in ways that express contemporary interests and preferences. The spiritual orientation represented by *Emet ve'emuna* preserves an essentially religious dimension in its discussion of prayer. This religious dimension involves personal and communal orientation toward God; structure and order in the prayers established by tradition; and *kavana*, the living and intending quality of prayers enhanced by modern creativity. This does not reduce the significance of prayers and services to spiritual meaning alone.

In attempting to characterize the Conservative service, with some guidance from religious and sociological interpretations, we repeatedly encounter the problem of how to balance pairs of contrasting phenomena (ones that can be juxtaposed and coordinated but do not yield to a single, coherent form of integration). Conservatism has historically characterized itself as a synthesis of the best in both Judaism and modernity. But as *Emet ve'emuna* confirms, the synthesis is not reduced to a single orientation. Alternative orientations are respected and balanced.

The balance between tradition and modernity is paralleled in a whole series of balances, which are open to varying formulations.

1. Established forms of observance are promoted within the synagogue; new forms of observance are promoted both within the synagogue (including attendance itself) and beyond.

2. Traditionalism indistinguishable from an Orthodox congregation (save for mixed seating) is common at early stages of the service; innovation is common at later stages.

3. Choosing a seat near the centre of liturgical drama allows people to be active participants; choosing a seat elsewhere (and the presence of a choir) allows them to be passive observers.

4. The service itself preserves traditional religious formulations; the rabbi's comments and sermons add moral, humanistic and personalistic interpretations—including those that depart from tradition.
5. Hebrew is used in almost every prayer; the vernacular is used for every other purpose.
6. Those who determine the nature of ritual at the synagogue maintain respect for rabbinic authority (that is, expertise); their committee is run, in effect, as a participatory democracy.
7. As ecclesiastical corporation, the congregation is formally established under provincial law and governed by its own by-laws in conjunction with the principles of Conservative Judaism; as a group of Jews, the congregation convenes more or less spontaneously for services and other communal or cultural events.
8. The service is distinctively Jewish, indeed highly traditional for a Conservative synagogue; it is also modified in various ways to be appealing, or at least tolerable, to a modern, largely secularized and well-educated community.
9. The synagogue is a house of worship; it is also a community centre.

The list could go on. Clearly, this community has a complex character, which is appropriate for people who identify themselves simultaneously with Judaism and the wider culture. The synagogue provides a liturgy that accommodates a wide range of orientations toward the performance of, and participation in, the liturgy.

## Conclusions

The morning service develops from a traditional form (mainly in the early morning prayers) to a more contemporary form (focused upon dramatic and engaging events such as the bar mitzvah, *haftara*, rabbi's talk and musical performances by cantor and choir).

The development of the service parallels the development of the congregation from a small core group to a far larger group composed of regular congregants, occasional congregants and guests. And it reflects the historical development of a more modern service, moving toward the mainstream of the Conservative movement though still traditionalist in comparison with most.

The main clues to what is interesting, engaging and meaningful in the service are (aside from personal comments) patterns of attendance, receptive attention and active participation by congregants. These patterns vary among congregants in ways that allow various classifications. I have classified in terms of the core group, regular congregants, occasional ones and guests.

The service develops to engage the attention, interest and involvement of larger numbers of modern Jews, attracted by friendly social contact, by bar mitzvahs and bat mitzvahs (social-transitional-initiating events), honours bestowed on members, musical performances by the cantor and choir, and the challenging and evocative talks of the rabbi, which express a whole cluster of closely related identifications, associations and values.

A decline in attention to the Torah reading, taken together with the avoidance of traditional authoritarian formulas in the rabbi's talks, indicate a decline in the traditional sense of belief and in the traditional attitude toward the authority of rabbinic traditions in people's personal lives. Yet the rabbi preserves a certain authority when it comes to the requirements and possibilities of Conservative Judaism; the religion committee, composed of congregants, respects this much. Thus, established Conservatism provides a kind of constitutional framework within which the congregation acts, more or less according to principles of participatory democracy. In this and several other aspects, Conservatism combines features common in modern secular and humanistic cultures with features distinctive to the Jewish religion and culture, a balance that preserves both particularistic and universalistic identifications. The rabbi's talk either reinforces attitudes and values common to the various socio-cultural formations represented in the congregation or it challenges them from a standpoint of moral and humanistic values that belong to a quest not only for a better life but for a more Jewish life.

Although traditional religiosity has declined with respect to both belief and practice, religious identification remains important to Conservative Jews. So does the maintenance of a religious institution that preserves traditional practices. But the meaning of these practices is less traditional. It is oriented instead toward meaningful identification, association, and involvement with a spiritual, moral and religious culture that preserves a traditional core but does not impose it.

**Note**

1   The formulation of a positive historical approach to Jewish religion is attributable to Zacharias Frankel, though his intent is a matter of divergent interpretations. See especially Ginzberg (1977, 1-10).

# PART 3

## Between Congregation and Family

# 10

# Contemporary Bar Mitzvah Rituals in Modern Orthodoxy

## SIMCHA FISHBANE

### Problematic

This paper sets forth a social anthropological analysis of the bar mitzvah[1] ritual as celebrated in a modern Orthodox synagogue situated in a suburb of a major Canadian city. Mary Douglas, in her discussion of death rituals, speaks of society's ruthlessness in its exploitation of the bereaved for group purposes (1979, 32). Without applying her harsh terminology, this same understanding of the social functions of ritual is applicable to the overall social order. In the Durkheimian tradition, social scientists have developed the hypothesis that ritual behaviour reflects the *Zeitgeist* of society. Douglas develops this theory further: "The analysis of ritual symbolism cannot begin until we recognize ritual as an attempt to create and maintain a particular culture, a particular set of assumptions by which experience is controlled" (1966, 128).

Most studies that apply these theories of rituals and collective needs have dealt with data from primitive societies. A review of the scholarly literature reveals that few attempts have been made to test the theory by applying it to established contemporary religions in general and Judaism specifically.[2]

The rite of bar mitzvah provides an example of change in contemporary Judaic ritual as well as a representation of the collective need. Not only does this ritual reflect the basic socio-religious "world" constructed by rabbinic Judaism, it also offers evidence of a ritual process developed in a North American context. My hypothesis is that the bar mitzvah ritual has come to serve the collective needs of the Jewish macro-social structure (as will be explained below). In addition, it contributes to the strengthening of the inner boundaries of the Jewish social order. Furthermore, the ritual fulfills the collective expression and needs of the micro-corporative synagogue's social and religious organization.

### Methodological perspective

The data for this study were gathered during a two-year period of participant observation. In addition to attending the daily morning and evening prayer services, I was involved in educational and social activities, including six bar mitzvah parties. Furthermore, 25 synagogue families and all the professional staff were interviewed. As I am an observant Jew, I was accepted by the synagogue members as an insider. This facilitated the task of gathering data. In addition, my status allowed me access to the group, its trust and its permission to conduct my research. There are scholars who argue that this method of gathering data is not objective. Nevertheless, I accept Samuel Heilman's approach to participant observation: ". . . as an insider I could supply, both through introspection and a sense of the relevant questions to ask, information about dimensions of inner life not readily available to pure researchers" (1976, xi).

I have divided this paper into three topics: a brief discussion of the bar mitzvah ritual in rabbinic literature and history; a discussion of the ritual in contemporary North American Jewish society and an analysis of the ritual.

In order to obtain a systematic ethnographic report of the bar mitzvah ritual, I will apply Arnold van Gennep's typology of the rites of passage. Van Gennep studied the order and content of the life-cycle rituals in primitive societies, and characterized these periods in the individual's life as rites of passage (1960). He indicated that to pass from one phase to another, the individual must fulfill certain conditions usually enveloped in ceremonial acts or rituals. "For every one of these events," he observed, "there are ceremonies whose essential purpose is to enable the individual to pass from one defined position to another which is equally well defined" (1960, 3). When crossing the order of each stage, the person is "unifying himself with a new world" (1960, 20). Van Gennep then sub-divided each life-cycle period, or rite of passage, into three phases; the separation from previous status, or pre-liminal phase; a transitional, or liminal, stage; and the reincorporation into the new, or post-liminal, stage. A phase might not be developed to the same extent in each specific set of society's ceremonies. This tripartite-structure theory bears direct relevance upon social change and the social consciousness of the society studied.

Van Gennep's concept of liminality has had significant influence upon studies of symbolism. Scholars such as Victor Turner (1964) and Mary Douglas (1966) have developed this theory in their own directions. For the purpose of this paper, I will focus on Douglas' analysis of the liminal phase (1966, 37). This phase, while being divorced from the previous stage and incorporated into the next, retains elements of both.[3]

Consider the following analogy. During the month of January, someone travels by train from New York to Montreal. He boards the train wearing his heavy winter coat unbuttoned and conversing freely in English. Crossing the border, with the weather becoming colder, he begins to button his coat. French is used more freely than before. During the entire trip, he retains elements of New York's weather and culture while incorporating "French Canada," but he is not in Montreal until he has stepped off the train. The anomalous stage is this train ride, which is not part of the past and is not yet incorporated into the future; it possesses elements of both periods.

## Bar mitzvah in classical rabbinic Judaism

The contemporary bar mitzvah ceremony is a phenomenon uniquely developed by North American Jewry. Consistent with most contemporary

Jewish religious rituals, it has been modified and developed from eighteenth- and nineteenth-century rabbinic Judaism, with its roots in Talmudic through mediaeval rabbinic law and custom.[4]

Although contemporary Judaism celebrates the bar mitzvah ritual on the thirteenth birthday of the male youth, the age of initiation into rabbinic adulthood was not formalized until later times. Early rabbinic literature attributed this initiation period to physiological puberty: the presence of two pubic hairs (Babylonian Talmud, Niddah 46a). According to the version of Elijah of Vilna, the Babylonian Talmud makes reference to this rite of passage during the period of the second Temple; "There was a beautiful custom in Jerusalem . . . that with a thirteen-year-old boy, his father would bring him in front of each elder to be blessed, strengthened, and to pray that he might be privileged to study Torah and perform good deeds" (Sofrim 18:5).

The boy's new status entailed obligations pertaining to vows (Babylonian Talmud on Nedarim 5:5) and required fasting on Yom Kippur (Babylonian Talmud, Yoma 82a). The only reference in early rabbinic documents to an initiation age with respect to rabbinic obligations is found in Mishnah Avot 5:21: "at thirteen for the *mitsvot*" (commandments).

As rabbinic Jewry evolved, the need for "social puberty" developed. Physical puberty signs were not palpable and could not be employed for the social need. Society required a uniform measure to signify this passage in the life cycle. In thirteenth-century France, Rabbi Tam alludes to 13 as the age of initiation *(Tosafot* Babylonian Talmud, Niddah 49a). In the fourteenth century, the age 13 ("social puberty") became accepted as the recognized time for initiation into Jewish adulthood (Abrahams 1969, 32). In sixteenth-century Italy, moreover, Rabbi Moses Isserles wrote explicitly of 13 as the age of bar mitzvah (*Orah Hayim* 55, 5) in his gloss to Rabbi Karo's *Shulhan Aruk*.

Bar mitzvah rituals developed according to the idiosyncrasies of diverse Jewish societies. These rituals, discussed in rabbinic literature, can be identified as:

1. Wearing phylacteries[5] for the first time (*Magen Avraham*, a commentary on the *Shulhan Aruk* from seventeenth-century Poland; *Orah Hayim* 37, 7);

2. Being "called up" to the Torah on Sabbath or during the week (*Levush*, a code of Jewish law from sixteenth-century eastern Europe; *Orah Hayim* 136);

3. Reciting the *maftir* (additional Torah portion) and any additional Torah sections (*Tzitz Eliezer*, responsa from twentieth-century Israel, vol. 7, sec. 1);

4. The father's public declaration that he is liberated from punishable halakic responsibilities for his son (Rabbi Isserles; *Orah Hayim* 225, 2);

5. A festive meal (*Magen Avraham*; *Orah Hayim* 225, 4);

6. Presents given to the boy (*Mishnah Brurah*, a commentary on the *Shulhan Aruk* from nineteenth-century Poland; *Orah Hayim* 306, 33);

7. Presentation of a rabbinic discourse (*Kaf Hahayim* 225, 11, a commentary on *Shulhan Aruk* from twentieth-century Israel); and

8. Printed invitations to the bar mitzvah reception (*Ketav Sofer*, responsa from nineteenth-century eastern Europe; *Even Ha'ezer* 22).[6]

Before twentieth-century Judaism, the major ritual related to this rite of passage seems to have been the first wearing of *tfilin* (small boxes strapped to the arm and head, each of which contains biblical inscriptions on parchment; called "phylacteries" in English).

Mark Zborowski and Elizabeth Herzog provide a partial report of the ritual in the *shtetl* (village inhabited partly or mainly by Jews) of Eastern Europe: " . . . Father and son go quietly to the synagogue and the boy, with no fanfare, puts on the phylacteries for his prayers, as he has learned to do during the preceding weeks of training. Elaborate gifts and parties are associated with less 'religious' observance. The social part of the truly Orthodox bar mitzvah is a simple reception, a *kidush* in the synagogue and at home, with brandy and cakes for all. The high point is the declamation of the speech during this celebration, with parents beaming, friends admiring while everyone prepares to discuss later the merits of the 'little piece of Torah' to which the boy treats them" (1952, 351).

Contemporary North American Jews continue to practise their own model of the rabbinic rituals. The structure and performance of the bar mitzvah rites can be identified as belonging to their North American Jewish milieu.

Before analyzing the bar mitzvah ritual, however, a brief discussion of the "stage" and "actors" is required.

## The setting

The synagogue under study, which I will refer to as M. Z., is a modern Orthodox synagogue located in a suburb of a major Canadian city. The demographic data published by the city's Jewish community services indicate that approximately 2,000 Jewish families reside in this suburb. The economic status of the community can be identified as middle and upper-middle class. This social stratum belongs to the managerial and entrepreneurial sector of society. The modal age of adults identified with the synagogue is between 30-45. A family with two or three children of elementary-school age is the norm.

There are 800 families registered as paid members of the M. Z. synagogue. Another synagogue in the community is affiliated with the Reform movement and claims a membership of 70 families. To acquire and maintain membership in M. Z., a family must pay an annual membership fee of $500. Single applicants have reduced rates. Membership means paying less for the educational, social and religious functions of the synagogue. For example, members pay substantially lower tuition fees when they enrol children in the Hebrew day-school that is affiliated with the synagogue. Furthermore, only a member is permitted to celebrate a son's bar mitzvah in M. Z. This privilege includes the rabbi's religious instruction and guidance on matters pertaining to the ceremony, the renting of a hall and any additional organizational services related to the social functions held in the synagogue.

M. Z. is identified with modern Orthodoxy's "left wing," which attempts to "bend" *halaka* to its maximum while retaining specific rituals such as the bar mitzvah. An example of compromise can be recognized in the fact that the halakic requirement for the height of the barrier that divides the sexes in the sanctuary, a barrier that might be said to define an Orthodox synagogue, is the halakic minimum. The liberalism is related to the fact that, of the 800 dues-paying families in the synagogue, no more than a dozen identify themselves as halakically observant (that is, Orthodox) Jews.

The synagogue is organized and functions as a corporate structure with an elected executive body headed by a president. It is dependent upon its members for financial support. In addition to dues, revenue is obtained through fund-raising functions, contributions and payment for services provided to its members, the bar mitzvah celebration among them.

M. Z.'s staff is hired by the executive body. This staff includes the rabbi, cantor, executive director, youth director and a party co-ordinator who also officiates as the *kashrut* supervisor. Functionally, the rabbi is the ultimate power in decision making. He is directly involved in all religious, educational, social, administrative and personnel decisions. His salary, the highest of the professional staff, is representative of his status. One of his functions is to assign an instructor to the bar mitzvah candidate, someone who will teach him his role in the bar mitzvah liturgy. The cantor and party co-ordinator, in addition to their titled roles, serve as instructors. The executive director is concerned with the technical and physical set-up in the synagogue. These functions include the technical arrangements for the bar mitzvah ceremony and party.

The synagogue architecture is symbolic of its members and their social allegiance. It is a modern structure studded with traditional Jewish symbols, pictures and artifacts. In addition to the sanctuary, chapel, reception hall and kitchen, its buildings encompass offices, two schools, meeting rooms and a store that sells Jewish artifacts. A brief description of the sanctuary is necessary to understand properly the symbolic representation of the bar mitzvah ritual.

The ark, containing the Torah scrolls, is situated against the eastern wall. On the northern side of the ark are positioned six "thronelike" seats. The rabbi sits closest to the ark, adjacent to the president, two sextons, and the cantor. The ark and the "thrones" are located on the *bima*, a platform. On the *bima* rests a *shulhan* (table) where the Torah scrolls are read and where the prayer reader stands. Two benches are located behind the *shulhan* at the edge of the *bima* farthest from the ark. This design is standard in Orthodox synagogues. M. Z., in adherence to rabbinic law, requires men and women to sit separately. The men's and women's areas are divided by a three-foot barrier termed a *mehitsa*. The men's section, positioned between two sections for women, is divided into three subsections. The middle subsection, directly facing the ark, is designated for the bar mitzvah family and guests. Female celebrants and guests sit in a raised section north of the *bima*, behind the northern subsection for men. Men and women use the same entrance to the sanctuary. The women, to reach their seats, must pass through the back rows of the men's area. This description of the sanctuary sets the stage for the bar mitzvah ritual.

## The bar mitzvah ritual

### The separation phase

The bar mitzvah candidate at M. Z. begins his preparations approximately one half year prior to the celebration of the ritual. The commencement of this preliminary period and the extent of the boy's future participation in the liturgy are ultimately determined by the rabbi. The nature of the boy's involvement is dependent upon his Hebrew academic background as well as musical talents. A prerequisite for the boy to be accepted as a bar mitzvah candidate is a minimum of four years of Jewish education.

The bar mitzvah family can choose a Saturday morning or afternoon ceremony. The afternoon liturgy, being less demanding, will attract the "weaker student." The morning service requires the boy to recite at least the *maftir* and *haftara*. The afternoon service demands, at most, the reading of a few Torah verses. In addition, the Saturday morning liturgy offers the boy a broad selection of additional choices. He might choose to lead the *shaharit* (morning) service, the *musaf* (additional) service, or the conclusion of the Saturday morning liturgy. Furthermore, he can elect to read any or all of the eight Torah selections. At the afternoon service, additional options include leading the succinct *minha* (afternoon service), the brief *ma'ariv* (evening service) and/or reciting the *havdala* (a service that concludes the Sabbath). The more numerous the portions he performs of the morning liturgy, the higher is the boy's social status. Qualified candidates are encouraged to execute the maximum.

As indicated above, the rabbi assigns an instructor to the boy. At first, the candidate meets with his mentor one evening a week. As the bar mitzvah date approaches, the classes might be held more frequently, contingent upon the boy's needs. All bar mitzvah lessons are taught in the synagogue. In addition to the sections he has chosen to perform, the boy is taught the blessings and how to don *tfilin*, the blessings for the "call up" to the Torah and the prayers when the Torah is removed from the ark. The rehearsals for the performance and the aspects that require Jewish knowledge are studied with the rabbi. The candidate's father periodically attends the lesson to view the boy's progress. Maternal participation in these preparations is virtually non-existent.

At M. Z., the "call up" ritual is celebrated during the week of the boy's thirteenth birthday (which might occur a number of weeks prior to the actual bar mitzvah ceremony). For the first time, on a Monday or Thursday morning, he dons the *tfilin* and is "called up" to read the Torah. It is customary for both parents to attend the ceremony. Prior to bar mitzvah age, rabbinic law does not firmly restrict the boy from sitting with the mother. Now, the mother sits behind the *mehitsa*, separated from her son. The symbolic weight of this act will be discussed later.

At the completion of the morning liturgy, the rabbi announces the boy's "call up" and impending bar mitzvah, thus proclaiming the first stage of the rite of passage, the separation phase. The congregation is then invited for refreshments provided by the bar mitzvah family. The family's preference governs the type of refreshments offered. It ranges from a seated and catered affair to cookies and a bottle of liquor. The former style also includes invited guests who might participate in the service. I cannot correlate the pattern of the "call up" ceremony with other variables related to the bar mitzvah. This conclusion of the "call up" ceremony to the Torah symbolically represents the boy's separation from his childhood and his entrance into a new phase.

*The transitory or anomalous phase*

Throughout the interval from the "call up" to the bar mitzvah ceremony, the boy continues to don the *tfilin* during the weekday morning services, although the rabbinic obligation begins only after his incorporation into Jewish adulthood. In addition, M. Z. requires the candidate and his father to attend Friday night and Sabbath morning services before the actual bar mitzvah date, under the pretension that they will become better acquainted with the liturgy. This participation ideally results in a clearer understanding of the liturgy and a superior performance. Attendance at four such services is customary. During these services, the boy is not "called up" to the Torah or awarded any other "adult" honours, although these were already rendered at the "call up" ceremony.

Bar mitzvah classes are intensified during the anomalous stage. The boy and his instructor can convene for up to three lessons weekly. At this time, rehearsals with the rabbi commence in the sanctuary. The parents attend only the final practices. During the rehearsals, the boy practises the following rites: transference of the Torah from the ark with the appropriate prayers, the Torah parade around the sanctuary, the reading of the Torah from the scrolls and the appropriate Torah blessings. At the time of the parents' involvement, the "staging" for the rabbi's blessing is rehearsed.

With the exception of the above-mentioned preparations during the anomalous period, there are no modifications in the social, religious and educational functions and obligations of the bar mitzvah candidate. He is treated by both parents and community as he was prior to the separation phase. The expected changes are to transpire subsequent to the incorporation phase.

*The incorporation phase*

For the purpose of this exercise, I will focus upon the Sabbath morning ritual, since dissimilarities from the afternoon service are minimal. Instances of relevant discrepancies will be identified.

The Saturday service commences at 9:00. The bar mitzvah family arrives beforehand to greet invited guests and confirm final technical arrangements. Male guests are offered *kipot* (skull-caps) embossed with the bar mitzvah boy's name and wool *talitot* (prayer-shawls) provided by the synagogue. The bar mitzvah boy wears his own *talit*, purchased especially for this ritual.[7] Female guests are offered the standard synagogue lace head covering.

The celebrating family dresses formally for the ritual. The men often wear tuxedos. This attire contrasts with the less formal dress code of the weekly participants. Sabbath morning guests adopt the less formal dress code. Afternoon bar mitzvah guests, however, might dress formally.[8] Male members of the family are seated in the first row of the bar mitzvah section. The mother and other female members of the family are guided to the centre of the front row of the women's area. Male ushers greet all the guests at the sanctuary door and direct them to their respective seating areas.

Contingent upon whether the boy has chosen to lead the morning service, he, his family and guests might or might not be involved in the execution of this liturgy. In any event, the bar mitzvah boy's role begins at the Torah-transferring ceremony. The rabbi, cantor, president, two sextons, four guests and the boy himself take their places on the *bima* facing the ark. The four guests are awarded the honour of opening the ark and presenting the Torah scroll to the bar mitzvah boy, who leads this section of the liturgy. Following his recital of the cantorial prayers, the boy, holding a scroll, leads a procession of the actors present on the stage through the aisles of the men's section of the sanctuary. This parade permits the congregation, including the women around the periphery, to kiss the Torah scrolls.

The procession concludes at the *bima*, where the Torah scroll is placed on the table and opened in preparation for its reading. Dependent on whether the bar mitzvah boy reads from the Torah portion immediately, he either returns to his seat or remains standing on the *bima* in order to proceed. In the majority of cases, the boy's Torah-reading role begins when his father is called to the Torah. The son's ritual participation in the father's honour is publicly emphasized and acknowledged by the rabbi.

At the final reading, the cantor (who has been chanting instead of the sexton) summons the bar mitzvah boy to the Torah. The boy recites the blessings and reads the *maftir*. Upon the completion of this portion and the second Torah blessing, the father formally declares from the *bima* his liberation from punishable halakic responsibilities for the actions of his son. The formula cited is "Thank (God) I am exempted from this one's punishment." This proclamation formally acknowledges the "separation" from childhood and incorporation into Jewish adulthood.

Prior to the reading of the *haftara*, the bar mitzvah boy faces the congregation and reads a short introduction and explanation of this appended reading. The short speech, prepared together with the rabbi, might be considered a replacement for the traditional "piece of Torah" presented by the bar mitzvah boy. The *haftara* is then chanted. At the conclusion, the boy returns to his seat. From his egress from the *bima* until he arrives at his seat, he is greeted by the congregants with cries of "*mazel tov*" (congratulations). At this point, one ought to note the symbolic significance of the bar mitzvah and the entire Torah ritual. This Torah ritual has a special meaning for the celebrants as well as for the social consciousness. The purpose of the ritual is conveyed in the symbolic representation of the exit and entrance rites of the ceremony. The boy turns his back on his previous status when he ascends the *bima* and faces the open ark with its majestic Torah scrolls revealed. He is symbolically entering the portal of his new role. The Torah, considered the basis of rabbinic law, is indicative of his new status as a Jewish adult, someone who is obliged to adhere to its laws. During the procession through the men's section of the sanctuary, the bar mitzvah boy displays the Torah scroll as he continues along this symbolic passageway. There is no retreat; he has symbolically closed the door. Throughout the entire ceremony, the Torah continues to be indicative of the new role and remains contiguous to the bar mitzvah boy. Subsequent to his egress from the *bima* and the Torah scroll, he is acknowledged and welcomed into his new role with the greeting of "*mazel tov*." The bar mitzvah boy has symbolically left the passageway and entered the Jewish adult social arena.

The service continues with the *musaf* liturgy. It commences with the return of the Torah to the ark but is interrupted for the rabbi's weekly sermon. The closing portion of the sermon is concerned with the bar mitzvah family and the boy. The rabbi acknowledges, when appropriate, the family's affiliation and participation in Jewish social, educational and communal affairs. Furthermore, the bar mitzvah boy's Jewish educational background and the extent of his role in the liturgy is formally recognized. The greater the participation and performance, the longer and more elaborate are the praises. These acknowledgements and praises are repeated by the president during his announcements at the conclusion of the services.

The rabbi then invites a "past" bar mitzvah boy to present the celebrant with the synagogue's gift: a prayer-book. The synagogue's bar mitzvah certificate is awarded by the rabbi. If the boy attends a Hebrew day-school, a second school certificate is presented. A third certificate, related to the State of Israel, might also be offered, depending upon the parents' wishes. All three certificates are presented by the rabbi after the prayer-book award.

The *musaf* prayers are concluded with the bar mitzvah boy chanting the final section, once again standing before the open ark. The congregation is then invited to participate in a *kidush* sponsored by the boy's family. The guests are invited for cocktails and a reception in the synagogue's hall. Prior to the departure of the participants from the sanctuary, but after the conclusion of the services, the rabbi invites the bar mitzvah boy and his immediate family to stand in a predesignated area of the men's section for the family benediction. This rite and its content are not found in rabbinic Judaism; it was initiated by M. Z.'s rabbi to compensate for the women's lack of participation in the bar mitzvah ritual.

The reception, or festive meal, does not explicitly subsume or continue the bar mitzvah rites. It cannot be identified as different from other festive meals. The rabbi introduces general religious rituals: blessings over the bread and wine, grace after meals. No desecration of the Sabbath is permitted. At a Sunday night reception, similar religious rituals are innovated but other elements—such as a band, photographers, and candle-lighting ceremonies—are incorporated. But the meal, as a total entity in itself, is relevant to the social consciousness, a subject to be explored further.

### Discussion and analysis

This discussion continues in keeping with the theoretical perspectives presented in the "problematic" of this study. The major focus is the application of the social anthropological theory of social collectivity to the modern North American bar mitzvah ritual as practised in M. Z.[9]

First, the bar mitzvah ritual must be viewed as a total, structured complex composed of individual rites. Each rite comes to serve society's collective needs. Although the bar mitzvah ceremony as a total complex serves this social function, it is also only one segment of the aggregate ritual model that composes the Jewish social structure. Whether it be the basic patterns of the segments of the individual ritual, the whole ritual or the total complex of rituals, all implicitly convey the same meaning.

The bar mitzvah ritual, as described above, mirrors the rites initiated by rabbinic Judaism. Modern-day society is not cut off from its religious culture, as religion is not cut off from modern-day society. I accept Douglas' definition that "anthropologists treat culture as autonomous when autonomy means more than independence, when it means initiative to move society" (1982b, 12). This influence is reflected and dramatized in the rituals practised by North American Jews. Rabbinic Judaism, the "life of Torah," has been abandoned by most contemporary Jewry. Instead, they have generated their own autonomous religious, Jewish social structure. Modern

Jews have rejected the "macro" rabbinic social religious system initiated in the second century. The religious rituals themselves were innovated to ensure the symbolic boundaries erected between themselves and the outside world. Social forces, not ideology, became the underlying current in the transformation of these beliefs and rituals.[10] Douglas' classification system of "high-group," "high-grid" society characterizes rabbinic society, while her "high-group," "low-grid" characterizes the North American Jewish milieu (1978).[11]

Rather than abandon all rituals, this Jewry has chosen, or been encouraged, to develop specific rites. Jack Lightstone argues that "contemporary Jewry has remained committed to maintaining in some significant sense this Jewish identity; on the other hand, they are equally intent upon participating fully in the larger Canadian milieu" (1987, 1). He continues with the emphasis on the social psychological influence in retaining expressed practices and therefore Jewish identity, "by telling themselves and one another stories of what it means to belong to the group and by encouraging the ritual behavior geared to the same end" (1988, 3).

I suggest that this concept can be carried further.[12] An additional variable in ritual purpose within the collective consciousness is the synagogue— the "micro" society of rabbinic Judaism. This collective structure, although greatly altered in its socio-religious form, has remained intact. The "synagogue," cognizant of the ethnic-national identity of the North American Jews as well as the rituals that they have selected to preserve, has incorporated these elements, emphasizing this identity into its collective structure and purpose.

Functioning as a corporate social structure, the synagogue sponsors social, political and educational activities that do not explicitly threaten the individuals' beliefs but, rather, allow each member to choose his or her "religious expression." Alternatively, the collective need is encouraged, developed and rendered through all the activities and rituals, whether "sacred" or "secular." This social organization has generated new rituals. These activities mould the patterns and forms manifested through the rituals, which are largely identified as uniquely North American. Thus the member achieves his religious fulfillment while the synagogue assumes the role, for the majority of North American Jews, as defender and preserver of rabbinic Judaism. The bar mitzvah is one ritual that illustrates this role.

A larger, more functional, synagogue means a greater opportunity to supply the services needed to perform the role of defender and preserver of the borders of rabbinic Judaism. As Emile Durkheim notes in his *Elementary Forms*, a stronger corporate order goes with a sense of power. The bar mitzvah ritual at M. Z., as part of a puzzle joining neatly together to form the total picture, serves these communal needs. The bar mitzvah requires four years of Jewish education. It is considered to be basic in invoking greater commitment to Jewish identity and its perceived effects. This commitment is further strengthened during the period of bar mitzvah preparations, especially the studies with the rabbi. The requirement to participate in services, the "call up" ceremony and the training occurring on the synagogue premises, all are additional factors leading to this goal. These actions produce social control over the individuals and thus, presumably, increase their Jewish commitment.

In addition to its symbolic representation, furthermore, the "call up" service requires the family to attend and participate in a weekday prayer service. This helps guarantee to the synagogue its ability to function religiously on a daily basis and, in turn, enhances its status. In addition, the boy becomes familiar with the weekday services. Familiarity reduces the threat of the unknown and induces further participation, even if only for specific future occasions such as reciting the *kadish* (doxology associated with mourning).

The ritual costumes (*kipa, talit* and *tfilin*) worn during the performance of the various prayer services represent the change of social status for the boy. To the father and other male participants, they evoke generic identity and sentiments that result in the reaffirmation of their collective identity. They might associate these costumes with earlier emotional Jewish experiences—their own bar mitzvahs, for example, or the deaths of their parents. Furthermore, the bar mitzvah boy now joins this social solidarity. His ritual clothes become for him a future code of social communication.[13]

The family and guests coming together at the bar mitzvah service are further reaffirming their collective identity. This ritual practice serves to reinforce the feeling of group boundary and to encourage, strengthen and foster attachments to the Jewish collectivity. The structured symbols—ritual language, music and motions of the liturgy—all contribute to communication and social solidarity.

On the practical level, the boy's familiarity with the prayer service means that he now becomes an added member of the potential pool of prospective liturgical leaders. This is significant in that it once again strengthens the functional ability of the synagogue while guaranteeing its future.

Festive meals are found to be part of the scenario of most rites of passage, and their nuances have been explored in detail by social scientists. The participants who attend the service and are invited to the reception are given an opportunity to strengthen their Jewish friendship bonds and therefore the "group." Although the service requires a minimal degree of Jewish learning, the festive meal does not. The guests do not, on the whole, frequent the synagogue on a regular basis. But in this setting, the service and then the meal are a proclamation and strengthening of their Jewish identification. Furthermore, invitations are reciprocal, thereby allowing this meeting to repeat itself.

The economic aspect of the bar mitzvah is an essential factor in the "maintenance" of the synagogue. The necessary membership dues, the service charge for the hall, as well as other financial considerations that must be attended to, provide an income for the synagogue's corporate structure. This income not only contributes significantly to the maintenance of the synagogue but also allows for development and growth. This results in more opportunities to serve the collective need. Thus the collective need enhances, strengthens and lays the groundwork for the maintenance of Jewish identity in the future.

## Notes

1. This paper is not concerned with bat mitzvah ritual, a theme that requires separate attention. In addition, I remind the reader of the remarks of J. Lightstone at the outset of this volume (p. 4). He notes, "In the context of this volume, with its focus on public liturgical ritual in the synagogue, the public communal aspects of . . . family rituals [such as bar mitzvah] are privileged." See also Lightstone's note at that point (chap. 1, n.3).

2. Work conducted by social scientists on contemporary Judaism has dealt overwhelmingly with demographic data (see Cohen 1983).

3. Turner develops van Gennep's transitional phase, claiming that the individual acquires in this status a certain autonomy from the rest of the ritual.

4. Rabbinism is a form of Judaism based upon rabbinic law that was codified in the Middle Ages. Today it is identified with the Orthodox sector of Judaism.

5. Religious paraphernalia worn by an adult man, usually during the morning prayer services.

6. See also Tzokensiki 1980.

7. In M. Z., prior to this ceremony a boy does not wear this religious garment.

8. Attire for women, which is not always in accordance with the Orthodox standards, might require compromises on the part of the synagogue participants and leadership.

9. This theory can be explored in Durkheim (1961; 1964; see Douglas 1978).

10. See Lightstone (1987; 1990) for a detailed discussion of early rabbinic Judaism and its transformation in the twentieth century.

11. I am aware that some scholars criticize Douglas' classifications but believe that they are applicable to rabbinic and modern Jewish societies.

12. I do not disagree with Lightstone's argument or his other sociological theories that might be applied to contemporary Jewish religious rituals. Rather, I identify other possible meanings that can be conveyed through this behaviour.

13. The discussions of Douglas (1970) and Bird (1979) concerning character and meaning of ritual behaviour have contributed greatly to this analysis.

# 11

## Jewish Mourning Rites: A Process of Resocialization

## SIMCHA FISHBANE

### Introduction

Social scientists have argued that religious rituals reflect the *Zeitgeist* of society. Emile Durkheim (1961) and his heirs Robert Hertz (1960), Alfred Reginald Radcliffe-Brown (1952), Mary Douglas (1970; 1975; 1978), Victor Turner (1979), Peter Berger (1969) and Berger and Thomas Luckmann (1984) have especially developed this argument. The Durkheimians argue that the unity of a society is maintained by means of its collective representations, including rituals. Not only does ritual reflect society, but it is an important variable in the creation and perpetuation of the social system. Moreover, these ritual acts, which are valued intrinsically by their actors (Bird 1979), are fraught with not only explicit but also implicit meanings (Douglas 1975a; 1975b; 1975c). All these aspects and functions of ritual are enhanced by the dramatic character of ritual behaviour (Turner 1969; 1974). In a cultural setting, one group of rituals will illuminate a wide range of related configurations in the overall cultural structure. Such a set of rituals can be termed a "ritual complex." Indeed, it is often the case that a ritual complex acts as a symbolic representation of the social system as a whole.

This paper first analyzes the mourning rites[1] *as prescribed* by rabbinic Judaism.[2] It attempts to demonstrate how mourning rites, which communicate explicit and implicit meaning, are structured to serve the welfare of the social unit. This analysis further supports the theoretical models proffered by Douglas, Turner and Berger. Second, the study of the rites in question is conducted in connection with their *actual* performance by persons affiliated with a modern Orthodox synagogue situated in the suburbs of a major Canadian city.

The socio-economic profile of this synagogue community can be described as middle to upper-middle class. Most of its 800 member families belong to the managerial and entrepreneurial class. No more than 10 families of the non-clerical synagogue members identify themselves as halakically observant Jews (popularly referred to as Orthodox Jews).[3]

### Problematic: Methodological and theoretical perspectives

Hertz states: "death has a specific meaning for the social consciousness; it is the object of collective representation" (1960, 38). In their studies of mourning rituals, social psychologists, sociologists and anthropologists have discussed the welfare of individual survivors. Hertz summarizes this discussion: "For the collective consciousness death is in normal circumstances a temporary exclusion of the individual from human society.... In the final analysis, death as a social phenomenon consists in a dual and painful process of mental disintegration and synthesis. It is only when this process is completed that society, its peace recovered, can triumph over death" (1960, 86).

Hertz's basic hypothesis is that mourning rites are concerned with the resocialization (whether psychological, or sociological) of the individual survivor as well as the body and soul of the deceased. The rituals concerned with death have a latent function: the intense emotions of individuals are socialized; that which has the potential for social disruption is channelled in communally approved directions.

There is a complementary level of analysis that concerns neither the survivor nor the disposition of the deceased but the welfare of society. In her concise, insightful survey of the facts surrounding the complex of death rituals, Douglas writes that "rituals of warm support for the bereaved are consistent with their status being ruthlessly exploited for group purposes in funerary rhetoric. Everyone goes to funerals; they are judged as a major ceremonial form and how to lay on a good one is common knowledge. By contrast, without strong *group*, death having no social place as such is no subject to celebrate publicly" (Douglas 1978, 32).

Douglas has chosen to view the complex of death or mourning rites within our complementary level of analysis. Moreover, one may perceive the "group's" exploitation of rituals as a means of implicitly conveying to the member its message of communal authority, thus reinforcing the boundaries of society. Therefore, mourning rites, an example of a ritual process performed within a group structure, serve to strengthen the group norms.

An additional hypothesis that must be considered in our discussion of mourning rites is Arnold van Gennep's processual analysis (1960) as developed by Turner. Turner's analysis emphasizes (as did van Gennep's) society's needs as well as the individual's. Although the rituals concerned with these rites of passage are performed most frequently for the individual rather than for the collective, Turner asserts that their implicit function serves the group as a whole. They give expression to the group's definition of itself. Death and the complex of mourning rites, a time of crisis for the individual and society, is an example of a rite of passage. Turner speaks of the period of transition as a liminal stage. He defines liminality as being located "where time and place of withdrawal from normal modes of social action can be seen as potentially a period of scrutinization of the central values and axioms of the culture in which it occurs" (1977, 167).

During the week of sitting *shiva* (described in detail below) the surviving relatives are graphically placed in a liminal status. Whether gathered in the deceased person's home (as enjoined by traditional rabbinic practice) or in their own, they do not carry out their ordinary home-based roles. They withdraw from many standard adult responsibilities and activities, such as those associated with food, work, grooming and participating in communal functions (including communal prayer in the synagogue). They are fed by others. While in this liminal state, they are in a position to comfort one another, and to acknowledge their new identities as survivors, without having to be distracted by their ordinary, daily activities. After the *shiva*, during two subsequent periods covering the next three weeks and the subsequent 11 months, the male survivors are expected to assume new religious responsibilities as *kadish*-sayers and *minyan* makers (both, again, explained below). During these periods, as a result, mourners assume a more active and vital role in the synagogue community. They become more closely related to other men who are mourners. They become more publicly acknowledged during the synagogue services. They gain greater skill as ritual participants and, if their level of skill permits, as lay leaders of the daily liturgy. In the process, they become more intertwined with the life of the synagogue.

As stated above, this paper will explore the historical development of Jewish mourning rites in rabbinic law (*halaka*) as well as their performance in contemporary Judaic society. The mourning rituals as codified in the *halaka* continue to be practised by rabbinic, or observant, Jews. To analyze the change in the ritual process as practised by non-Orthodox Jews, therefore, it is imperative that we explore the ritual's history. In this paper, we assume the halakic laws of mourning to represent this history. Turner, who advocates the appropriation of history as a means to explain ritual, states in his discussion of the Franciscan Order: "In considering the early history of the Franciscan Order, it becomes clear that the social structure is intimately connected with history, because it is the way a group maintains its form over time. Structureless communitas can bind and bond people only momentarily" (Turner 1977, 153). Jack Lightstone, in his discussion of Douglas' "Cultural Bias," further develops this concept and writes: "Viewing variation in ritual patterns as movement along an historically given continuum seems particularly salient in the study of contemporary religions. In the modern period a community's ritual forms often arise in a context which stresses an historical consciousness and self-awareness of how one does things differently than another closely related community" (Lightstone 1988, 8).

Before proceeding, let me provide a brief account of how the ethnographic data were collected. This study of mourning rituals is part of a larger collaborative research project concerning the meaning and function of ritual for contemporary members of the synagogue. The author attended weekday and Sabbath services at the subject synagogue for approximately two years. Furthermore, he participated in 10 funerals and attendant rites at the mourners' homes. In addition to such participant observation, mourners and the rabbi of the synagogue were interviewed regarding the members' religious observance and beliefs. The occupational and social involvements of the subjects and their attitudes to the synagogue, to the Jewish community, and to its institutions, complemented the data on mourning rites.

## Mourning rites in Judaism

*Rabbinic Judaism*

For the purpose of this analysis, I will use Douglas' social structural typology (1970; 1979). Rabbinic Judaism can be equated with what she identifies as "strong-grid, strong-group," or otherwise terms "a bounded structure system" (1978, 20).[4] Rabbinism created tight group boundaries that constrained the exit of its members and the entrance of strangers. This tight social structure offers "a life support system" (1978) as well as direction for the behaviour of its members. But to retain this social structure, strict control of members is a necessity.

In a bounded structure system, stratification, leadership and sub-grouping must be developed. Clear definition of roles is demanded. At the same time, society's security necessitates involvement of the individual within the group. Significantly, observance of rabbinic law requires Jews to live in areas of dense Jewish population, thereby promoting intense social and religious interaction. In addition, this public social relationship places the member in open view of society, thus allowing the Jew's role to develop and be reinforced by social recognition. This role and status is also enhanced by means of the members' public proclamation through religious ritual. In the subject community, the members, although they are not Orthodox, have chosen to reside in close proximity to the synagogue and are thus subject to the above social pressure, support, reinforcement and involvement. Thus the implicit intent of the rabbinic law and ritual apply also to these non-Orthodox Jews who retain enough identification with rabbinic tradition to affiliate with an Orthodox synagogue.

This social map was developed in view of the rabbinic authorities' perception of the diaspora milieu and of Jewish needs therein. Rituals evolved as tools of rabbinic leadership, thus defining the articulated social structure. The religious rites then enabled the authorities to retain the "tight" social structure. Ritual symbols, accordingly, expressed and set a high value upon control. The purpose of these rituals or codes, taken for granted by adherents, was not expressed in explicit terms. The rites implicitly conveyed a message or substantiated a specific need. "It is a system of control," writes Douglas, "as well as a system of communication" (1973, 55).

*The family*

The rabbinic Jew's society is divided into compartments consisting of family units. These are the parts that constitute the whole, the building blocks of society. Family roles are clearly defined, with parents located at the apex of the hierarchy. In addition, this unit has its own set of rites and rituals, which differ from those of society as a whole. The family thus diverges in its social construction from the total social map. Halakic obligations for the observant Jew, in the family context, differ from his requirements in the larger social matrix. Rabbinic society, however, retained for itself the power to define, create and reinforce the roles and rites of the family. Exercising such social religious power was necessary for rabbinic Judaism to survive as a whole, for any threat to the compartment would thus be seen as a threat to society. A threat to the part is a threat to the whole. Social scientists studying contemporary North American Jews have also emphasized family solidarity as a factor serving to guarantee the traditional Jewish structure.[5]

One example is the death of a parent. This results in a leadership role being vacated. Society must identify new actors to fill the role of leadership in the family, thus securing its structure. Not to fill this role or to allow it to evolve its own hierarchy would leave Jewish society partly undefined and at risk.

## Funeral rites

The mourner commences observation of the Jewish mourning rites (in contrast to *onen* rituals) immediately following the interment ceremony at the cemetery. *Halaka* recognizes the identity of the survivor according to two distinct time periods. Prior to the burial (*ste'emat hagolel*), one is designated as an *onen* or as someone "in the period of *aninut*." The survivor is not yet classified as a mourner (*avel*). Only following the burial does one become a mourner, thus commencing the period of mourning (*avelut*). Although the focus of my study is the period of mourning, specific *onen* rituals prepare the survivor and society for a later identification of roles. Redefinition of the new role begins with the public proclamation of a new status. This declaration first entails rending of the survivor's outer garment (*kriya*) at the moment of awareness of the death. Halakah further requires that, if clothes are not torn at the moment the relative becomes aware of the death, the rite should be observed either immediately prior to the funeral service or before interment at the cemetery. The mourners of our subject synagogue perform this ritual at the funeral home immediately prior to the funeral service. A representative of the funeral home offers the women a black kerchief and the men a black tie which he directs them to tear. This behaviour, although it is not in accordance with the traditional custom (in which one tears one's own garment), still does not negate halakah. The Christian influence of wearing "black" garments has been introduced.

The *kriya* ritual is observed by and for seven types of relatives: father, mother, brother, sister, son, daughter, and spouse. The tear, which must be plainly visible, is made over the heart at least on the outer garment. It should not be torn along the seam and must be a "purposeful scar" (Lamm 1969, 42). Those mourning for parents sever the garment in public and on the left side of the body. Persons mourning for other relatives may rend their vestment in private and on the right side. As mentioned above, the subjects of our study perform the ritual at the funeral home. It is done in private and on the appropriate side of their body. The torn garment is worn until the completion of the seven-day mourning period. The *kriya* ritual, which is executed during the *aninut* period, has publicly singled out the survivor, still an *onen*, as having a special social status.

During the period of *aninut,* additional rules and rites can be identified as a public announcement of the new status. *Onenim* are forbidden to shave (for males),[6] cut their hair or bathe. They are forbidden to study Torah or to work, thereby making them conspicuously absent from daily public social involvement. Furthermore, they are forbidden to attend parties or participate in public merrymaking. They are even exempted from specific religious rituals, whether attributed to Torah or rabbinic law.[7] The exemption from Torah law includes the wearing of phylacteries (*tfilin*) and the reciting of "Hear O Israel." The suspended rabbinic laws incorporate general daily prayers and food blessings. The exclusion of *onenim* from the accepted religious patterns is normative for the liminal state and is therefore both their own personal and their society's declaration of the change in social status. This exclusion is emphasized by suspension of the male *onen*'s right to complete the prayer quorum (*minyan*) or to congregate with the required number of Jews to recite the public blessing after meals (*zimun*).

As discussed earlier, the *onenim* studied are affiliated with an Orthodox synagogue, but they are not "committed," observant Jews. They do not practise the *halaka* strictly on a regular basis. Thus the suspended laws of phylacteries, prayers and blessing are irrelevant. On the other hand, *halakot* for the *onenim*, such as those that forbid them to cut their hair or require that they abstain from merrymaking, are observed. The subject synagogue's rabbi usually visits with survivors prior to the funeral and instructs them in these laws. The rabbi also presents *onenim* with a book that states and explains the laws and rituals concerned with death and mourning. The time prior to the funeral is usually spent by the soon-to-be mourners with preparations for the burial. The funeral home is visited, a coffin is chosen and other technical details are concluded. This might include meeting incoming visitors at the airport. Thus, although only the newly introduced rituals are practised, the *onenim* have entered the state of liminality.

*Aninut* is climaxed at the funeral ceremony. Rabbinic Judaism requires the interment to be completed within a day of death. *Halaka* also stresses the importance of all Jews participating in the funeral service. The performance of many Judaic commandments is deferred to permit them to attend the service. To encourage attendance, rabbinic sources state that the Jew's participation in the funeral service will gain him the right to the "next (post-mortem) world" (Levine 1985, 389).

Attendance at the funerals studied varied in the number of participants. The popularity of the deceased and his or her family seemed to be the criterion for attendance. On one occasion, in addition to the immediate family of the deceased, approximately 125 additional participants were present. The rabbi explained that on the rare occasions, when there are fewer than 10 men, either he or the funeral home will organize a quorum (*minyan*). In this way, the group's "life support" system is maintained.

Much importance is attached to the eulogy during the funeral service. Aaron Levine, in his discussion of rabbinic eulogies, enumerates the themes incorporated by the eulogizer (1985, 343-45). Suggested motifs include the family, the role of the husband and children. The eulogizer, society's spokesman, and in our case the synagogue rabbi, implicitly informs survivors that they stand at the threshold of a new role with new duties. The rabbi explained this: "I speak about the person and his family the way they should remember the deceased." Thus, as Douglas rightly states, "rituals of warm support for the bereaved are consistent with their status being ruthlessly exploited for the group purposes in funerary rhetoric" (1979, 32). A society structured as "strong-group, strong-grid," such as rabbinic Judaism, and considered to be so by the leadership of the modern Orthodox synagogue studied, demands that its members make the funeral a public affair; in this way, rabbinic society or its leadership serves its own needs. At the funerals I observed, the eulogy followed the same model discussed, but was delivered by the rabbi in the funeral chapel, not at the graveside as is often done in Orthodox Jewish communities.

A society might choose to stress one or more of the various points in the process of death, burial and mourning in the encoding of liminality. For example, Hertz argues that among the Dayaks the period between the first and second burial is particularly important. Rabbinic authority, by naming the *aninut* period, has marked the gap between death and burial as worthy of special attention. According to Hertz, collective representations and collective ritual activity surrounding death are related directly to the body and soul of the deceased. Rabbinic mourning rituals begin immediately after the corpse is covered. Maurice Lamm, in his guide to Jewish mourning rites, speaks of the recessional from the graveside as a redirecting of the concerns of society from the deceased to the mourners: "It marks the transition from *aninut* to *avelut*, the new state of mourning which now commences" (1969, 66-67).

## Exit and entrance rituals

The *kadish*, thought by the uninformed to be a prayer for the dead, is to the rabbinic Jew a prayer to celebrate the glory of God. Of the five forms of *kadish* that exist, only one deals with death—and that obliquely. The other forms are used in the general everyday services, but the death-oriented *kadish* is recited by a male survivor at the graveside immediately after the deceased has been interred. The burial *kadish* differs in its opening lines:

> Magnified and sanctified be His great name. In the world which He will renew, reviving the dead and raising them to life eternal, rebuilding the city of Jerusalem and establishing therein His sanctuary; uprooting idol worship from the land and replacing it with the Divine worship—May the Holy One, blessed be he, reign in His majestic glory (Lamm 1969, 172).

This particular *kadish* engages the topic of death but avoids any mention of the deceased in question. Instead, it transcends the immediate situation and links a generalized concept of the death to messianic ideals: "In the world which He will renew, reviving the dead, and raising them to life eternal, rebuilding the city of Jerusalem and establishing therein His sanctuary." Furthermore, the reference to the Jerusalem temple and the glory of God in the burial *kadish* reaffirms God's authority and therefore rabbinic authority as a timeless entity supported by society into the most distant future.

At the onset of the recital of the burial *kadish*, the *onen* is declared a mourner. Through this prayer, he formulates and pronounces his acceptance of the new leadership role bestowed upon him by society. In leading this recital, he appears to take upon himself a new role, as leader. The deceased symbolizes society's acceptance of that chapter of life and the renewal of structure through the new speaker who is reciting the prayer. The mention of death in the burial *kadish* reflects the acceptance of the exit role by the survivor.

The fact that this speaker begins a new leadership role in society explains why, in traditional rabbinic Judaism, only men recite the *kadish*. However, reflecting the social dialectics of modern society, some women now recite the *kadish*, a result of the changes in the social map of North America. Among the mourners I observed were two women who recited the *kadish* on a regular basis during the synagogue's daily prayers. The rabbi informed me that since the *halaka* does not forbid this behaviour (though it does not encourage it), he allows the women to recite the *kadish*. At the cemetery, he invites *all* mourners to recite. During the year of obligation (to be discussed later), women recite the *kadish* from their section of the sanctuary.

The exit-entrance ritual at the cemetery comes to a close when all present form two lines facing inward, and the mourners walk away from the graveside between the lines. Turning their backs on death, the mourners pass through a symbolic portal into their newly adopted role. The people present close ranks behind the mourners and the social units can concentrate on the restoration and maintenance of the prior structures.

*Shiva: The first period of mourning*

The mourners are taken directly from the cemetery to the house of the deceased or to the *shiva* house. Before entering the home, hands are ritually washed in water prepared by "supporters." This ritual might also be performed at the outside borders of the cemetery. The totality of the experience of death and contact with the pollution of the dead is placed behind the mourners in symbolic closure as the pollution is ritually washed away from their hands after departing from the cemetery and before entering the house of mourning. In contrast to mourners in many other religions,[8] Jewish mourners do not undergo any specific rituals before entering the house of mourning. The entrance rites were completed at the cemetery when they passed between the two lines of participants. The mourners remain in the *shiva* house for seven days as they proceed through the process of confirming their new roles. The *shiva* or mourning house is preferably located in the home of the deceased rather than that of the survivor. If this is not possible, then one of the survivors' houses is used. The emphasis upon the home of the deceased rather than that of the mourner symbolizes the transfer of the mantle of the deceased's role onto the shoulders of the survivor.

Immediately after entering the *shiva* house, the mourners remove their shoes. The mourners, who have symbolically altered the accepted norm in this way, cannot leave until this stage of the process is brought to a close. While thus incarcerated, the mourners' attention is focused on the demands of their new role in society. Others proceed with the task of reinforcing these roles. This procedure of confinement for the mourners is not strange in religious mourning rites, but the uniquely Judaic activities that take place in the *shiva* house are significant. The core activities and functions involve food.[9] Food is seen as a convenient catalyst through which the main events can be played out.

Immediately after entering the house and removing their shoes, the mourners are served the meal of condolence (*se'udat havra*). The food is provided and served by neighbours or friends. Thus we see the introduction of outsiders into the house of mourning. Since the mourners are not yet perceived as being fully integrated into their new roles, they are not yet ready for incorporation into society. They are established, therefore, in their liminal status. Furthermore, the mourners are supposed to eat alone lest they form the quorum that would require them to recite the public blessing after the meal (*zimun*). Because the mourners interviewed are not Orthodox (despite their affiliation with an Orthodox synagogue), they do not recite this prayer at any time, nor are they careful about sitting separately.

The menu of the meal consists of bread and eggs. Eggs are often seen in rabbinic literature as associated with the Temple or the destruction of the Temple. They serve as a constant reminder that rabbinic authority derives its power through the "Bible" and the Temple, God's manifestation on earth. This allusion to rabbinic authority and its derivation from Temple society are persistent themes in the rituals of mourning. They are also found in the rituals related to the fast of Tisha B'av and the passover *seder*. This motif was already seen in the *kadish* at the cemetery. Additional examples of the concept include, first, the expression used to comfort mourners: "May the Lord comfort you among the other mourners of Zion and Jerusalem." This statement is first recited while the mourners pass between the two lines at the cemetery. The rabbi articulates the "comfort" in both Hebrew and English. It is continually employed whenever one takes leave of the mourner during the *shiva* interim.

Second, there is a reference to the Temple in the portion added to the blessing after meals when (if) recited in the house of mourning. It reads:

O comfort, Lord, our God, the mourners of Jerusalem and those who mourn this sad event. Console them from their mourning and gladden them from their grief, as it is said "Like a man whose mother consoles him so I will console you, and in Jerusalem you will be consoled." Blessed are you Lord, Comforter of Zion through the rebuilding of Jerusalem. Amen (Scherman 1984, 199).

Visiting by neighbours and friends is not fortuitous. Rabbinic Judaism emphasizes the obligation of all Jews to visit the mourners' house and offer comfort, a ritual that continues to be widely practised even among today's non-observant Jews. During these seven days of *shiva*, the mourners alter their normative pattern of sitting; they sit on low stools, even on the floor, while the influx of visitors continues. Beyond providing comfort, this procedure of differentiation provides both mourners and visitors with an opportunity for the collectivity to apply group reinforcement in adopting their new roles.

In addition, a further series of rites is in force. Some of these are brought forward from the *onen* period, but several other ones are added. A partial list of *shiva* rites, laws and prohibitions is provided by Meir Krentzman (1986, 5-18). Every item listed is derived from the normative patterns of Jewish ritual. They include location of *shiva*; burning of *shiva* candles; covering mirrors; meal of condolence; sitting on low stools or floor; prohibition of cohabitation; prohibition of anointing; prohibition of bathing; prohibition of marriage; study of Torah; prohibition of wearing shoes; prohibition of work; prohibition of *tfilin*; prohibition of *talit*; prayer held in *shiva* house, instead of synagogue; and ending the *shiva*. The mourners I observed adhered to the "public" rites. I assume that others, such as avoidance of cohabitation and bathing, were not observed.

The confinement of the mourner to the *shiva* house precludes his attendance at daily prayers at the synagogue. Therefore, additional visitors must come to the house of mourning. These comforters are required to be present at specified times each day to fulfill rabbinic prayer obligations and constitute the *minyan*. Whereas the survivor was not included in the *minyan* during the *onen* period, he is not only included at the *shiva* house but encouraged to lead the prayers. Thus the mourner, by his participation in the prayer service, continues to proclaim his newly adopted status in public. The visitors, in turn, encourage and reinforce the incorporation of these roles by the mourner. Most of the mourners studied had led the *minyan* in their house of *shiva*. When 10 men were not present, the rabbi either provided the missing number of persons or permitted the mourners to attend the synagogue. If the mourners could not read Hebrew and were therefore not able to lead the prayers, transliterations were supplied by the synagogue to enable them to recite the *kadish*.

The forty-ninth psalm is added at the completion of the liturgy in the house of mourning. Even though this prayer refers to death in general, it

## Completion of shiva

*Halaka* does not stipulate any entrance or exit rituals at this point. The entrance rituals into the new status were completed by the mourner at the cemetery site. This new status is perceived as enduring and unbridgeable. Therefore, with the mourner entrenched in this new status, there is likewise no stipulation for exit rituals at the completion of the two additional mourning periods.

As with many North American Jews, our subjects perform a ritual to end the *shiva* with a "walk around the block." Krentzman states that this is "a formal act to demonstrate their rejoining the community" (1986, 18). In my discussion with Rabbi Krentzman, he pointed to research indicating that this ritual, which originated in eastern European Jewish communities, was adopted mainly by the non-Orthodox community in North America. Since many of these Jews (but not our subjects) end their mourning rites with *shiva*, they have introduced an exit ritual. I suggest that, furthering this interpretation, the non-observant Jews do subscribe to the full authority of rabbinic Judaism. They are, however, selective with regard to their observance and do not fully incorporate the roles required by the social unit as defined by rabbinic Judaism. Hence, the exit rite serves to signify the completion of their involvement with rabbinic mourning rituals. However, the mourners observed for this study did not terminate the mourning rites with the completion of *shiva* and did perform the ritual "walk around the block." I will further discuss the implications of this phenomenon in the conclusion of the paper.

## Shloshim and the "year-long" period of mourning

The *shloshim* period begins at the completion of the *shiva* and extends for 30 days after burial. The "year-long" period continues for an additional 11 months (12 from the date of the burial).

As the survivor moves from one period to the next there is a corresponding reduction in number of required mourning rituals practised. In accordance with Lamm (1969, 145; 148), the following prohibitions continue in force, under normal circumstances, during *shiva* and during *shloshim*:

- haircutting, shaving, nailcutting, bathing and the wearing of new clothes or newly laundered clothes

- getting married

- attending parties

The following is a brief survey of the observances for the entire 12-month period:

- Haircutting, technically prohibited for 12 months, is permitted upon the occasion of social reproach after the *shloshim*, as indicated above.

- Similarly, the wearing of new clothes is permitted upon "social reproach" after the *shloshim* and after being worn for a brief period of time by others, although, technically it is a 12-month observance.

- The mourner should change his usual seat in the synagogue at prayer. On the Sabbath he may sit in his usual place.

- According to regulation, the *kadish* is recited.

These rites are almost all public in nature and continually serve to mark the mourner as a person learning to adopt new roles. The subject mourners, as in the period of *shiva*, adhere to the public rites, thereby receiving community exposure, support and encouragement.

## Kadish

The *kadish* is not a prayer for the dead but a glorification of God. It is recited during prayer services. Recitation of this prayer requires a *minyan* and must be recited standing. In the observed synagogue, the mourners assemble as a group close to the ark and in full view of the congregation for the recital of the *kadish* prayer. Within the liturgy, four variations of the *kadish* appear, all of them being concerned with the glorification of God. These need not be expanded upon here. Some of them are recited by the mourner, and the remainder are chanted by the prayer leader (*shaliah tzibur*) alone. Rabbinic Judaism, therefore, encourages the mourners to lead the prayers, thus enabling the mourners to gain multiple opportunities to recite the *kadish*. The mourners are asked to lead the services depending upon which stage of mourning they are observing. Even in the case of our subject mourners, who have weak Hebrew-reading skills, the service is led by a *kadish*-sayer. The survivors with limited skills make a conscious effort during the year of mourning to improve their Hebrew and thus be able to lead services. They will usually begin with leading the short afternoon prayers and then they will attempt the lengthy morning service. The adult education program in the synagogue offers Hebrew and prayer classes that are often visited by the mourners. Once again, these public rituals confirm my hypothesis that society publicly and manifestly singles out the mourner.

Rabbinic Judaism differentiates between mourning for parents and doing so for the other five types of relatives mentioned (brother, sister, son, daughter and spouse). Mourning rites including a recitation of the *kadish*, are concluded at the end of one month in the case of the five relatives, but they are maintained throughout the "year" after the loss of a parent. This differentiation can be understood if we examine the level of threat to the social fabric after the loss of relatives in each category. The loss of a parent, who provides a leadership role in the social unit, causes a serious rupture in the social network; hence, the social necessity of ensuring that a replacement has adopted each of the vacant roles, both functionally and structurally. This necessity is reflected in the fact that mourning rites and the evolving emphasis on saying the *kadish* are extended to "one year." In the modern context, the death of a parent is a particular threat to an individual's continued participation in Jewish observance, because many Jews attend synagogue and maintain other traditional rituals and practices mainly for the sake of aging or elderly parents. The loss of a relative in any of the other five categories engenders a less severe threat to the cohesion of the social unit; therefore, it requires a less extensive ritual.

In support of my hypothesis that mourning rites serve to re-establish the pre-death social order, I point to the prescription of rabbinic Judaism that only males are required to recite the *kadish*. Krentzman writes: "A daughter should not recite the *kadish* in the synagogue, but should answer 'amen' from the women's section" (1986, 32). This stipulation is based upon the rabbinic intention that the male survivors adopt the leadership roles lost to society as a result of the death; hence it is the man that society must "incorporate" into these roles. I have already noted that, as a result of the values of contemporary society, the female subjects are permitted to recite the *kadish*, and do so, in synagogue. The implication of this modification will be discussed below.

Since rabbinic Judaism is based on male-dominated leadership, women represent a threat to the structure. This might explain why the woman is accorded by *halaka* equal ritual status to the man only when she is dead. No longer a threat to the social system, she is buried in the same ritual way as a man. The male-dominated structure is further strengthened through the death of the woman because it is the male survivor who recites the *kadish* for her, thus publicly emphasizing his role. Synagogue services in contemporary North American Judaism are more dependent upon female attendance and participation than was the case in the past. Accordingly, women have been granted a greater ritual role in recent years and, in some orthodox synagogues, have been encouraged to recite the *kadish*.

## Discussion

During the Jewish mourning period, the group has maintained and supported the mourners, through the symbolism of ritual and public dissonant behaviour, as they enter their new roles. I have argued that, in rabbinic Judaism, the initiate or mourner is elevated to a new status. However, under the influence of contemporary society, most Jewish families have adopted a modern structure in which roles are not clearly defined. These mourning rites were intended to facilitate passage of the mourner to a new status. This new status, however, is ambiguous in our modern society. Therefore, mourning rituals are in danger of being transformed into a ritualism[10] or of simply becoming defunct. But Jewish society has not disregarded the mourning rites; instead, it has subtly (but by no means consciously) reoriented them and thus allowed them to have an impact upon the family and Jewish community. The retention of mourning rites is effected through the community, which informs its members what to do and how they must conform to what is considered proper practice. Jewish mourners attribute importance to the mourning rites because the community tells them to do so, and there is a public consensus that this is proper behaviour. However, Jews in our subject synagogue accept the funeral rites only as long as they do not infringe more than minimally upon the family's lifestyle.

In the civil religion of North American Jews, as practised in the observed synagogue, the family remains a constant in the continuation of Jewish identity.[11] Jews today are aware that the dilution of the family unit threatens their continuity. The construction of the mourning rituals, as I have said, continues to foster family solidarity and to emphasize communal needs. The rabbi explained to me that, during the *shiva*, he encourages the mourners to discuss their changed family relationships and obligations resulting from the death. Thus Judaism continues to emphasize the observance of the mourning rites but takes into consideration the changed family structure. It does not discourage women, for example, from reciting the *kadish*.

## A concluding observation

Following the model proposed by Robert King Merton in his analysis of functionalism (1957, 77), I would like to note additional latent or implicit functions of Jewish mourning rites. These functions, which are not necessarily intended or recognized by the survivor, operate so as to fulfill the needs and support the continuation of Jewish society in general and the subject synagogue in particular. The study of mourning rituals for this purpose does not exclude the possibility that community exigencies can be served by additional rituals. In the case of mourning rites, however, significance must be attached to what Merton defines in his discussion of Durkheim as a "recurrent activity . . . [that is] the part [the activity] plays in the social life as a whole and therefore the contribution it makes to the maintenance of the structural continuity" (Merton 1957, 77).

Rabbinic Judaism is aware that the collectivity is no longer the Jewish communal world, but specifically the synagogue. Rituals that have previously served the social consciousness of the macro-rabbinic society now are directed to function for the micro-rabbinical social structure, namely, the synagogue. The ritual of reciting the *kadish* is employed for this purpose; other mourning rites are considered less compelling after the *shiva*. Those who say the *kadish* and participate in daily and Sabbath services at the synagogue, after all, actually help to strengthen the life of the congregation.

The subject synagogue and its mourners were chosen to validate the hypothesis that mourning rites cohere with the contemporary Jewish social map. The synagogue achieves its religious legitimacy through prayer services held daily, both morning and evening. The *kadish*-sayers constitute the majority of the *minyan* group, thereby helping to legitimate the religious aspect of the synagogue. The synagogue, then, functions not only as a weekend religious gathering place, or as an office for the rabbi, but also endeavours to develop its complementary social and educational services and to act as a community centre. Without the foundation of the daily *minyan*, the wider synagogue activities might not have a legitimate base from which to function. It is the *kadish*-sayers, in essence, who maintain this ongoing service. Rabbinism promotes the psychological appeal of reciting the *kadish*; as people continue to die, the continuation of the synagogue through the collectivity of the survivors is guaranteed.

The strength of the synagogue society is furthered by a reduction in fees for "new members." The synagogue society recognizes these *kadish*-sayers in their roles as skilled participants in the liturgy. Classes are offered in prayer as well as in written and spoken Hebrew. A system of "honours" motivates skilled participation. The most skillful participants are proffered reinforcements such as the following: leading services, honours related to the reading of the Torah, and publicly reading the prescribed Torah portions.

My research has also shown that most members who have a greater involvement in the synagogue have been recruited from the *kadish*-sayers. The *kadish* period is for them a liminal period after which they are incorporated as active participants in the synagogue community. Furthermore, the incorporation of the *kadish*-sayer will attract his immediate family; they too become involved in synagogue activities, thus augmenting the committed synagogue membership.

A dynamic based on "positive feedback" evolves. Increased membership enhances the status of the synagogue in the wider Jewish society. The latter, in turn, attracts more synagogue adherents. The greater the population base of the synagogue community, the more likely its function is to succeed, further enhancing its membership. A larger population base also increases the financial capacity of the synagogue to mount services. This, in turn, attracts new adherents.

To conclude, I have shown how the mourning rituals of rabbinic Judaism cohere with a specific social structure: the rituals can be seen as a particular model of the "strong-grid," "strong-group" society as presented by Douglas. Moreover, I have shown that they are enacted during a period of liminality as conceived of by Turner. Lastly, I have shown how rabbinic Judaism has utilized the mourning rituals within a contemporary North American Jewish society to enhance synagogue life. The latter has been transformed from an encompassing rabbinic "world" to a Jewish "corporation."

## Notes

1. For the purposes of this paper I do not differentiate the terms rites and rituals. I refer the reader to Fred Bird's (1979) characterization of ritual action.
2. The halakic sources I researched for mourning rites were *Tur Yoreh De'ah; Shulhan Aruk Yor'eh Deah; Aruk Hashulhan Yoreh De'ah* (sections on mourning laws); Tzokensiki 1980; Lamm 1969; Levine 1985; and Krentzman 1986.
3. For additional data and analysis of the subject of synagogue, see Fishbane 1987.
4. Scholars have argued that Douglas' hypothesis is not applicable to modern, pluralistic and industrialized societies. I suggest Berger and Luckmann's (1984) discussion of socialization as a complement to Douglas' mapping of society as an answer to this criticism.
5. For example, see Goldscheider 1986.
6. The topic of women shaving their legs is absent from rabbinic literature. The subject rabbi, when asked if this type of shaving was permitted replied, "It is not appropriate, but I would not prohibit it."
7. Rabbinic Judaism attributes a greater importance, and thus encourages stricter adherence, to laws stated to be either explicit or deduced from the Torah.
8. See Huntington and Metcalf 1980.
9. See Douglas 1975, 249-74.
10. See Bird 1979.
11. J. Hirschberg's (1988) multivariate analysis of parental and educational factors in the development of Jewish identity included many of the same subjects as this study. He concluded that, on all measures, the most significant predictors of the children's ethnicity were parental and family factors. For a discussion of the family-centred nature of rituals retained in the "civil religion" of Canada's Jews, see J. Lightstone 1986, revised and published for the first time in English as chapter 3 of this volume.

# 12

# Family Rituals and Religion: A Functional Analysis of Jewish and Christian Family Ritual Practices

## FREDERICK B. BIRD

All families with any cohesion and self-identity engage in ritual acts that reinforce these qualities. They can be quite diverse: traditional or newly created, religious or secular, elaborate or simple, acknowledged as such or not. In this paper, I explore the functions of ritual in family life and the impact on it of religious commitment.

Families engage in varied ritual acts. One family[1] has developed an elaborate ceremony, including a huge bonfire on the beach, to mark the opening of their summer cottage each year. Another family, at the urging of the children, becomes more observant with respect to Sabbath evening meals. Several families invest considerable time, material and effort into house decorations, gifts, parties, festive meals and greeting cards to mark the Christmas season. One couple has developed a very personal and private ceremony for Saturday mornings, which include sexual intimacies and breakfast in bed. Many families have developed their own particular ways of celebrating birthdays, anniversaries and secular holidays.

Many occasions in everyday life, from weddings that bring families into being to the funerals that mark the end of particular individuals' lives within these families, can inspire rituals. The number of occasions that families ritualize and the elaborateness of these rituals vary with the existence and forms of religious involvement. Religious traditions provide as ready resources basic ritual scripts for family occasions such as births, weekend activities, mealtimes and seasonal festivities. These religion-based repertoires of ritual scripts vary from the austere and simple offerings in the United Church of Canada to quite extensive and elaborate offerings in Jewish Orthodoxy. In the paragraphs that follow, I compare and analyze the rituals of Jews and Christians by examining how these traditions respond to the occasions that provoke ritual dramas. More specifically, I analyze the extent to which, and the ways by which, diverse Jewish and Christian families have established rituals in connection with mealtimes, weekends, the seasons of the year and events of the life cycle.[2]

Most families make at least some of their daily or weekly meals into ritual occasions. They establish customs about how they prepare food, set tables, bless meals and eat. Many of these customs are closely connected with ethnic and religious traditions. For centuries, Catholics substituted fish for meat on Fridays. Jews still avoid shellfish and pork; they also distinguish between meat and milk meals. Several Mishnaic tractates are concerned with the proper ways of harvesting, preparing, serving and consuming food at meals. Many families establish their own customs with respect to meals. They might eat their evening meals in dining rooms and breakfasts in kitchens, for example, or have elaborate meals on weekends and simpler meals during the week. Families ritualize their weekly meals in two complementary ways: setting aside certain times for meals and accompanying them with ceremonies.

Typically, special importance is placed on specific meals during the week. Even if family members are unable to eat other meals together, they come together for Sunday dinner, or Sabbath evening, or Saturday night or whatever other time is deemed particularly valuable. For these occasions, they dress in nicer or more elaborate clothes, and the meals themselves will involve more preparations, additional courses, special drinks and fancier desserts (Douglas 1975a).

Religious families often accompany their meals with grace (prayers or readings). They vary considerably in this regard. At one time, Protestant families often included Bible readings and prayers with breakfast. Several of the families we interviewed held hands and sang graces for evening meals. Some Jewish and Christian families provided liturgical accompaniment to their meals only once a week: a special dinner on Friday evening or Sunday.

By means of rituals, families turn mealtime into something more than simply an occasion for receiving nourishment. Insofar as they use scripts associated with given traditions, they acknowledge and reconfirm their connectedness with much larger communities. They thereby signal to themselves that they are, indeed, part of a people identified as being Jewish or Catholic or Protestant. They also present themselves to each other as a group of people deserving special recognition. Indirectly, they recognize themselves as a group that, at least for some meals or parts of meals, takes time to express the sense of being a special group. Moreover, conversations at ritualized meals differ from those at other meals. Discursive conversations about business and personal confessions are discouraged or eliminated in favour of conversations about family activities, memories, hopes and humourous events.

Weekends, too, provide occasions for families to develop rituals. Viewed as a whole, families develop quite a number of rituals to establish weekends as a time different from the rest of the week. Observant Jewish families set aside a day to interact. So do families in which distracting influences of the secular order, such as business, are minimized if not altogether excluded. After six days in which family members are going hither and thither, interacting with diverse others, interacting with each other only long enough to keep the show on the road, families reconstitute themselves as families on weekends. They take off to country cottages or on family outings, for instance, or retreat into their own homes. Many families relax certain norms on weekends: they sleep in, wear more casual clothes, order in prepared food or go out to eat. Consider the special clothing worn on weekends.

Family members might wear clothes that are more informal than usual, even casual. For specific events, though, they might wear clothes that are more formal, even festive. Going to church on Sunday morning was for a number of interviewed families the mid-point of a series of ritualized acts: baths on Saturday night, fasts on Sunday morning, followed by visiting and eating dinner with friends and/or relatives. Several Reconstructionist Jewish families alternate between secular weekends in the country and fairly observant weekends in town.

Most interviewed families considered going to church or attending synagogue as a kind of family ritual, although they differed on the relation between attending these congregational rites and family life. Many Orthodox Jews considered attending synagogue something individual family members do—sometimes only the men on Friday evening and everyone on Saturday morning—but seldom considered it as their own family ritual (unless it involved the bar mitzvah or bat mitzvah of a relative or friend). Except for the Reconstructionists, moreover, they did not sit together in the synagogue as members of a family. They sat as women and men representing the women and men of the congregation and interacting with friends and associates. In contrast, several families from the United Church, which is a liberal Protestant denomination, regarded going to church as one of the more important family rituals—even when not all of them sat together because some family members were in the choir or taught church school. They considered going to church an important ritual partly because they recognized so few other family rituals and this was one thing they could all do together; they got dressed up specially for the occasion, went out together and came home together. For Jewish and Christian families, attending religious services constitute one part of a larger set of rituals by which families establish weekends as special times.

Most families use ritual forms to mark and celebrate different seasons or days over the course of the year. The number and variety of these can be quite extensive even if we include only legal holidays, birthdays and semi-secular celebrations for Hallowe'en and St. Valentine's day. Although adults view most of these days off from work as occasions for leisure, children often view them as occasions for the enactment of ritual dramas incorporating special meals and festivities; these, of course, involve the family as a whole.[3] Aside from birthdays and anniversaries, most families choose not to take part in much ritual activity on these secular holidays and events. Unless dates gain an explicitly religious aura, families rarely mark them with special family celebrations. President's Day, Labour Day, May Day, Hallowe'en, St. Valentine's Day and New Year's Eve, for example, are not usually occasions for family rituals in Canada and the United States. Thanksgiving is the exception. Interestingly, though, this holiday still retains a coherent religious character; it is an occasion for extended family gatherings. For many traditional Catholics in Quebec, New Year's Day served as a focus for family life: on this occasion, fathers assumed a priestly/patriarchal role and formally blessed family members. Families sometimes use the secular holidays for family activities such as trips, picnics or more elaborate meals. But rarely do they associate these trips or meals with scripted words or gestures.

In contrast, the calendars of religious holidays, both Jewish and Christian, often provide occasions for special family celebrations. To be sure, some holidays—Yom Kippur, Good Friday, Pentecost—have hardly any significance for family life. But other dates—Christmas, Hanuka, Passover—do; religious traditions provide basic scripts for what are, *par excellence*, family rather than congregational rituals. Especially with respect to Passover for Jews and Christmas for Christians, families undertake extensive and elaborate preparations. Houses are decorated. Special foods are prepared. The eventual enjoyment of the holiday is connected with the preparations undertaken. All family members are involved in these preparations. Some activities take place at the church or synagogue, it is true, but the celebrations take place primarily at home and involve relatives—uncles and aunts, cousins, sisters, brothers. The individual family celebration becomes, simultaneously, an extended family celebration and a communal celebration. Although religion provides these celebrations with basic scripts, more extensive and detailed for Jews than for Christians, families develop their own variations. Hanuka, Christmas and Passover are seasons, moreover, not just specific days; as such, they encourage elaborate celebrations.

Seasonal rituals mark the passage of time. But they are not strictly rites of passage, which mark changes in status or social circumstance. These celebrations symbolize the ongoing characteristics of family life rather than transformations. They provide ways for families to affirm the givenness of their being. In symbolic terms, they recall the founding events in religious history; in practical terms, though, they provide occasions for the expression of mutual affection through the giving of gifts or other exchanges.

Life-cycle events also provide occasions for family rituals. Family rituals are usually enacted to dramatize and celebrate birth, growing up, marriage and death. Almost always, these celebrations involve members of the extended family in addition to those of the nuclear family. The rituals developed by Christians and Jews differ considerably, except in the case of weddings. Most families find some way to celebrate births. The formal rituals for baptism or circumcision are often treated as communal rites more than family rites, because they are performed in churches or hospitals or because family members are typically overwhelmed by non-family guests. Still, these are occasions for family celebrations. The same is true of marriages and deaths. Christians generally lack any dramatic way of celebrating or dramatizing growing up. Catholic children celebrate first communion, it is true, but they are second-graders; the ritual does not symbolizing maturation. Confirmation exercises are more like rites for inducting new members than genuine rites of passage. This is not true of bar mitzvahs or bat mitzvahs. They are far more elaborate and require far more preparation. Even though children of 12 or 13 do not mark the passage into adulthood, they do dramatize the passage from childhood to adolescence. Moreover, these rites involve not only the adolescents themselves. In a fundamental sense, they involve both families and communities: families call attention to themselves both individually and collectively; congregations celebrate and reaffirm their own collective identity.

There are many occasions, therefore, with regard to which families can engage in ritual dramas or enactments. Families can devise their own rites, of course. To a considerable degree, though, religious traditions provide the basic scripts for these rites. Some traditions have specialized in this, but others have not; United Church families have far fewer ritual scripts, and far less elaborate ones, than Orthodox Jewish families. As far as families are concerned, the United Church provides them with just a few basic scripts for family rituals and celebrations: going to church, grace at meals, Christmas celebrations and weddings. More than Orthodox Jewish families or even Catholic families, therefore, these families have to create their own scripts. The United Church families we interviewed were, not surprisingly, largely unaware of the family rituals they regularly enacted. Even though they recognized going to church as a kind of a ritual, they thought about this activity not in terms of drama or ritual performance but in terms of cognitive content and the quality of performances offered by choirs and ministers.

The Catholic and Anglican families we interviewed, on the other hand, differed in this respect. Not only did they regard church services primarily as ritual events, but they also developed their own family rituals to celebrate both religious holidays and secular ones. One Anglican couple, for example, developed a ritual including a walk in the woods to celebrate fall. Another celebrated spring with a special planting day. Still another arranged a whole set of stylized family activities in connection with the annual parade on St. Patrick's Day. Having associated religion with ritual performances, they seemed readier to incorporate ritual drama into family life.

Orthodox traditions provide Jewish families with the most extensive repertoire of ritual scripts in connection with weekly meals, weekends, seasons, holidays and life-cycle events. More than other families, therefore, these are given opportunities to perform rituals. This is true even among Reconstructionist families, moreover, many of which perform their rites only now and then. In order to perform their little dramas well, people must both learn their lines and put some feeling into their stylized roles. Jewish family members, in particular, need to be prepared. They are trained formally at the synagogue before their bar mitzvahs and bat mitzvahs. They are also trained informally by imitating their parents. To the extent that families participate in these rituals, they also connect their own identities as families with religious tradition.

So far, I have engaged in a preliminary discussion, the major purpose of which has been to note two things: the occasions in relation to which families might enact ritual performances; and the ways in which families, whether Jewish or Christian, characteristically develop their own rituals. The major point has been that oral and written scripts for most family rituals have been set by religious traditions but are modified and augmented by families. In other words, families typically use standardized scripts in order to symbolize their own unique identities as families.

But why do families develop or use rituals of this kind? And how do religious commitments affect their performances? Typically, people answer the first question in terms of theology or history. They invoke theological rationales, for example, to explain the symbolic importance of their rites. They refer to the supposed historical origins of specific rituals. And they talk about the history of their own family's involvement with particular celebrative acts. Some talk about eating goose every Christmas. Others talk about waking their children with a song on birthdays. Still others talk about visiting their grandparents on the high holidays.

From a social scientific perspective, their answers are not really adequate. They do not really *explain* why these families continue to enact particular rituals. At best, they do so indirectly. These accounts are invoked to affirm the symbolic value of specific rituals and to reaffirm commitment to them. What I am looking for, on the other hand, are statements that would make sense to others as well. I am looking for public accounts, functional explanations, that identify the personal *good* of these performances for family rites as such. To argue that families perform these rites because they are traditional begs the question. What must still be explained are the benefits gained by virtue of acts that invoke traditions—benefits that might well include the ones I shall analyze.

It is possible and sometimes insightful to examine the particular functional benefits of specific rituals. This can be done for taboos, funeral rites, weddings and so forth. It is important to examine not only the obvious or manifest functions and benefits of specific rites but also the less obvious or latent ones. One of the latent functions of a bar mitzvah or bat mitzvah, for example, is the way that both preparing for it and celebrating of it reintegrate lax parents into congregational life by requiring them to provide direct support for their own children and, at the same time, to increase their involvement with parents of other children at the same stage (see Fishbane in chapter 10 of this volume; Schoenfeld 1988; 1990; 1992).

When we examine the specific functions of family rituals, it is possible to observe several patterns. Different rituals often have the same or equivalent functions. Farewells, birthdays and ritual hugs all enable people to express strong emotional feelings in acceptable ways. Then, too, most rituals recall and reaffirm specific sets of normative expectations. For comparative analytic purposes, I have identified four general functions that well-performed family rituals help fulfill. Even as families enact rituals, I argue, they enjoy the benefits associated with these functions. I have identified these functions partly to provide standards against which to assess the overall impact of ritual performances on the lives of different families and partly to establish bench-marks that distinguish well-staged ritual performances from lifeless, tawdry or hackneyed ones. The impact of ritual enactments on family life is a result not only of the number and character of the scripts they provide, after all, but also of the ways they are put into play.

First, rituals allow people to express strong feelings that they might otherwise either silence or express in a confused jumble. Thomas Scheff has argued that good ritual enactments facilitate the fitting aesthetic distancing of emotions. As a consequence, rituals enable people to express strong feelings but without being overpowered by them (Scheff 1977). For example, funeral rites provide vehicles both to express pent-up feelings of guilt, sadness, anger, loss and love but to keep these feelings from getting out of hand. The same might well be said of weddings or handshakes. Although the rituals accompanying meals may have been tacked on indirectly, they might well function as ways for family members to express their deepest affections for each other but in ways that do not seem affected and insincere. Even stereotyped symbolic forms often help family members express feelings more articulately than they might if forced to speak spontaneously. At times of grief, crisis or intimacy, spontaneous speech often goes astray. It devolves into a babbling or stumbling torrent of mere words or embarrassed pauses—as people search unsuccessfully for the right words and often end up with words that communicate either more or less than they intend. Standardized expressions, on the other hand, offer simple and ready-made vehicles for communicating strong feelings.

Second, rituals provide ways for families to acknowledge and affirm basic expectations. These vary from respecting traditions to honouring parents, from affirming norms of cooperation to invoking ideals of serving others. Weddings call attention to standards of loyalty and keeping promises, funerals to gratitude and faith, circumcision to communal commitments, and all in ways that emphasize moral virtues suitable for a vibrant family life. This function of ritual enactments is often acknowledged. What still needs to be acknowledged is that families decidedly benefit from this communication, that rituals provide regular and persuasive ways both for socializing children or young people and for resocializing older people with regard to basic family standards. This kind of normative communication is in many ways more persuasive than lectures or overt moral instruction, mainly because it directly connects moral expectations with both respected ideals and personal identifications.

Third, rituals allow families to represent who they really are to themselves. This kind of internal communication, like personal reflection at an individual level, is very important for family life. Families engage in many different activities. As individuals, people frequently go quite separate ways: to work, to school, to parties and so on. Although it is easy for them to recognize their co-existence as a family, it is quite a different matter for them to identify and affirm their unique character as a family. Whatever else they do through ritual, they hold up an image for themselves of who they are. Although communicated in compact form, this image is often quite complex. Take the Sabbath evening candle-lighting and meal. What are families representing? They are acknowledging their worldwide connection with all other Jewish families in both contemporary and preceding generations (those who either did or are doing the same things). They also confirm that this religious-ethnic identification is an integral dimension of who they are as a family. Through ritual, they acknowledge that family members are expected to play different roles based on gender and generation (since sex and age presuppose specific ritual roles). Through different symbolic gestures, they represent themselves as caring for one another. By participating in these rites as a group, they represent themselves as a distinct collectivity or community. By having foods already prepared, and by disallowing other activities aside from participation in synagogue, they signal that they have set aside time simply for each other as a family. Through these ritual gestures, Jewish families do not just hold up a mirror to themselves. As Emile Durkheim argued (albeit for society as a whole), they represent normative images of themselves to which they recommit themselves. This strengthens their sense of collective identity.

The same kind of analysis might well be pursued for Christmas or Hanuka, for birthdays or going-to-bed rituals. Whatever else they might do, whatever commitments they might address to God, whatever ancestral deeds they might recall, these rites allow participants to re-present themselves, as any theatrical company would, with a sense of ownership in the scripts.

Rarely is this representational communication self-conscious. In part, as I will argue, this is because communication loses some of its force when too overt. Intragroup communication is something like dream communication. According to current theories, dreams allow individuals to sort out their lives unconsciously. Deprived of sleep and thus of dream-time, they become disoriented. But dream communication, while very compact and multidimensional, is indirect. Recalled or not, dreams let individuals represent to themselves dimensions of their lives that they would not otherwise acknowledge. The same things are true of ritual. Groups of people represent to themselves dimensions of their collective life that they would not otherwise acknowledge. And they can do so without sounding preachy, without babbling, without becoming self-righteous, without putting people on the defensive. What they acknowledge is the reality of ideal images of themselves, their larger interconnections, their distinct values, their important promises and their form of indebtedness. As a result, these images continue to play a vital role in their lives, without having to be presented orally, overtly or discursively.

Four, rituals allow families to celebrate. Celebrating is like playing games and having fun. Its mode of communication is distinct from that which is used at work, say, or at school. It involves relaxation of other attitudes and dispositions along with concentration on alternative rules and expectations. Minimally and characteristically, most family rituals provide occasions for families to express personal gratitude for what and who they are, whatever their status in secular terms. At weddings, funerals, baptismal parties and at grace, this is a characteristic motif. But these rituals usually go further. They provide ways of making festivals out of these occasions.

By including extra food or wine for their special meals, they allow people to rejoice. When friends greet with a hug, this ritualized act enables them not only to express mutual recognition and gratitude but also to express real affection and happiness at meeting each other. Rituals, as I have argued right along, help us dramatize our lives in ways that make them more festive, interesting and multidimensional.

Families do try to celebrate apart from ritual enactments. They have parties, entertain, go on outings. But notice the considerable degree to which ritual-like gestures accompany these activities.

I have reviewed several functions of family ritual practices, in general terms. My aim is to explain, from a social scientific perspective, why families engage in these acts. To be sure, there are other factors. My list of general functions is not exhaustive. Throughout this part of the argument, I have made an assumption that is only partly valid. That is, I have assumed that families perform these rituals expectantly and with feeling. Very often, though, this is certainly not the case. Nonetheless, this major exception confirms my basic argument. If families do not perform these rites well, they might be worse off than if they had attempted to organize their family lives without any celebrations or rites at all. Like any dramatized enactment, a poor performance is alienating. It is impossible to get a sense of drama from the first reading of an unskilled and insensitive performer. It is not rituals as such that sustain the function but well-performed ones. Not all attempts at ritual sustain the functions I have analyzed. Ritual practices come and go, wax and wane, for several reasons. (1) Families might make no real attempt to find a fit between recommended ritual scripts and their own lives. They might fail to augment, edit or modify the script or the staging in ways that relate sensitively to the lives and histories of participants. These adjustments might be made by adding ritual ceremonies for birthdays, weekends, weddings and mealtimes as well as subtracting or abridging given scripts. (2) Participants might be unprepared for their roles. Good ritual performances require both preparation and practice. Just because initial enactments are stilted, though, it does not follow that subsequent performances will be. (3) Ritual enactments fail to the extent that participants approach them not as mini-dramas but as obligatory formulae that must be mouthed and walked through in order to please people who would otherwise be offended. It is difficult to experience such forced enactments as other than arbitrary and meaningless charades. Newcomers might well experience ritual enactments in these terms, but this feeling often diminishes to the extent that others communicate their own sense of drama.

Religious commitments influence family rites partly by affecting the ways families enact rituals as part of their common life. Specific religious traditions influence the ritual practices of families in at least four major ways. These can be analyzed while reviewing some major differences between the Protestant, Catholic and Jewish families we interviewed.

First, religious traditions provide the basic repertoire of ritual scripts, which families can use, augment and amend as they fashion their own practices. Traditional Jewish and Catholic environments offer much fuller representations of seasonal and weekend rites than does the Protestant. Liberal Protestants and Reform Jews were most likely to either make up their own rituals or have no rituals at all to mark seasons, weekends or meals. Reconstructionist Jews, Catholics and Anglicans were most likely to treat their traditions as resources to be drawn upon, from time to time, without necessarily following them in detail.

Two, religious groups as organized communities encourage families to perform rituals and train them to do so competently and easily. Traditionally, both Christians and Jews have sent their children to religious classes after school or on weekends. And these classes have often been seen as opportunities to encourage greater religious observance by parents. When it comes to teaching parents, religious classes have been very effective in using seasonal ceremonies as the subject matter for class activities. Catholic families have been encouraged to fast on Fridays and Jewish ones to light candles on Friday evenings. In recent years, self-consciously Catholic education has declined, however, and self-consciously Jewish education increased. The results are worth noting: a decline in family ritual among Catholics and an increase among Jews.

Organized religious communities not only encourage greater use of traditional scripts for family rituals, however, they also train parents to participate comfortably. This is decisive. As they prepare for their bar mitzvahs or bat mitzvahs, for example, children are trained in language skills. Parents, too, are either trained or retrained as they help their children. A similar kind of training, at a more elementary level, is provided for Catholic second-graders as they prepare for first communion. Anglican and Catholic lay people typically make a virtue of learning the words to written liturgies. The same is true of men and some women in Jewish congregations. As a result, they use their prayer-books as references for their parts rather than scripts to be read. Because they have learned their scripts, Jews, Anglicans and Catholics are more likely than Protestants to appreciate them, gain a sense of drama from their enactment and use them to express their feelings.

Three, congregational rituals provide models for family rituals. The congregation presents images of how to treat ritual scripts. In Reconstructionist synagogues, men and women sit together. Together, they follow traditional rituals while trying to redefine their meanings in contemporary terms. Ritual scripts are seen as valued and honoured resources but ones that must be updated. Families are encouraged to construct their own ways of staging rituals for weekends, meals and even bar mitzvahs or bat mitzvahs. In Orthodox synagogues, on the other hand, men, women and children play quite different roles. Families are encouraged to maintain these differences. Family identity is closely connected with both the extended family and the congregation. Rituals are considered scripts to be learned and followed, not as resources or models to be modified.

It is interesting to contrast a Reform Jewish congregation and a Presbyterian one. In their congregational worship services, platform parties in both performed their ritual roles with great competence. The rabbi, the minister, the cantors, the choirs—all acted as skilled dramatis personae. Lay people were transformed into largely passive members of an audience. They came to assume that rituals were performed only by skilled actors, people who cannot be considered normative models for family life. They came to associate rituals with performances they watched rather than acted out for themselves. They assumed that normative expectations were primarily communicated discursively rather than by means of ritual drama.

Four, religion influences the character of family rituals by the ways theological messages direct the forms onto something other than family itself. When people engage in playing a game because they believe it is good or functional for them to do so, their play is not so much fun. It has become therapy. Playing is most fun when done for the sake of playing well. At times, this might involve winning. Always, however, it involves putting one's heart and mind fully into the game. The same can be said for family rituals; they are most fun (and most like drama) when people engage in them simply for the sake of doing them well.

Some theological arguments foster precisely this kind of attitude; others do not. If we are observing the Sabbath because God commands us to do so, we might do so in any of the following ways: (1) observing it, because it has always been done, but without much sense of drama or sport; (2) looking over our shoulder, as it were, and worrying so much about God's judgment that we forget our lines or only mouth them; (3) deciding to make up our own lines but leaving others to stumble, miss the cues or not know what to say; or (4) attempting to perform the script well, as something like a good game to be played in keeping with its rules and objectives. Traditionally, committed Christians and Jews have assumed this latter attitude and their rituals have acquired a sense of drama. This approach contrasts with the attitude of at least half the United Church families interviewed, who cited sociological and psychological explanations for why they went to church as families. There was much truth in their explanations. But the fact remained that they no longer experienced their rituals as dramas.

## Notes

1   These and other examples cited in this essay correspond to actual ritual practices among the approximately 45 families interviewed in the course of this research project.

2   I use possible ritual occasions rather than actual ritual practices as a reference because this allows me to analyze comparatively both the range and types of actual rituals affected by different religious traditions.

3   Both Hallowe'en and many children's birthdays have become not so much family as neighbourhood rituals, in which parents take turns in helping to sponsor activities involving groups of children.

# Glossary: Selected Terms

**Adom olam:** a hymn

**Alenu:** a hymn

**Aliya (aliyot):** the honour of "ascending" the platform (*bima*) to recite blessings over the reading of a section of the Torah scrolls; "ascending," or migrating to the land of Israel

**Amida:** the silent prayer said while "standing," then repeated by the cantor with the *kedusha* ("sanctus")

**Aninut:** the state of mourning between death and interment[1]

**Aron hakodesh:** the ark, or cupboard, containing the Torah scrolls

**Atara:** the collar of a *talit*

**Avel (avelim):** mourner(s)

**Avelut:** the period of mourning

**Ba'al tshuva:** someone who returns to Judaism

**Bar mitzvah:** a boy who comes of age (that is, takes on the adult responsibility for fulfilling the commandments); the ceremony marking this event

**Barku:** the call to prayer, which opens *shaharit* (morning prayers) as well as *ma'ariv* (evening prayers)

**Bet midrash:** the "house of study" (which has traditionally referred to one of the synagogue's primary functions)

**Bima:** the platform on which stand the *shulhan* (reading table) and *aron hakodesh* or *hekal* (ark containing the Torah scrolls) along with, in most contemporary synagogues, the rabbi's pulpit and a number of throne-like chairs for the rabbi, cantor(s) and several officers of the synagogue

**Birkot hashahar:** "blessings of the dawn" recited at the beginning of *shaharit* (morning prayers)

**Daven:** to pray

**En kelohenu:** a hymn

**Gabai:** liturgical coordinator

**Haftara (haftarot):** passage(s) from the Prophets usually chanted by knowledgeable congregants (or bar mitzvah boys) after the Torah reading

**Halaka (halakot):** rabbinic law(s)

**Haredi (haredut):** modern ultra-orthodox(y)

**Hazan (hazanim):** professional cantor(s)

**Hazan sheni:** "second," or assistant, cantor

**Hazanit:** a female cantor

**Hevra mishnayos:** Mishna study group

**Hevra shas:** Talmud study group

**Hekal:** the term sometimes used in a Sephardi synagogues for ark of the Torah scrolls (known in Ashkenazi synagogues as *aron hakodesh*)

**Kadish:** doxology (one version of which is recited in connection with mourning)

**Kavana:** intention, focus (usually with respect to prayer)

**Kedusha:** the "sanctus" said during the repetition of the *amida*

**Kehila:** community

**Kibbutz (kibbutzim):** cooperative agricultural settlement(s) in Israel

**Kidush:** the blessing over wine said to sanctify the Sabbath and festivals; often used to include the light meal or snack that accompanies this blessing when said at synagogue after the service

**Kipa (kipot):** skull-cap(s)

**Kriya:** rending of garments by mourners

**Ma'ariv:** daily liturgy for evening prayer

**Magen david:** the "shield of David" that is an emblem of Jews, Judaism and (by virtue of its appearance on the flag) of Israel

**Matbe'a tfila:** the basics of prayer

**Mazal (or mazel) tov:** congratulations (literally: "good luck")

**Mehitsa:** barrier dividing the seating areas of men and women in the synagogue

**Menora:** candelabrum used on Hanuka (and often found on both sides of the arks in synagogues)

**Minha:** daily liturgy for afternoon prayer

**Minhag:** custom, usage, conduct (as distinct from *halaka*)

**Minyan:** a quorum (10 men over the age of 13) required for a public worship (as distinct from private worship)

**Mitsva (mitsvot):** commandment(s)

**Musaf:** concluding part of a liturgy, including the "additional" *amida* that commemorates the additional sacrifices offered in the Temple on Sabbaths, festivals and new moons

**Ner tamid:** the "eternal light," a small, perpetually burning lamp suspended above and immediately in front of *aron hakodesh* or *hekal* (ark)

**Oneg shabat:** a reception, often following a Friday evening service, in honour of the Sabbath

**Onen (onenim):** mourner(s) during the interval between a relative's death and burial

**Psuke dezimra:** "hymns of praise" recited during morning prayers after *birkat hashahar* but before *shaharit* proper

**Parnas:** a lay officer of the synagogue who distributes various honours to congregants during the public liturgy and/or supervises the reading of the Torah scrolls

**Rav musmak:** an ordained rabbi

**Rosh yeshiva:** head of a rabbinical academy

**Seder:** a religious feast, having its own special liturgy, that is held at home on the first two nights of Passover

**Se'udat havra:** meal of condolence at the *shiva* house

**Shabat shalom:** Sabbath greeting

**Shaharit:** daily liturgy for morning prayer, which includes: the *barku* (call to prayer), *shma* (the "Hear O' Israel" with attendant blessings), *amida* (the silent prayer said while "standing") and (on Sabbaths, festivals, new moons, fasts, Mondays and Thursdays) the Torah reading

**Shaliah tzibur:** the one who leads public prayer, usually a lay member of the congregation rather than a *hazan* (professional cantor)

**Shamash:** the beadle

**Shavu'ot:** the festival of "weeks" commemorating the revelation at Mount Sinai (sometimes called the Jewish Pentecost)

**Shloshim:** the period of "30" days following burial

**Shma:** a focal point of morning and evening liturgies (and of personal prayer at bedtime) that begins with "Hear O Israel" and includes passages from Numbers and Deuteronomy along with attendant blessings

**Shtibl:** small synagogue

**Shmone esre:** part of the *amida* (the "18" benedictions)

**Shul:** Yiddish for synagogue

**Shulhan:** the "table" from which the *hazan* (cantor) or *shaliah tzibur* leads the service and on which the Torah scroll is placed to be read

**Sidur (sidurim):** the prayer-book(s) used during the liturgy

**Ste'emat hagolel:** burial, or "covering of the grave"

**Smika:** ordination

**Sukot:** autumn festival of "booths" or "tabernacles"

**Talit (talitot):** prayer-shawl(s)

**Tfilin:** small boxes strapped to the arm and head, each containing passages from scripture (often called "phylacteries" in English)

**Tisha B'av:** fast day on the ninth of Av to commemorate the destruction of both ancient Temples

**Trop:** melody, traditional cantillation

**Yeshiva (yeshivot):** rabbinical academy(ies)

**Yishuv:** pioneering settlement in Palestine

**Yom Ha'atzma'ut:** Israel's Independence Day

**Yom Hasho'a:** Holocaust Memorial Day

**Yortsait:** anniversary of a death

**Zimun:** a quorum (three men over the age of 13) permitting the public recitation of *birkat hamazon* (grace after meals)

# Note

1   Definitions for terms pertaining to funerary and mourning rites are adapted from Lamm (1969, 25-257).

# References

Abrahams, Israel
    1969    *Jewish Life in the Middle Ages.* 1896. Reprint, New York: Atheneum.

Abramson, Harold J.
    1980    Religion. In *Harvard Encyclopedia of American Ethnic Groups,* edited by S. Thernstrom et al. Cambridge, MA: Belknap Press.

Austin, John Langshaw
    1962    *How To Do Things With Words.* Cambridge: Harvard University Press.

Barth, Frederik, ed.
    1969    *Ethnic Groups and Boundaries: The Social Organization of Culture Difference.* Boston: Little, Brown.

Bellah, Robert Norbert
    1970    *Beyond Belief: Essays on Religion in a Post-traditional World.* New York: Harper & Row.

Bellah, Robert Norbert, et al.
    1991    *The Good Society.* New York: Knopf.

Berger, Peter
    1967    *The Sacred Canopy: Elements of a Sociological Theory of Religion.* Garden City, NY: Doubleday.

———, and Thomas Luckmann
    1984    *The Social Construction of Reality: A Treatise in the Sociology of Knowledge.* 1966. Reprint, New York: Anchor Books.

Bernstein, Basil
    1971    *Class, Codes, and Control,* vol. 1. London: Routledge and Kegan Paul.

Bird, Frederick B.
    1979    The Nature and Function of Ritual Forms: A Sociological Discussion. *Studies in Religion* 9, 1:387-402.

Blau, Joseph Leon
    1966    *Modern Varieties of Judaism.* Lectures on the History of Religions, n. s., vol. 8. New York: Columbia University Press.
    1976    *Judaism in America: From Curiosity to Third Faith.* Chicago History of American Religion. Chicago: University of Chicago Press.

[Borowitz, Eugene, ed.]
    1976    *Reform Judaism: A Centenary Perspective.* New York: Central Conference of American Rabbis, Ad Hoc Committee on the President's Message.

Bourguignon, Erika
    1974    Cross-Cultural Perspectives on the Religious Uses of Altered States of Consciousness. In *Religious Movements in Contemporary America*, edited by Irving I. Zaretsky and Mark P. Leone. Princeton: Princeton University Press.

Broadbar-Nemzer, Jay, et al.
    1993    An Overview of the Canadian Jewish Community. In *The Jews in Canada*, edited by Robert J.Brym, William Shaffir and Morton Weinfeld. Toronto: Oxford University Press.

Brym, Robert J.
    1993    The Rise and Decline of Canadian Jewry? A Socio-Demographic Profile. In *Canadian Jewry Today: Who's Who in Canadian Jewry*, edited by E. Lipsitz. Downsview, ON: JES Educational Products. 1989. Reprinted in *The Jews in Canada*, edited by Robert J.Brym, William Shaffir and Morton Weinfeld. Toronto: Oxford University Press.

———, William Shaffir, and Morton Weinfeld, eds.
    1993    *The Jews in Canada*. Toronto: Oxford University Press.

Bulka, Reuven P.
    1984    *The Coming Cataclysm: The Orthodox-Reform Rift and the Future of the Jewish People*. Oakville, ON: Mosaic Press.

Burkert, Walter
    1983    *Homo Necans: The Anthropology of Ancient Greek Sacrificial Ritual and Myth*. Translated by Peter Bing. Berkeley: University of California Press.

Castiglioni, Baldassarre
    1959    *The Book of the Courtier*. Translated by Charles S. Singleton. Garden City, NY: Doubleday.

Cohen, Steven M.
    1983    *American Modernity and Jewish Identity*. London: Tavistock.

———, and Calvin Goldscheider
    1984    Jews, More or Less. *Moment* 9, 8 (Sept. 1984)): 41-46.

Crossan, John Dominic
    1975    *The Dark Interval: Toward a Theology of Story*. Niles, IL: Argus Communications.

Dashefsky, Arnold, ed.
    1976    *Ethnic Identity in Society*. Chicago: Rand McNally.

Douglas, Mary
    1966    *Purity and Danger: An Analysis of Concepts of Pollution and Taboo*. London: Routledge and Kegan Paul.
    1970    *Natural Symbols: Explorations in Cosmology*. London: Barrie and Rockliff.
    1973    *Natural Symbols: Explorations in Cosmology*. 2d ed. London: Barrie and Jenkins.
    1975a    Deciphering a Meal. In *Implicit Meanings: Essays in Anthropology*. London: Routledge and Kegan Paul.

| | |
|---|---|
| 1975b | In the Nature of Things. In *Implicit Meanings: Essays in Anthropology*. London: Routledge and Kegan Paul. |
| 1975c | Self-evidence. In *Implicit Meanings: Essays in Anthropology*. London: Routledge and Kegan Paul. |
| 1978 | *Cultural Bias*. Occasional Papers of the Royal Anthropological Institute of Great Britain and Ireland, vol. 35. London: Royal Anthropological Society. |
| 1982a | The Effects of Modernization on Religious Change. *Daedalus* 111, 1:1-20. |
| 1982b | *In the Active Voice*. London: Routledge and Kegan Paul. |

———, ed.

1984   *Food in the Social Order: Studies of Food and Festivities in Three American Communities*. New York: Russell Sage Foundation.

Durkheim, Emile

1961   *The Elementary Forms of the Religious Life*. Translated by Joseph Ward Swain. 1915. Reprint, New York: Collier Books.

1964   *The Rules of Sociological Method*. 8th ed. Edited by George E. G. Catlin. Translated by Sarah A. Solovay and John H. Mueller. 1938. Reprint, New York: Free Press of Glencoe.

1974   *Sociology and Philosophy*. Translated by D. F. Pocock. London: Routledge & Kegan Paul, n.d. Reprint, New York: Free Press.

Edwards, Jonathan

1959   *The Religious Affections*. Works of Jonathan Edwards, edited by John E. Smith, vol 2. New Haven: Yale University Press.

Elazar, Daniel J.

1976   *Community and Polity: The Organization Dynamics of American Jewry*. Philadelphia: Jewish Publication Society.

———, and Harold M. Waller

1990   *Maintaining Consensus: The Canadian Jewish Polity in the Postwar World*. Lanthan, MD: University Press of America, and Jerusalem: Centre for Public Affairs.

Eliade, Mircea

1957   *Cosmos and History: The Myth of the Eternal Return*. Translated by Willard R. Trask. New York: Harper & Row.

Elias, Norbert

1978   *The Civilizing Process*. Translated by Edmund Jephcott. New York: Urizon Books.

Elinon, J., P. Haberman, and C. Cell

1967   *Ethnic and Educational Data on Adults in New York City, 1963-1964*. New York: Columbia University Press.

*Emet ve-emunah: Statement of Principles of Conservative Judaism.*

1988   New York: Jewish Theological Seminary of America; Rabbinical Assembly; United Synagogue of America; Women's League for Conservative Judaism; Federation of Jewish Men's Clubs.

Epstein, A. H.

n.d.   *Aruh Hashulhan*. Jerusalem: n. p.

Erikson, Erik
- 1977 *Toys and Reason: Stages in the Rationalization of Experience.* New York: Norton.

Fein, Leonard
- 1988 *Where Are We? The Inner Life of America's Jews.* New York: Harper & Row.

Feinstein, Moshe
- 1959-85 *Igrot Moshe.* New York: n. p.

Fingarette, Herbert
- 1971 *Confucius: The Secular as Sacred.* New York: Harper & Row.

Finkelstein, Louis
- 1977 Judaism as a System of Symbols. 1954. In *Conservative Judaism and Jewish Law*, edited by Seymour Siegel and Elliot Gertel. Studies in Conservative Jewish Thought, vol. 1. New York: Rabbinical Assembly; Ktav.

Fishbane, Simcha
- 1987 Contemporary Bar Mitzvah Rituals in Modern Orthodoxy. *Journal of Religion and Culture* 2, 1 (Fall): 166-189. Reprinted with minor revisions in chap. 10 of this volume.
- 1989 Jewish Mourning Rites: A Process of Resocialization. *Anthropologica* 31, 1:65-85.

Freedman, Maurice
- 1978 Social and Cultural Anthropology. Chap. 1 of *Main Trends in the Social and Human Sciences*, ed. Jacques Havet, pt. 2, vol. 1. New Babylon: Studies in the Social Sciences, vol. 21. The Hague: Mouton; UNESCO.

Freud, Sigmund
- 1950 *Totem and Taboo: Resemblances between the Psychic Lives of Savages and Neurotics.* Translated by James Strachey. 1918. Reprint, New York: Norton.
- 1973 *New Introductory Lectures on Psychoanalysis.* Translated by James Strachey. 1933. Reprint, Harmondsworth, Eng.: Penguin.

———, and Joseph Breuer
- 1974 *Studies in Hysteria.* Translated by James and Alix Strachey. [Original dates?]. Reprint, Harmondsworth, Eng.: Penguin.

Friedman, Menachem
- 1987 Life Tradition and Book Tradition in the Development of Ultraorthodox Judaism. In *Judaism Viewed from Within and from Without*, edited by Harvey E. Goldberg. Albany: State University of New York Press.

Furman, Frida
- 1987 *Beyond Yiddishkeit: The Construction of the American Jewish Identity.* Albany: State University of New York Press.

Gans, Herbert J.
- 1979 Symbolic Ethnicity: The Future of Ethnic Groups and Cultures in America. *Ethnic and Racial Studies* 2, 1 (1979): 1-20.

Ganzfried, Solomon
- 1961 *Code of Jewish Law: A Compilation of Jewish Laws and Customs.* Translated by Hyman E. Goldin. New York: Hebrew Publishing Company.

Geertz, Clifford
- 1966 Religion as a Cultural System. In *Anthropological Approaches to the Study of Religion*, edited by Michael Banton. London: Tavistock.
- 1973 *The Interpretation of Cultures: Selected Essays.* New York: Basic Books.

Ginzberg, Louis
- 1977 Zechariah Frankel: Positive-historical Judaism. 1938. In *Conservative Judaism and Jewish Law*, edited by Seymour Siegel and Elliot Gertel. Studies in Conservative Jewish Thought, vol. 1. New York: Rabbinical Assembly; Ktav.

Girard, Rene
- 1977 *Violence and the Sacred.* Translated by Patrick Gregory. Baltimore: Johns Hopkins University Press.

Glazer, Nathan, and Daniel Moynihan
- 1970 *Beyond The Melting Pot: The Negroes, Puerto Ricans, Jews and Italians of New York City.* 1963. Reprint, Cambridge: MIT Press.

Goffman, Erving
- 1963 *Behavior in Public Places: Notes on the Social Organization of Gatherings.* New York: Free Press of Glencoe.
- 1967 *Interaction Ritual: Essays on Face-to-face Behavior.* Garden City, NY: Anchor Books.
- 1969 *Strategic Interaction.* Philadelphia: University of Pennsylvania Press.

Goldscheider, Calvin
- 1986a *The American Jewish Community: Social Science Research and Policy Implications.* Atlanta: Scholars Press.
- 1986b *Jewish Continuity and Change: Emerging Patterns in America.* Bloomington: Indiana University Press.

——, and Alan Zuckerman
- 1984 *The Transformation of the Jews.* Chicago: University of Chicago Press.

Goldstein, Sidney, and Calvin Goldscheider
- 1968 *Jewish Americans: Three Generations in a Jewish Community.* Englewood Cliffs, NJ: Prentice-Hall.

Goodman, Felicitas D.
- 1972 *Speaking in Tongues: A Cross-cultural Study of Glossolalia.* Chicago: University of Chicago Press.

Gordis, Robert
- 1978 *Understanding Conservative Judaism.* Edited by Max Gelb. New York: Rabbinical Assembly.

Gouldner, Alvin
    1960      The Norm of Reciprocity. *American Sociological Review* 25, no. 2:161-178 (April).
Grimes, Ronald L.
    1990      *Ritual Criticism*. Columbia: University of South Carolina Press.
    1992      Reinventing Ritual. *Soundings* 75, 1:21-41.
Gurock, Jeffrey S.
    1987      The Orthodox Synagogue. In *The American Synagogue, A Sanctuary Transformed*, edited by Jack Wertheimer. Cambridge, Eng.: Cambridge University Press.
Habermas, Jürgen
    1984      *The Theory of Communicative Action*. Translated by Thomas McCarthy. Boston: Beacon Press.
    1990      *Moral Consciousness and Communicative Action*. Translated by Christian Lenhardt and Shierry Weber Nicholsen. Studies in Contemporary German Social Thought. Cambridge: MIT Press.
Hammond, Phillip E.
    1988      Religion and the Persistence of Identity. *Journal for the Scientific Study of Religion* 27, 1 (March):1-12.
Handlin, Oscar
    1973      *The Uprooted*. 2d ed. Boston: Little, Brown.
Harrington, Michael
    1962      *The Other America: Poverty in the United States*. New York: Macmillan Company.
Hayes, Richard
    1992      Ritual, Self-deception and Make-Believe: A Classical Buddhist Perspective. Paper presented at the Conference on Self and Deception, called by the East-West Center, at University of Hawaii, Honolulu, 23-29 August 1992.
Heilman, Samuel C.
    1976      *Synagogue Life: A Study in Symbolic Interaction*. Chicago: University of Chicago Press.
    1983      *The People of the Book: Drama, Fellowship and Religion*. Chicago: University of Chicago Press.
——, and Steven M. Cohen
    1989      *Cosmopolitans and Parochials: Modern Orthodox Jews in America*. Chicago and London: University of Chicago Press.
Helmreich, William B.
    1982      *The World of the Yeshiva: An Intimate Portrait of Orthodox Jewry*. London: Collier Macmillan.
Hertz, Robert
    1960      A Contribution to the Collective Representation of Death. 1907. In *Death and the Right Hand*, edited by Rodney and Claudia Needham. Glencoe, IL: Free Press.

Hirschberg, Jack
    1988    Secular and Parochial Education of Ashkenazi and Sephardi Jewish Children in Montreal: A Study in Ethnicity. PhD. diss., Faculty of Education, McGill University, Montreal.

Huntington, Richard, and Peter Metcalf
    1979    *Celebrations of Death: The Anthropology of Mortuary Rituals.* Cambridge: Cambridge University Press.

James, William
    1961    *The Varieties of Religious Experience: A Study in Human Nature.* 1902. Reprint, New York: Collier Books.

Jay, Nancy
    1992    *Throughout Your Generations Forever: Sacrifice, Religion and Paternity.* Chicago: University of Chicago Press.

Jick, Leon A.
    1987    The Reform Synagogue. In *The American Synagogue, A Sanctuary Transformed,* edited by Jack Wertheimer. Cambridge, Eng.: Cambridge University Press.

Kallen, Evelyn
    1977    *Spanning the Generations: A Study of Jewish Identity.* Canadian Social Problems Series. Toronto: Longmans Canada.

Kaplan, Mordecai
    1960    *The Greater Judaism in the Making, A Study of the Modern Evolution of Judaism.* New York: Reconstructionist Press.
    1967    *Judaism as a Civilization: Toward a Reconstruction of American-Jewish Life.* 1935. Reprint, New York: Schocken.

Katz, Jacob
    1971    *Tradition and Crisis: Jewish Society at the End of the Middle Ages.* New York: Free Press of Glencoe, 1961. Reprint, New York: Schocken.

Kliger, Hannah
    1988    A Home Away from Home: Participation in Jewish Immigrant Associations in America. In *Persistence and Flexibility: Anthropological Perspectives on the American Jewish Experience,* edited by Walter P. Zenner. Albany: State University of New York Press.

Krentzman, Meir
    1986    *Jewish Laws and Customs and Mourning.* Montreal: Kehila Consultants.

Kugelmas, Jack, ed.
    1988    *Between Two Worlds: Ethnographic Essays on American Jewry.* Ithaca, NY: Cornell University Press.

Lamm, Maurice
    1969    *The Jewish Way in Death and Mourning.* New York: Jonathan David.

Leach, Edmund Ronald
    1976    *Culture and Communication: The Logic by which Symbols Are Connected: An Introduction to the Use of Structural Analysis in*

*Social Anthropology*. Themes in the Social Sciences. Cambridge: Cambridge University Press.

Levine, Aaron
 1985 *Sefer Zichron Meir on Aveilus*. Vol. 1. Toronto: A Levine, Zichron Meir Publications.

Lévi-Strauss, Claude
 1958 *Anthropologie structurale*. Paris: Plon.
 1979a The Structural Study of Myth. *Journal of American Folklore* 67 (1955): 428-444. Reprinted in *Reader in Comparative Religion*, edited by William A. Lessa and Evon Z. Vogt, 185-197. 4th ed. New York: Harper & Row.
 1979b The Effectiveness of Symbols. In *Structural Anthropology*, translated by Claire Jacobson and Brook Grundfest Scheepf. New York: Basic Books, 1963. Reprinted in *Reader in Comparative Religion*, edited by William A. Lessa and Evon Z. Vogt, 318-327. 4th ed. New York: Harper & Row.

Liebman, Charles S.
 1965 *Aspects of the Religious Behavior of American Jews*. New York: Ktav.
 1973 *The Ambivalent American Jew: Politics, Religion and Family in American Jewish Life*. Philadelphia: Jewish Publication Society of America.
 1975 A Sociological Analysis of Contemporary Orthodoxy. Judaism 13 (1964): 285-304. Reprinted in *Understanding American Judaism: Toward the Description of a Modern Religion. Vol. 2. Sectors of American Judaism: Reform, Orthodox, Conservative and Reconstructionism*, edited by Jacob Neusner. New York: Ktav.
 1988 *Deceptive Images: Toward a Redefinition of American Judaism*. New Brunswick, NJ and Oxford. Transaction Books.

Lightstone, Jack N.
 1986 Mythe, rituels et institutions de la religion civile de la communauté juive canadienne. In *Religion et culture au Québec: figures contemporaines du sacré*, edited by Y. Desrosiers et al. Montréal: Fides. With minor revisions, appearing in English for the first time in chapter three of this volume.
 1988 Ritual, Reality and Contemporary Society. *Journal of Ritual Studies* 2, 2: 195-216.

Luckmann, Thomas
 1967 *The Invisible Religion: The Problem of Religion in Modern Society*. New York: Macmillan.

Mack, Burton
 1987 Religion and Ritual. Introduction to *Violent Origins: Walter Burkert, René Girard and Jonathan Z. Smith on Ritual Killing and Cultural Formation*, edited by Robert G. Hamerton-Kelly. Stanford, CA: Stanford University Press.

Marty, Martin E.
　1984　　*Pilgrims in Their Own Land: Five Hundred Years of Religion in America*. Boston: Little, Brown.

Mauss, Marcel
　1967　　*The Gift: Forms and Functions of Exchange in Archaic Societies*. Translated by Ian Cunnison. London: n. p., 1954. Reprint, New York: Norton.

Mcbrearty, Madeleine
　1987　　The Uses of Non-vernacular Language in the Sabbath Morning Services of a Reconstructionist Synagogue. *Journal of Religion and Culture* 2, 1: 202-15. Revised version printed in chap. 5 of this volume.

Merton, Robert King
　1957　　*Social Theory and Social Structure*. Rev. and enl. ed. Glencoe, IL.: Free Press.

Morgan, Thomas B.
　1964a　A Threat to Survival. *Time*, 17 January, 41.
　1964b　The Vanishing American Jews. *Look*, May, 42-46.

Murphy, Robert Francis
　1971　　*The Dialectics of Social Life, Alarms and Excursions in Anthropological Theory*. New York: Basic Books.

Neusner, Jacob
　1965-69　*A History of the Jews in Babylonia*. 5 vols. Studia Post-Biblica, vol. 9. Leiden: Brill.
　1972　　*American Judaism: Adventure in Modernity*. Englewood Cliffs, NJ: Prentice-Hall.
　1981a　*Judaism: The Evidence of the Mishnah*. Chicago: University of Chicago Press.
　1981b　*Stranger at Home: "The Holocaust," Zionism and American Judaism*. Chicago: University of Chicago Press.
　1984　　*Torah in Context*. Philadelphia: Fortress Press.
　1987　　*The Death and Birth of Judaism: The Impact of Christianity, Secularism, and the Holocaust on Jewish Faith*. New York: Basic Books.

——, ed.
　1975　　*Understanding American Judaism: Toward the Description of a Modern Religion*. 2 vols. New York: Ktav; Anti-Defamation League.

Petuchowski, Jacob
　1975　　The Limits of Liberal Judaism. *Judaism* 14 (1965):146-58. Reprinted in *Understanding American Judaism: Toward the Description of a Modern Religion*. Vol. 2. *Sectors of American Judaism: Reform, Orthodox, Conservative and Reconstructionism*, edited by Jacob Neusner. New York: Ktav.

Prell, Riv-Ellen
   1987     Sacred Categories and Social Relations: The Visibility and Invisibility of Gender in the American Jewish Community. In *Judaism as Viewed from Within and from Without: Anthropological Studies*, edited by Harvey E. Goldberg. Albany: State University of New York Press.
   1989     *Prayer and Community: The Havurah in American Judaism.* Detroit: Wayne State University Press.

Radcliffe-Brown, Alfred Reginald
   1952     Religion and Society. In *Structure and Function in Primitive Society: Essays and Addresses*. London: Cohen and West.
   1979     *Taboo.* Frazer Lectures. 1939. Reprinted in *Reader in Comparative Religion*, edited by William A. Lessa and Evon Z. Vogt, 46-56. 4th ed. New York: Harper & Row.

Raphael, Marc Lee
   1984     *Profiles in American Judaism: The Reform, Conservative, Orthodox, and Reconstructionist Traditions in Historical Perspective.* San Francisco: Harper & Row.

Rappaport, Roy A.
   1971     Ritual, Sanctity and Cybernetics. *American Anthropologist* 73: 59-76.

Routtenberg, Max J.
   1973     *Decades of Decision, An Appraisal of American Jewish Life.* New York: Bloch.

Schechter, S. Solomon
   1945     *Studies in Judaism: Third Series.* 1896. Reprint, Philadelphia: Jewish Publication Society of America.

Scheff, Thomas J.
   1977     The Distancing of Emotions in Rituals. *Cultural Anthropology* 18, 3: 483-89.

Scherman, Nosson, ed.
   1955     *Shulhan Aruh, Yoreh De'ah.* Jerusalem: Mahon Hatam Sofer.
   1984     *The Complete Art Scroll Siddur: Weekday, Sabbath, Festival: Nusach Ashkenaz: A New and Anthologized Commentary.* New York: Mesorah Press.

Schoem, David
   1988     Learning to be a Part-Time Jew. In *Persistence and Flexibility: Anthropological Perspectives on the American Jewish Experience*, edited by Walter P. Zenner. Albany: State University of New York Press.

Schoenfeld, Stuart
   1981     Canadian Judaism Today. In *The Canadian Jewish Mosaic*, edited by Morton Weinfeld, William Shaffir and Irwin Cotler. Toronto: Wiley.
   1988     Integration into the Group and Sacred Uniqueness: Analysis of an Adult Bar Mitzvah. In *Persistence and Flexibility: Anthropological*

*Perspectives on the American Jewish Experience*, edited by Walter P. Zenner. Albany: State University of New York Press.

1990 Some Aspects of the Social Significance of Bar/Bat Mitzvah Celebrations. In *Essays in the Social Scientific Study of Judaism and Jewish Society*, edited by Simcha Fishbane and Jack N. Lightstone. Montreal: Department of Religion, Concordia University.

1992 Ritual and Role Transition: Adult Bat Mitzvah as a Successful Rite of Passage. In *The Uses of Tradition: Jewish Continuity in the Modern Era*, edited by Jack Wertheimer. New York and Jerusalem: The Jewish Theological Seminary of America.

Schwartz, Paul
1977 Testimonial Speech and Self-image: An Analysis of the Testimonial Ritual in New Religious Groups. Master's thesis, Concordia University, Montreal.

Searle, John R.
1969 *Speech Acts: An Essay in the Philosophy of Language*. London: Cambridge University Press.

Siegel, Seymour, ed.
1977 *Conservative Judaism and Jewish Law*. New York: Rabbinical Assembly.

Silverman, Myrna
1988 Family, Kinship, and Ethnicity: Strategies for Social Mobility: In *Persistence and Flexibility: Anthropological Perspectives on the American Jewish Experience*, edited by Walter P. Zenner. Albany: State University of New York Press.

Sklare, Marshall
1971 *America's Jews*. Ethnic Groups in Comparative Perspective. New York: Random House.
1972 *Conservative Judaism, An American Religious Movement*. New and augmented edition. New York: Schocken.

Taras, David, and Morton Weinfeld
1993 Continuity and Criticism: North American Jews and Israel. *International Journal*. Canadian Institute of International Affairs. Summer 1990. Reprinted in *The Jews in Canada*, edited by Robert J. Brym, William Shaffir and Morton Weinfeld. Toronto: Oxford University Press.

Tambiah, Stanley Jeyaraja
1979 A Performative Approach to Ritual. *Proceedings of the British Academy*, vol. 65. London: Oxford University Press.

Tillich, Paul
1957 *Dynamics of Faith*. Planned and edited by Ruth Nanda Anshen. World Perspectives, vol. 10. New York: Harper.

Titmuss, Richard Morris
1970 *The Gift Relationship: From Human Blood to Social Policy*. London: Allen and Unwin.

Turner, Victor W.
    1964    Betwixt and Between: The Liminal Period in Rites de Passage. In *Reader in Comparative Religion: An Anthropological Approach*, ed. William A. Lessa and Evon Z. Vogt. 3rd ed. New York: Harper & Row, 1972. Originally in *Proceedings of the American Ethnological Society*. Symposium on New Approaches to the Study of Religion. Seattle: American Ethnological Society; University of Washington Press, 1964.
    1974    *Dramas, Fields and Metaphors: Symbolic Action in Human Society. Symbol, Myth, and Ritual*. Ithaca, NY: Cornell University Press.
    1977    *The Ritual Process: Structure and Anti-structure*. Chicago: Aldine Press, 1969. Reprint, Ithaca, NY: Cornell University Press, 1977.

Tzokensiki, N. A.
    1980    *Gesher Hahayim*. Jerusalem: Solomon Printing.

van Gennep, Arnold
    1960    *The Rites of Passage*. Translated by Monika B. Vizedom and Gabrielle L. Caffee. Chicago: University of Chicago Press.

Waller, Harold M.
    1981a    A Re-examination of Zionism in Canada. In *The Canadian Jewish Mosaic*, edited by Morton Weinfeld, William Shaffir and Irwin Cotler. Toronto: Wiley.
    1981b    Power in the Jewish Community. In *The Canadian Jewish Mosaic*, edited by Morton Weinfeld, William Shaffir and Irwin Cotler. Toronto: Wiley.
    1993    The Canadian Jewish Polity: Power and Leadership in the Jewish Community. In *The Jews in Canada*, edited by Robert J. Brym, William Shaffir and Morton Weinfeld. Toronto: Oxford University Press.

Weber, Max
    1978    *Economy and Society: An Outline of Interpretive Sociology*. Based on 4th German edition. 1956, revised 1964. Edited by Guenther Roth and Claus Wittich. 2 vols. Berkeley: University of California Press.

Weinfeld, Morton
    1981    Intermarriage: Agony and Adaptation. In *The Canadian Jewish Mosaic*, edited by Morton Weinfeld, William Shaffir and Irwin Cotler. Toronto: Wiley.

Welch, Holmes
    1967    *The Practice of Chinese Buddhism*. Harvard East Asian Series, vol. 26. Cambridge: Harvard University Press.

Wertheimer, Jack
    1987    The Conservative Synagogue. In *The American Synagogue, A Sanctuary Transformed*, edited by Jack Wertheimer. Cambridge, Eng.: Cambridge University Press.
    1993    *A People Divided: Judaism in Contemporary America*. New York: Basic Books.

Westley, Frances
   1978      Searching for Surrender: A Catholic Charismatic Renewal Group's Attempt to Become Glossolalic. *American Behavioral Scientist* 20, 6 (July-August 1977): 925-40.

Wilson, Bryan R.
   1969      *Religion in Secular Society*. 1966. Reprint, Harmondsworth, Eng.: Penguin, 1969.

Woocher, Jonathan S.
   1986      *Sacred Survival: The Civil Religion of American Jews*. Bloomington and Indianapolis: Indiana University Press.

Wuthnow, Robert
   1987      *Meaning and Moral Order: Explorations in Cultural Analysis*. Berkeley: University of California Press.

Zborowski, Mark, and Elizabeth Herzog
   1952      *Life is with People: The Culture of the Shtetl*. New York Schocken Books.

Zenner, Walter P., and Janet S. Belcove-Shalin
   1988      The Cultural Anthropology of American Jewry. In *Persistence and Flexibility: Anthropological Perspectives on the American Jewish Experience*, edited by Walter P. Zenner. Albany: State University of New York Press.

# Index

Abelson, Kassel, 148
Abraham Ibn Daud, 55
Abrahams, Israel, 157
Abramson, Harold J., 112
Acculturation, 109-10
*Adon olam*, 76, 86
Afternoon prayers: *see Minha*
*Alenu*, 76, 102
Aliya, 7; in Conservative Judaism, 138, 141, 147; in Orthodox Judaism, 161, 166; in Orthodox Judaism (Sephardim), 113, 114, 116-17, 121-22n. 17; in Orthodox Judaism (*shtibl*), 129; Reconstructionist Judaism, 74, 87, 88n. 5; in Reform Judaism, 104
*Aliya* (Israel): *see* Israel
*Amida*: in Conservative Judaism, 138, 140, 143; in Orthodox Judaism, 72; in Orthodox Judaism (Sephardim), 116; in Orthodox Judaism (*shtibl*), 124, 129; in Reconstructionist Judaism, 73, 74, 79, 84, 86
*Aninut*, 173, 174, 175, 176, 178
Anti-Semitism, 59, 86, 98, 118
Aramaic, 35, 84
Architecture: in Conservative Judaism, 84, 137; in Orthodox Judaism, 84, 125, 159; in Orthodox Judaism (Sephardim), 113, 118; in Orthodox Judaism (*shtibl*), 123, 126; in Reconstructionist Judaism, 20, 69-71, 78, 79, 84; in Reform Judaism, 17, 95, 111-12
Ark, 5; in Conservative Judaism, 137, 141, 142; in Orthodox Judaism, 160, 162, 163, 164; in Orthodox Judaism (Sephardim), 113, 115, 116, 120; in Orthodox Judaism (*shtibl*), 13, 126; in Reconstructionist Judaism, 21, 70, 78, 79, 85; in Reform Judaism, 17, 18, 95, 101
*Aron hakodesh: see* Ark
*Aruk Hashulhan*, 184n. 2
Ashkenazim, 62n. 1, 116, 121n. 15
Assimilation, 53, 59, 109-10; in Orthodox Judaism (Sephardim), 120; in Reconstructionist Judaism, 79; in Reform Judaism, 97
*Atara*, 72
Austin, John Langshaw, 43, 48-49, 50
Authority: in Conservative Judaism, 143, 144, 146-47, 150, 151, 152; in Orthodox Judaism, 177, 179
*Avelut*, 173, 175
*Avot derabi Natan*, 55

*Ba'al tshuva*, 66
Bar mitzvah, 22, 38, 39, 43, 189, 190; in Conservative Judaism, 138, 139, 141, 142, 143; in Orthodox Judaism, 155-57, 166, 167n. 1; in Orthodox Judaism (Sephardim), 121-22n. 8, 121-122 n. 13, 121-22n. 17, 122 n.27; phase 1 (separation), 160-61; phase 2 (transition), 161-62; phase 3 (incorporation), 162-64; in Reconstructionist Judaism, 73, 86
Barth, Frederik, 121n. 4
Bat mitzvah, 38, 39, 189, 190; in Conservative Judaism, 138, 139,

141, 143; in Reconstructionist Judaism, 73, 86
Belcove-Shalin, J. S., 22 n.2
Bellah, Robert Norbert, 39
Berger, Peter, 121 n. 1, 124, 130-32, 169, 184
Bernstein, Basil, 25, 32, 77, 79, 81, 82 n. 4
*Bet midrash*, 13, 14
*Bima*: in Conservative Judaism, 137, 141; in Orthodox Judaism, 71, 160, 162; in Orthodox Judaism (Sephardim), 113, 115, 117, 119, 120; in Orthodox Judaism (*shtibl*), 125; in Reconstructionist Judaism, 70, 73-74, 78, 85, 87; in Reform Judaism, 17, 18
Bird, Frederick B., 31, 81, 101, 111, 167n. 13, 169, 183n. 1, 184n. 10
*Birkot hashahar: see* Blessings
Blessing, 36-37
Blessings: in Conservative Judaism, 139; in Orthodox Judaism, 161, 162, 164; in Orthodox Judaism (Sephardim), 117; in Reconstructionist Judaism, 74, 87
Booths: *see* Sukot
Borowitz, Eugene, 102, 103
Boundaries, Social, 10-11, 78, 84, 85-86, 118-20
Bourguignon, Erika, 46
*Brahot: see* Blessings
Breuer, Joseph, 32
*Brit mila: see* Circumcision
Broadbar-Nemzer, Jay, 53, 56, 62n.1
Brym, Robert J., 53, 62n. 1
Burial: *see Ste'emat hagolel*
Burkert, Walter, 34

Canadian Zionist Federation, 61
Candles, Sabbath, 96, 99, 191-92
Cantor: *see Hazan*; *Hazanit*
Caste, 20, 73-74, 77, 78, 79, 116
Castiglioni, Baldassarre, 24
Cell, C., 56

Central Conference of American Rabbis, 102
Children, 188-89; in Orthodox Judaism, 71, 158, 159, 184n. 11; in Orthodox Judaism (*shtibl*), 128; in Reconstructionist Judaism, 71, 73; in Reform Judaism, 101
Choir: *see* Music
Chosen people: *see* Peoplehood, Chosen
Christians: *see* Gentiles
Circumcision, 38, 39
Civil religion, 53-62
Class: in Orthodox Judaism, 169; in Orthodox Judaism (Sephardim), 110; in Orthodox Judaism (*shtibl*), 12, 15; in Reconstructionist Judaism, 20, 21-22, 77, 78, 80, 86
Clergy, 18, 19, 99, 103, 104
Cohen, Steven M., 53, 56, 62 n. 1, 65, 109
Combined Jewish Appeal, 60
Communication: *see* Ritual
Community centre, 68-69, 151
Congregation: *see* Synagogue
Conservative Judaism, 68-69, 135-52; and Orthodox Judaism, 91, 97, 140, 144, 147; and Orthodox Judaism (Sephardim), 120; and Reconstructionist Judaism, 83; and Reform Judaism, 140
Custom: *see Minhag*

Day of Atonement, 56, 188
Decorum: in Conservative Judaism, 74, 86, 139-40, 142, 143, 144; in Orthodox Judaism, 72, 75, 86; in Orthodox Judaism (Sephardim), 116; in Orthodox Judaism (*shtibl*), 125; in Reconstructionist Judaism, 74, 86; in Reform Judaism, 100
Democracy, 47, 152
Dietary laws, 16, 56, 159, 185

Douglas, Mary, 11, 32, 38, 40, 49, 54, 65, 66, 67, 77, 81, 82, 111, 155, 156, 164, 165, 167n. 11, 167n. 13, 169, 170, 171, 175, 183, 184n. 4, 184n. 9, 186
Dress, 56; in Orthodox Judaism, 72, 162, 167 n. 8, 173-74; in Orthodox Judaism (Sephardim), 114, 115, 119, 121n. 11; in Orthodox Judaism (*shtibl*), 13, 14, 123-24, 126, 127, 128, 129, 130, 132; in Reconstructionist Judaism, 73, 78-79; in Reform Judaism, 96, 99
Durkheim, Emile, 26, 27, 37, 38, 45, 49, 54, 68, 83, 90, 111, 155, 165, 169, 182, 192

Education, 76, 159, 160, 163, 165, 194
Edwards, Jonathan, 46
Egalitarianism, 21, 77
Eliade, Mircea, 25
Elias, Norbert, 24
Elijah of Vilna, 157
Elinon, J., 56
*Emet ve'emuna*, 135, 148, 150
*En kelohenu*, 76
English: *see* Vernacular
Erikson, Erik, 43
Eternal flame: *see Ner tamid*
*Ets hayim hi*, 142
*Even Ha'ezer*, 158
Evening prayers: *see Ma'ariv*

Family, 29, 39, 180-81, 185-95; and festivals, 188, 194; and identity, 189; and liturgy, 19; in Orthodox Judaism, 159, 160, 161, 162, 163, 164, 166, 172-73, 175, 180-81, 181-82, 184n. 11; and peoplehood, 59; and ritual, 185-95; and Sabbath, 56, 59; in Reconstructionist Judaism, 187; in Reform Judaism, 19, 103
Father, 161, 162, 163

Feinstein, Moses, 79, 121n. 7
Fingarette, Herbert, 33
Finkelstein, Louis, 148, 149
Fishbane, Simcha, 184n. 3, 190
Food: *see Kidush; Ritual; Seder; Shiva*
Frankel, Zacharias, 147, 152
French: *see* Vernacular
Freud, Sigmund, 32, 33, 34, 44, 45
Friedman, Menachem, 124, 132
Funeral, 173-75
Furman, Frida, 18

*Gabai*, 141
Gans, Herbert J., 109, 121n. 6
Geertz, Clifford, 11, 30, 32, 54, 81, 89, 90, 91, 102, 111
Gender, 5, 7, 192, 194; in Conservative Judaism, 138, 141, 144, 146, 147; in Orthodox Judaism, 17, 71, 72, 159, 160, 162, 164, 166, 167 n. 8, 175, 176, 181, 194; in Orthodox Judaism (Sephardim), 113, 115, 116, 119, 121n. 12, 121n. 13, 122n. 18, 122n. 26, 122n. 27; in Orthodox Judaism (*shtibl*), 13, 14, 125, 126, 127-28; in Reconstructionist Judaism, 20, 71, 73, 77, 78, 80n. 2, 83, 87; in Reform Judaism, 16, 66, 99
Gentiles: in Conservative Judaism, 144; in Orthodox Judaism (Sephardim), 118, 120, 122n. 22, 122n. 23; in Orthodox Judaism (*shtibl*), 13, 14-15; in Reconstructionist Judaism, 20, 22, 79, 85; in Reform Judaism, 19, 92, 98, 99-100, 104
Ginzberg, Louis, 152n.1
Girard, René, 34, 49
Glazer, Nathan, 110
God, 29, 39-40, 48, 57, 61-62, 180; in Conservative Judaism), 144, 147-50; in Orthodox Judaism, 175, 176, 177, 180; in

Reconstructionist Judaism, 68, 83-84
Goffman, Erving, 24, 27, 33
Goldscheider, Calvin, 53, 56, 62n. 1, 184n. 5
Goldstein, Sidney, 53, 62n. 1
Goodman, Felicitas D., 48
Gouldner, Alvin, 39
Grimes, Ronald L., 27, 43, 44
Gurock, Jeffrey S., 22n.2

Haberman, P., 56
Habermas, Jürgen, 25, 26
Hafets Haim: see Kagan, Israel Meyer Hacohen
*Haftara*: in Conservative Judaism, 138, 141, 142, 144; in Orthodox Judaism, 159, 160, 163; in Orthodox Judaism (Sephardim), 114, 116; in Reconstructionist Judaism, 73, 74, 84, 86; in Reform Judaism, 99, 101
*Halaka*, 56, 57, 157-158; in Orthodox Judaism (*shtibl*), 15, 16, 124, 129, 132, 169, 171, 173-75; in Reconstructionist Judaism, 86; in Reform Judaism, 66
Hammond, Phillip E., 110
Handlin, Oscar, 55
Handshaking, 117, 122n. 20
Hanuka, 56, 188, 192
Haredim, 124
Harrington, Michael, 53
Hasidim, 57
*Havadala*, 160
Hayes, Richard, 27, 43
*Hazan*: in Conservative Judaism, 137, 138, 141, 143-44; in Orthodox Judaism, 125, 159, 163, 177, 178, 180, 183; in Orthodox Judaism (Sephardim), 113, 114, 116, 117, 121n. 10, 121n. 11; in Orthodox Judaism (*shtibl*), 13, 124, 129; in Reconstructionist Judaism, 71, 73, 86
*Hazanit*, 16, 95, 96, 98-99, 101, 103

Hebrew, 60
Hebrew: in Conservative Judaism, 138, 139, 140, 142, 143, 150; in Orthodox Judaism, 125; in Orthodox Judaism (Sephardim), 117, 118, 119, 122n. 18; in Orthodox Judaism (*shtibl*), 124; in Reconstructionist Judaism, 69, 73, 75, 78, 81-82; in Reform Judaism, 95, 97, 98, 103
Hebrew Union College-Jewish Institute of Religion, 66
Heilman, Samuel C., 4, 27-28, 124, 130, 132, 156
*Hekal:* see Ark
Helmreich, William B., 124, 130
Hertz, Robert, 169-70, 175
Herzog, Elizabeth, 109, 158
*Hevra mishnayos*, 15
*Hevra shas*, 15
Hirschberg, Jack, 184n. 11
Holocaust, 57-59, 101, 143
Holocaust Memorial Day: see Yom Hasho'a
Home, 29, 30; in Orthodox Judaism, 176-77, 178; in Reform Judaism, 18, 19, 99
Huntington, Richard, 184 n. 8

Identity, 53-62, 110-12, 189; and anti-Semitism, 59; in Conservative Judaism, 150, 152, 165-66; and family, 189; in Orthodox Judaism), 165, 166-67, 182; in Orthodox Judaism (Sephardim), 118, 120, 122n. 24, 122n. 28; in Orthodox Judaism (*shtibl*), 130-33; in Reconstructionist Judaism, 22, 80, 85; in Reform Judaism, 18, 103; and ritual, 189
Individualism, 103, 104
Intermarriage, 53, 56, 58, 62n.1; among Ashkenazim, 62n. 1; in Orthodox Judaism (Sephardim), 62n. 1; in Reconstructionist Ju-

daism, 75, 85; in Reform Judaism, 19, 92, 104
Israel, 57-59, 61; in Conservative Judaism, 142, 144; in Orthodox Judaism, 164; in Orthodox Judaism (Sephardim), 122n. 21; in Reconstructionist Judaism, 75; in Reform Judaism, 101
Israel Independence Day: *see* Yom Ha'atzma'ut
Isserles, Moses, 157, 158

James, William, 29, 38
Jay, Nancy, 30, 34, 48, 49
Jewish Theological Seminary of America, 68
Jick, Leon, 22n. 2
Judaism, Rabbinic, 15, 54-58, 62, 164, 165, 167n. 4, 167n. 10, 167n. 11, 169-84, 172

*Kadish*, 35, 36; in Conservative Judaism, 140; in Orthodox Judaism, 166, 171, 175-76, 177, 178, 180-81, 182, 183; in Orthodox Judaism (Sephardim), 117; in Reconstructionist Judaism, 73, 76, 84; in Reform Judaism, 17, 102
*Kaf Hahayim*, 158
Kagan, Israel Meyer Hacohen, 124
Kallen, Evelyn, 53, 56
Kaplan, Mordecai, 68-69, 83, 85
Karo, Joseph, 157
*Kashrut: see* Dietary laws
Katz, Jacob, 55
*Kedusha*, 72, 73, 74, 79, 116
*Ketav Sofer*, 158
*Kibutz*, 59
*Kidush* 38, 43; in Conservative Judaism, 145; in Orthodox Judaism, 158, 161, 164; in Orthodox Judaism (Sephardim), 114, 117-18, 121n. 9; in Reconstructionist Judaism, 67, 70, 76, 84; in Reform Judaism, 96, 102

*Kipa*: in Conservative Judaism, 138; in Orthodox Judaism, 162, 166; in Orthodox Judaism (Sephardim), 114, 115, 121-22n. 17; in Orthodox Judaism (*shtibl*), 14, 72, 124, 127, 128, 132; in Reconstructionist Judaism, 66, 73; in Reform Judaism, 96, 99
Krentzman, Meir, 178, 179, 181
*Kriya*, 173

Lag Ba'omer, 60
Laity, 42-43; in Conservative Judaism, 143, 150; in Orthodox Judaism (Sephardim), 114, 115; in Orthodox Judaism (*shtibl*), 127-28; in Reconstructionist Judaism, 68, 71; in Reform Judaism, 98, 99-100, 103-4
Lamm, Maurice, 175, 179
Langer, Susan, 81
Law, Jewish: *see* Halaka
Leach, Edmund Ronald, 30, 81
Lévi-Strauss, Claude, 34, 36, 38, 82
Levine, Aaron, 174, 175
Levites: *see* Caste
*Levush*, 157
Liberalism, 21, 47, 77, 145-47, 150-51, 159
Liebman, Charles S., 53, 55, 112
Life-cycle: *see* Bar mitzvah; Bat mitzvah; Funeral; Mourning; Ritual, Family
Lightstone, Jack N., 83, 110, 165, 167n. 1, 167n. 10, 167n. 12, 171, 184n. 11
Lineage, 20
Liturgy, 3-22; active and passive participation in, 17, 20; attendance at, 19; cadence in, 20, 21; change in, 7-8, 17, 18; and communication, 7, 8, 12; in Conservative Judaism, 150; and custom, 5; and expectations, 5; and family, 19; and gender, 5, 7; and identity, 8, 11; implicit meanings

of, 7, 8, 9-10, 12; imports from home, 18; multivocality of, 8-9; in Orthodox Judaism, 33, 71-76; in Orthodox Judaism (Sephardim), 116-18; participants in, 18; in Reconstructionist Judaism, 20, 71-76; in Reform Judaism, 17-19; social cogency of, 9-11; social mapping in, 10-22; and theology, 8, 9; variation in, 5, 9, 11-12; vernacular in, 8;
Luckmann, Thomas, 53, 121n. 1, 124, 130-32, 169, 184n. 4

*Ma'ariv*, 160
Mack, Burton, 34
*Maftir*, 157, 160
*Magen Avraham*, 157, 158
Mapping, Social, 111; in Orthodox Judaism, 172, 176, 182; in Orthodox Judaism (*shtibl*), 12-16; in Reconstructionist Judaism, 20-22; in Reform Judaism, 16-20, 104-5
Marriage, Mixed: *see* Intermarriage
Marty, Martin E., 46
Marx, Karl, 49
Matrilineality: *see* Lineage
Mauss, Marcel, 39
Mcbrearty, Madeleine, 37, 67
*Mehitsa*, 17, 71, 113, 119-20, 159, 160
Men: *see* Gender
Menstrual blood: *see* Purity laws
Merton, Robert King, 182
Metcalf, Peter, 184 n. 8
*Minha*, 160
*Minhag*, 83
*Minyan*, 35, 36, 43; in Conservative Judaism, 138; in Orthodox Judaism, 174, 171, 178, 180, 182, 183; in Orthodox Judaism (Sephardim), 121n. 14; in Orthodox Judaism (*shtibl*), 127, 128, 129
Mishnah, 55, 157, 185-86
*Mishnah Brurah*, 158
Mixed marriage: *see* Intermarriage

Modernity, 55-57, 61-62; in Conservative Judaism, 136, 144, 150; in Orthodox Judaism, 164-65; in Orthodox Judaism (Sephardim), 109-11; in Reconstructionist Judaism, 68-69; in Reform Judaism, 97-98, 104-5
Mol, Hans, 110
Morgan, Thomas B., 53
Morning prayers: *see* Shaharit
Mourning: in Orthodox Judaism, 169-84; in Orthodox Judaism (Sephardim), 116-17; in Reform Judaism, 17
Moynihan, Daniel, 110
*Musaf*: in Conservative Judaism, 138, 143-45; in Orthodox Judaism, 72, 160, 163, 164; in Orthodox Judaism (Sephardim), 116; in Orthodox Judaism (*shtibl*), 129; in Reconstructionist Judaism, 76
Music: in Conservative Judaism, 16, 138, 139, 140, 141, 142, 143-44, 145; in Orthodox Judaism, 16; in Orthodox Judaism (Sephardim), 113, 116, 119; in Orthodox Judaism (*shtibl*), 124; in Reconstructionist Judaism, 82; in Reform Judaism, 16, 98-99, 100, 101
Myth, 57-61

*Ner tamid*, 70, 95, 113
Neusner, Jacob, 55, 56, 61
New Year, 56
Non-Jews: *see* Gentiles

*Oneg shabat*, 99
*Onen*: *see* Aninut
*Orah Hayim*, 157, 158
Orthodox Judaism, 125, 132-33; and Conservative Judaism, 91, 97, 140, 144, 147; and Reconstructionist Judaism, 76, 78, 79, 83, 91; and Reform Judaism, 90-91,

97-98, 103; and Sephardim, 112-20; and *shtibl*, 12, 15, 122-23

*Parnas*, 87, 115
Particularism, 152
Passover, 24, 25, 35, 41, 48, 188
Patrilineality: *see* Lineage
Pentateuch: *see* Torah
Peoplehood, 53-62, 112
Peoplehood, Chosen, 77, 83, 85, 112
Pesah: *see* Passover
Petuchowski, Jacob, 66
Phylacteries: *see* Tfilin
Pluralism, 55, 110; in Orthodox Judaism (Sephardim), 120; in Orthodox Judaism (*shtibl*), 15-16; in Reform Judaism, 104
Prayer, 56, 148
Prayer-book: *see* Sidur
Prayer-shawl: *see* Talit
Prell, Riv-Ellen, 22n. 2
Priests: *see* Caste
Prophets: *see* Haftara
*Psuke dezimra*, 129, 139
Purim, 24, 56
Purity laws, 56

Rabbi: in Conservative Judaism), 137, 141, 143, 144-47, 152; in Orthodox Judaism, 125, 159, 163, 164, 165, 174, 175; in Orthodox Judaism (Sephardim), 114, 121n. 11; in Orthodox Judaism (*shtibl*), 14, 124, 126-27, 128-30; in Reconstructionist Judaism, 20, 21, 71, 75-76, 78-79, 80n. 3, 87; in Reform Judaism, 16, 18, 96-97, 101, 103
Rabbinical Assembly, 148
Radcliffe-Brown, Alfred Reginald, 49, 169
Rappaport, Roy A., 81
Reconstructionist Judaism, 20-22, 65-80, 83-84; and Conservative Judaism, 83; and Orthodox Judaism, 76, 78, 79, 83, 91; and Orthodox Judaism (Sephardim), 120; and Reform Judaism, 68-69, 83
Reconstructionist Rabbinical College, 68, 69, 83
Reform Judaism, 89-108; and Conservative Judaism, 140; and Orthodox Judaism, 90-91, 97-98, 103; and Orthodox Judaism (Sephardim), 120; and Reconstructionist Judaism, 68-69, 83
Reitzes, Allan, 53, 56, 62n. 1
Remembrance Day, 101
Ritual: and civil religion, 58-59; and communication, 28-41; 81, 89, 191-92; constitutive, 28-30;definition of, 23; as drama, 23-28; elements of, 82; expressive, 31-35; and food, 38-39, 51n. 5, 185-86, 191-92; and identity, 189; interpretation of, 48-51; invocative, 36-38; and obsession, 44; regulative, 35-36; replaces theology, 66; self-representative, 30-31; variation in, 41-48
Ritual, Family, 185-95; and children, 188-89; and control, 172, as drama, 189; duration of, 193; expectations of, 191; explanations of, 190; and feelings, 191; and food, 166-67, 185-86; functions of, 190, 191-93; and gender, 192; Jewish and Christian, 193-94; in life-cycle events, 188-89; in Orthodox Judaism, 194; in Reconstructionist Judaism, 194; in Reform Judaism, 194, 195; and seasons, 187-88; and synagogue, 187; and weekends, 186-87
Rosh Hashana: *see* New Year
Routtenberg, Max J., 146

Sabbath, 48, 56, 56, 195, 191-92
Sacred: in Orthodox Judaism, 165; in Orthodox Judaism (Sephardim), 116, 119; in Reconstructionist

Judaism, 78, 79, 82, 84, 85; in Reform Judaism, 89-90, 104
*Sanctus: see* Kedusha
Saussure, Ferdinand de, 111
Schechter, S. Solomon, 55, 147
Scheff, Thomas J., 32, 41, 191
Scherman, Nosson, 177
Schoenfeld, Stuart, 53, 55, 56, 57, 190
Schwartz, Paul, 46
Searle, John R., 29, 48-49
Seating: in Conservative Judaism, 16, 138, 150; in Orthodox Judaism, 160, 161, 162; in Orthodox Judaism (Sephardim), 113, 121n. 16; in Orthodox Judaism (*shtibl*), 127-128; in Reconstructionist Judaism, 16, 20, 73, 78; in Reform Judaism, 16
Secularity, 57, 66, 165; in Conservative Judaism, 144, 145, 152; in Orthodox Judaism (Sephardim), 109; in Orthodox Judaism (*shtibl*), 13, 14-15; in Reconstructionist Judaism, 77; in Reform Judaism, 90
*Seder*, 41, 48, 49, 56, 177
Sephardim, 62n. 1, 112-22; and Conservative Judaism, 120; and Reconstructionist Judaism, 120; and Reform Judaism, 120
Sermon: in Conservative Judaism, 138; in Orthodox Judaism, 125, 163; in Orthodox Judaism (Sephardim), 120; in Orthodox Judaism (*shtibl*), 129; in Reconstructionist Judaism, 20, 21, 72, 75-76; in Reform Judaism, 97, 101, 103
*Se'udat havra*, 177
Shabat: *see* Sabbath
Shahar, Charles, 53, 56, 62n. 1
*Shaharit*: in Conservative Judaism, 138-39; in Orthodox Judaism, 160; in Orthodox Judaism (Sephardim), 116; in Orthodox Judaism (*shtibl*), 129
*Shaliah tzibur*, 129, 180
*Shamash*, 114, 115
Shavu'ot, 59
*Shiva*, 170, 177-79, 182
*Shloshim*, 179-180
*Shma*: in Conservative Judaism, 138, 140; in Orthodox Judaism, 72, 174; in Orthodox Judaism (*shtibl*), 124, 129; in Reconstructionist Judaism, 73, 74, 79, 84, 86; in Reform Judaism, 102
*Shmone esre: see* Amida
*Shtand*, 123
*Shtibl*, 12-16, 123-33
*Shulhan*: in Orthodox Judaism (Sephardim), 113; in Orthodox Judaism, 160; in Orthodox Judaism (*shtibl*), 13, 126; in Reconstructionist Judaism, 70, 74, 78, 79, 84, 87; in Reform Judaism, 17, 95
Shulhan Aruk, 157, 158, 184 n. 2
*Sidur*, 5-6; in Conservative Judaism, 137, 138, 146; in Orthodox Judaism, 125, 163; in Orthodox Judaism (Sephardim), 114; in Reconstructionist Judaism, 21, 69, 73, 74, 76, 84, 86; in Reform Judaism, 96, 101
Siegel, Seymour, 148, 149
Sklare, Marshall, 53, 55
Skull-cap: *see* Kipa
*Smika*, 14
Socialization, 130-133
*Ste'emat hagolel*, 173
Sukot, 24
Supernatural: *see* God
Synagogue, 56, 58
Synagogue: in Conservative Judaism, 146-47, 151; in Orthodox Judaism, 109, 159, 165, 182-83; in Reconstructionist Judaism 68-69

Tabernacles: *see* Sukot

*Talit*: in Conservative Judaism, 138; in Orthodox Judaism, 72, 125, 162, 166, 178; in Orthodox Judaism (Sephardim), 114, 115, 117, 119; in Orthodox Judaism (*shtibl*), 126, 129; in Reconstructionist Judaism, 73, 78; in Reform Judaism, 66, 96, 99, 104
Talmud, 55, 157
Tam, 157
Tambiah, Stanley Jeyaraja, 28, 38, 51n. 4
Taras, David, 59
Temple (Jerusalem), 177
*Tfila: see Amida*
*Tfilin*, 158, 161, 166, 174, 178
Theology, 9, 33, 39, 61-62
Tillich, Paul, 37
Tisha B'av, 177
Titmuss, Richard Morris, 39
Tobin, Gary, 53, 56, 62n. 1
Torah, 55, 57, 59, 62, 144, 149, 164; oral, 55, 57-59; study of 12-3, 14-5, 16, 56
Torah reading: in Conservative Judaism, 138, 141, 142, 152; in Orthodox Judaism, 72, 162-63; in Orthodox Judaism (Sephardim), 114, 116; in Orthodox Judaism (*shtibl*), 129; in Reconstructionist Judaism, 73, 74-75, 78, 86; in Reform Judaism, 97, 99, 101
Torah scrolls, 5, 37; in Conservative Judaism, 141, 142; in Orthodox Judaism, 160, 162, 163; in Orthodox Judaism (Sephardim), 117; in Orthodox Judaism (*shtibl*), 13; in Reconstructionist Judaism, 21, 74, 75, 78, 85; Reform Judaism, 17, 95, 101, 104
Torczyner, J., 62 n. 1
Traditionalism, 145-47, 150-51, 152
Tzokensiki, N. A., 167, 184n. 2
Tu Bishvat, 60
*Tur*, 184n. 2

Turner, Victor W., 36, 156, 167n. 3, 169, 170, 171, 183
*Tzitz Eliezer*, 157

United Jewish Appeal, 60
United Synagogue of America, 68
Unity, Congregational, 145-51
Universalism, 103-4, 152

Van Gennep, Arnold, 156, 167n. 3, 170
Vernacular, 8; in Conservative Judaism, 16, 140, 142, 151; in Orthodox Judaism, 16, 125, 177; in Orthodox Judaism (Sephardim), 117; in Orthodox Judaism (*shtibl*), 120, 124, 127, 128; in Reconstructionist Judaism, 16, 73, 75, 78, 84; in Reform Judaism, 16, 97, 103
Veterans Day: *see* Remembrance Day

Waller, Harold M., 59, 61,
Weber, Max, 25, 26, 49
Weinfeld, Morton, 53, 59, 62n. 1
Welch, Holmes, 52n. 6
Wertheimer, Jack, 22n. 2
Westley, Frances, 46
Wilson, Bryan R., 65
Women: *see* Gender
Woocher, Jonathan, 53, 57, 59, 62
World Zionist Organization, 61
Wuthnow, Robert, 23, 51n. 2

*Yeshiva*, 12-15, 123, 130-33
Yiddish: *see* Vernacular
Yom Ha'atzma'ut, 57, 60, 101, 103
Yom Hasho'a, 57
Yom Kipur: *see* Day of Atonement
*Yortsait*, 139

Zborowski, Mark, 109, 158
Zenner, Walter P., 22n. 2
*Zimun*, 174, 177
Zionism, 59-61, 142, 144
Zuckerman, Alan, 56